TRANSPORTED TO THE PRESENT FROM AN ALTERNATE TIMELINE WHERE VILLAINS TRIUMPHED AND THE WORLD DEVOLVED INTO LAWLESS WASTELANDS, LOGAN USED HIS SECOND CHANCE AT LIFE TO REJOIN THE X-MEN AND AVERT CATASTROPHES LIKE THE ONES THAT BEFELL HIS WORLD. HOWEVER, HIS ADVANCED AGE HAS CAUGHT UP WITH HIM AND HIS FAMED HEALING FACTOR IS SEVERELY REDUCED, LEAVING HIM SLOWLY DYING OF ADAMANTIUM POISONING...

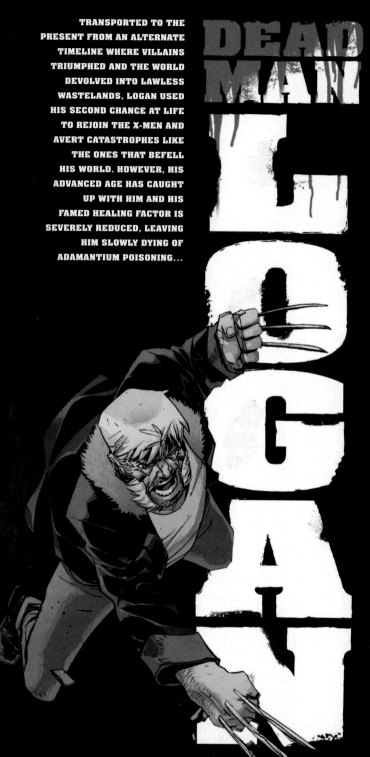

DEAD MAN LOGAN

ED BRISSON
WRITER

MIKE HENDERSON
ARTIST

NOLAN WOODARD
COLOR ARTIST

VC's CORY PETIT
LETTERER

DECLAN SHALVEY
COVER ARTIST

CHRIS ROBINSON
EDITOR

JORDAN WHITE
X-MEN GROUP EDITOR

P9-CDO-918

COLLECTION EDITOR **MARK D. BEAZLEY**
ASSISTANT EDITOR **CAITLIN O'CONNELL**
ASSOCIATE MANAGING EDITOR **KATERI WOODY**
SENIOR EDITOR, SPECIAL PROJECTS
JENNIFER GRÜNWALD
VP PRODUCTION & SPECIAL PROJECTS
JEFF YOUNGQUIST

BOOK DESIGNERS **SALENA MAHINA**,
ADAM DEL RE & **ANTHONY GAMBINO**

SVP PRINT, SALES & MARKETING **DAVID GABRIEL**
DIRECTOR, LICENSED PUBLISHING **SVEN LARSEN**
EDITOR IN CHIEF **C.B. CEBULSKI**
CHIEF CREATIVE OFFICER **JOE QUESADA**
PRESIDENT **DAN BUCKLEY**
EXECUTIVE PRODUCER **ALAN FINE**

SINS OF THE FATHER

DEAD MAN LOGAN VOL. 1: SINS OF THE FATHER. Contains material originally published in magazine form as DEAD MAN LOGAN #1-6. First printing 2019. ISBN 978-1-302-91465-3. Published by MARVEL WORLDWIDE, INC., a subsidiary of MARVEL ENTERTAINMENT, LLC. OFFICE OF PUBLICATION: 135 West 50th Street, New York, NY 10020. © 2019 MARVEL No similarity between any of the names, characters, persons, and/or institutions in this magazine with those of any living or dead person or institution is intended, and any such similarity which may exist is purely coincidental. **Printed in the U.S.A.** DAN BUCKLEY, President, Marvel Entertainment; JOHN NEE, Publisher; JOE QUESADA, Chief Creative Officer; TOM BREVOORT, SVP of Publishing; DAVID BOGART, Associate Publisher & SVP of Talent Affairs; DAVID GABRIEL, SVP of Sales & Marketing, Publishing; JEFF YOUNGQUIST, VP of Production & Special Projects; DAN CARR, Executive Director of Publishing Technology; ALEX MORALES, Director of Publishing Operations; DAN EDINGTON, Managing Editor; SUSAN CRESPI, Production Manager; STAN LEE, Chairman Emeritus. For information regarding advertising in Marvel Comics or on Marvel.com, please contact Vit DeBellis, Custom Solutions & Integrated Advertising Manager, at vdebellis@marvel.com. For Marvel subscription inquiries, please call 888-511-5480. **Manufactured between 4/19/2019 and 5/21/2019 by LSC COMMUNICATIONS INC., KENDALLVILLE, IN, USA.**

10 9 8 7 6 5 4 3 2 1

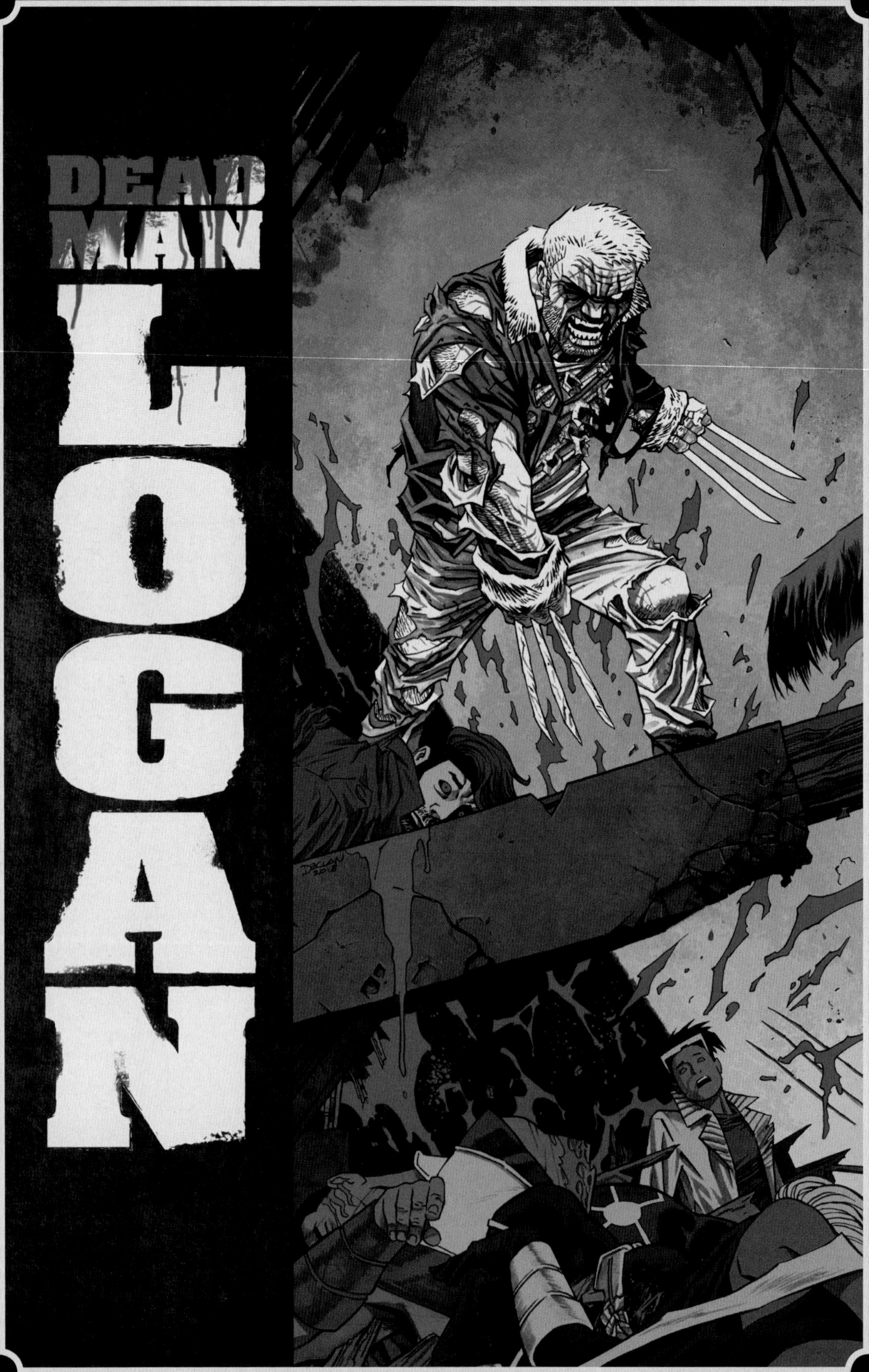
DEAD MAN
LOGAN

1

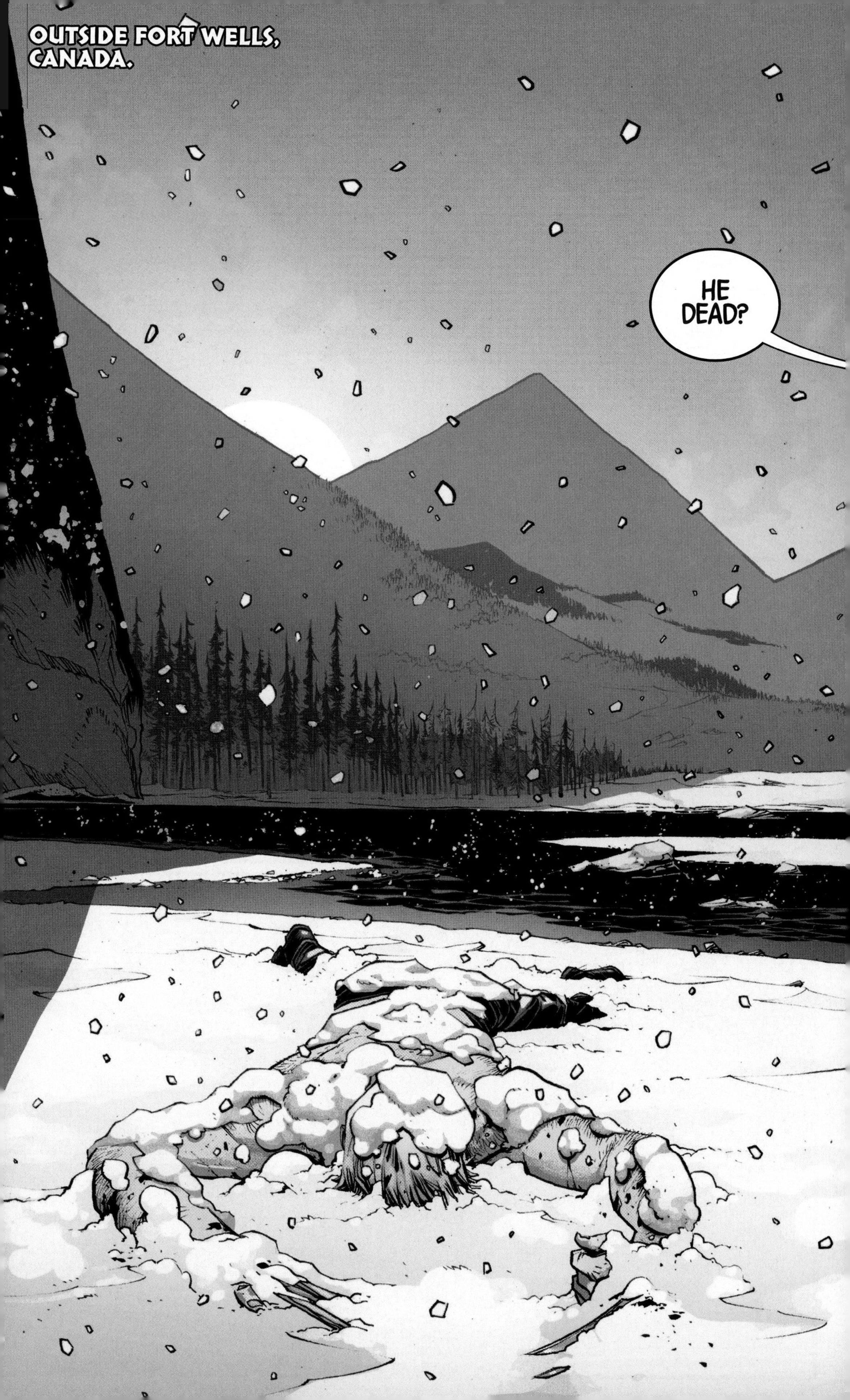
OUTSIDE FORT WELLS, CANADA.
HE DEAD?

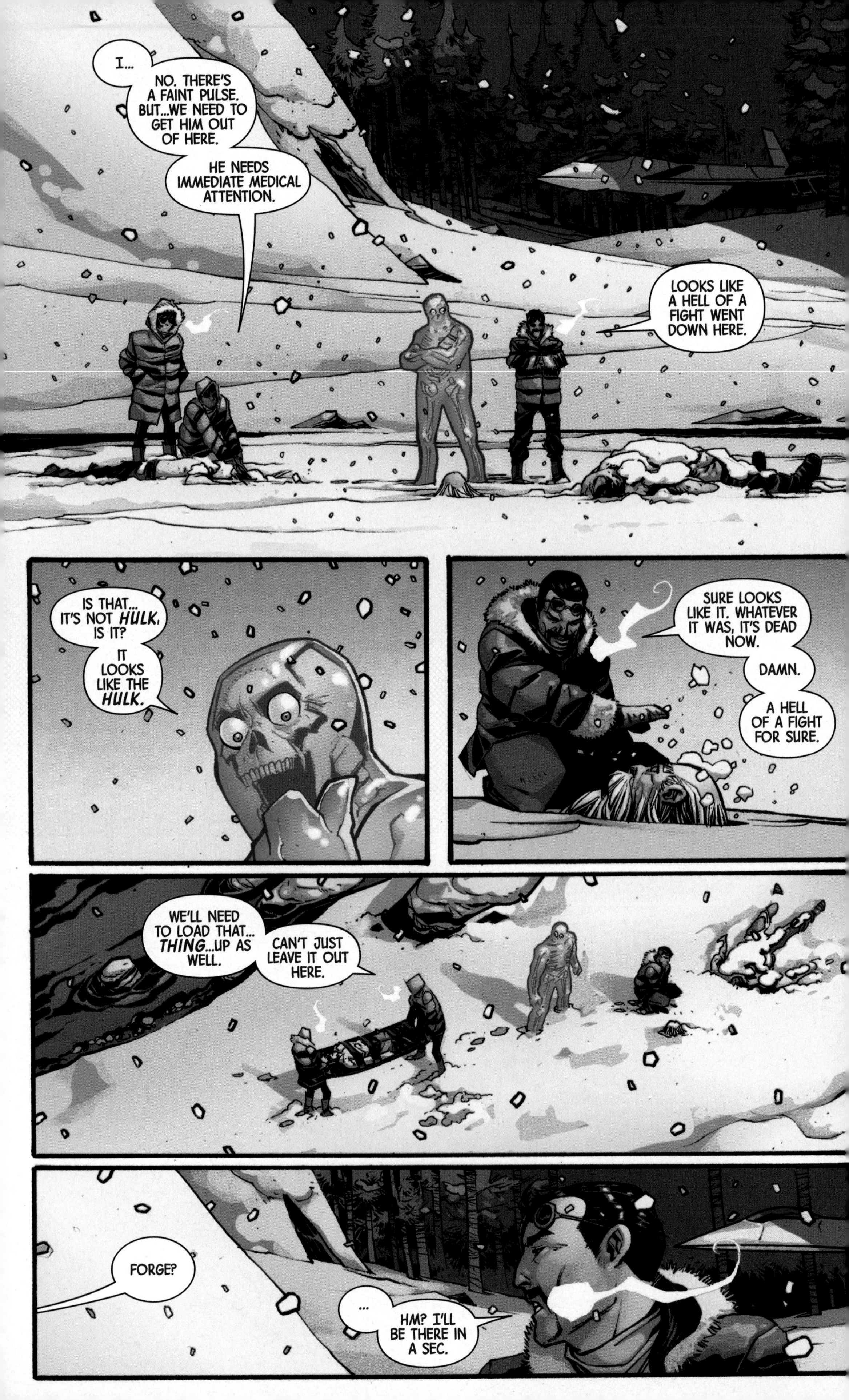

I...
NO. THERE'S A FAINT PULSE. BUT...WE NEED TO GET HIM OUT OF HERE.
HE NEEDS IMMEDIATE MEDICAL ATTENTION.
LOOKS LIKE A HELL OF A FIGHT WENT DOWN HERE.
IS THAT... IT'S NOT HULK, IS IT?
IT LOOKS LIKE THE HULK.
SURE LOOKS LIKE IT. WHATEVER IT WAS, IT'S DEAD NOW.
DAMN.
A HELL OF A FIGHT FOR SURE.
WE'LL NEED TO LOAD THAT... THING...UP AS WELL.
CAN'T JUST LEAVE IT OUT HERE.
FORGE?
...
HM? I'LL BE THERE IN A SEC.

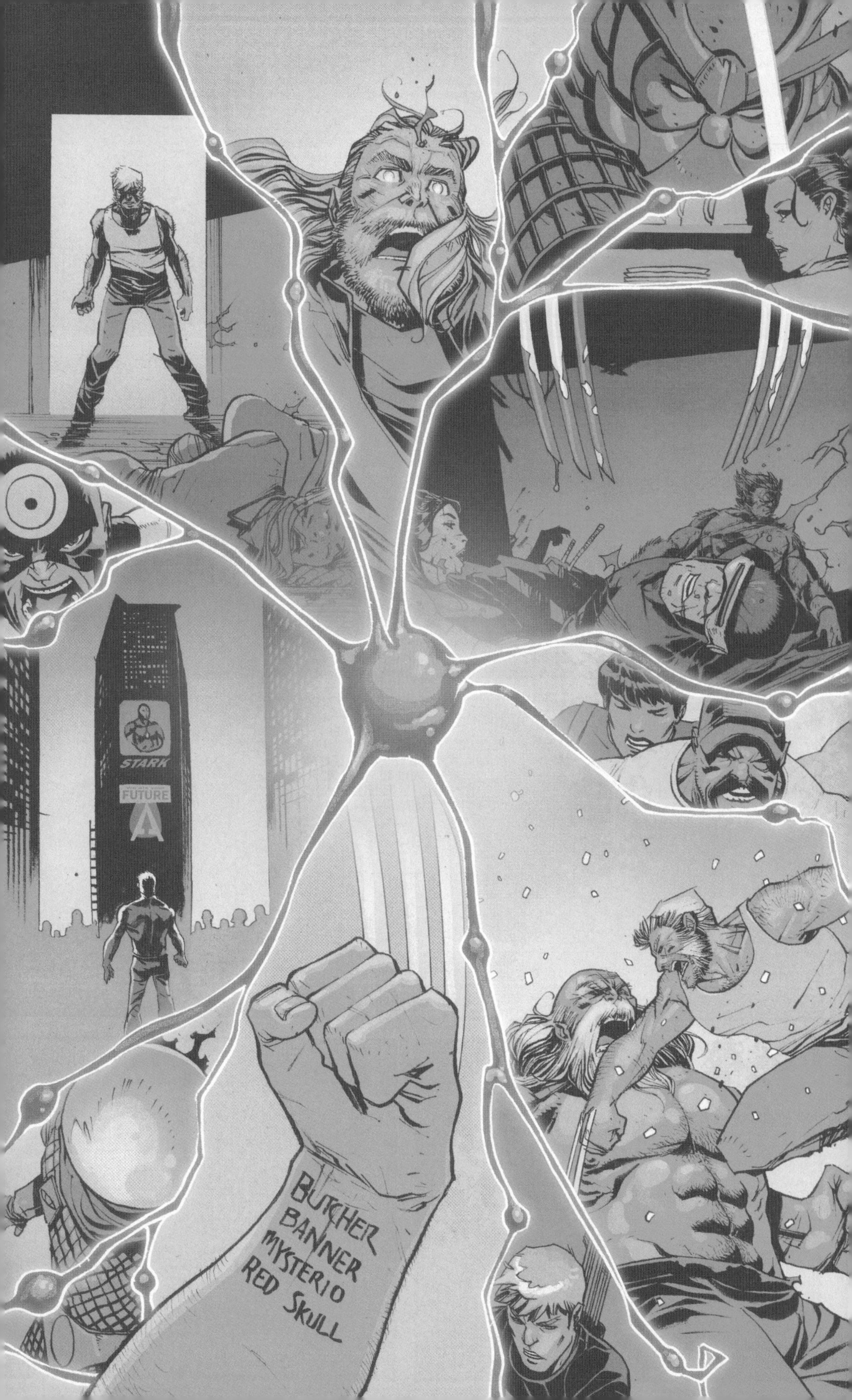
STARK
FUTURE
BUTCHER
BANNER
MYSTERIO
RED SKULL

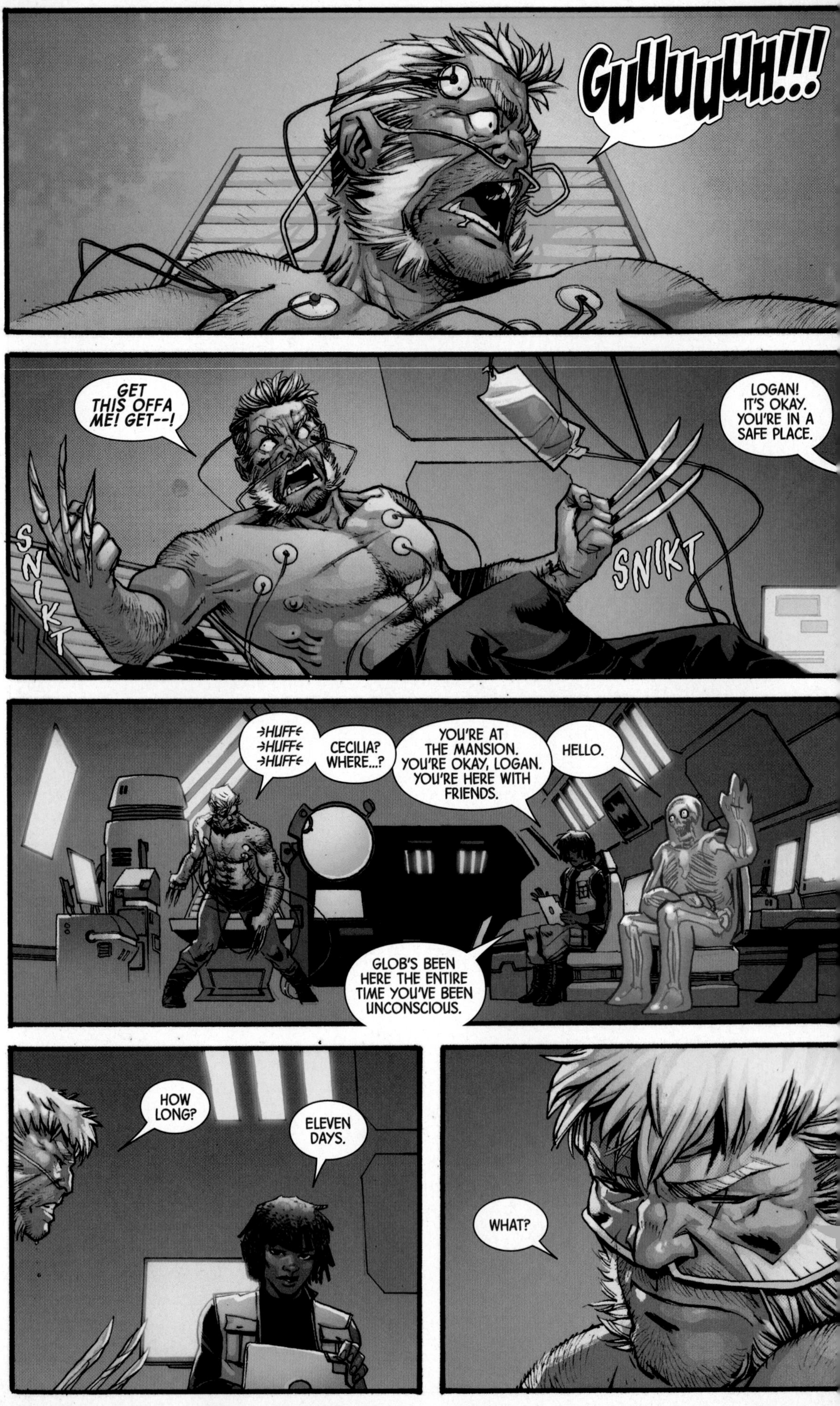
GUUUUUH!!!
GET THIS OFFA ME! GET--!
SNIKT
SNIKT
LOGAN! IT'S OKAY. YOU'RE IN A SAFE PLACE.
→HUFF← →HUFF← →HUFF←
CECILIA? WHERE...?
YOU'RE AT THE MANSION. YOU'RE OKAY, LOGAN. YOU'RE HERE WITH FRIENDS.
HELLO.
GLOB'S BEEN HERE THE ENTIRE TIME YOU'VE BEEN UNCONSCIOUS.
HOW LONG?
ELEVEN DAYS.
WHAT?

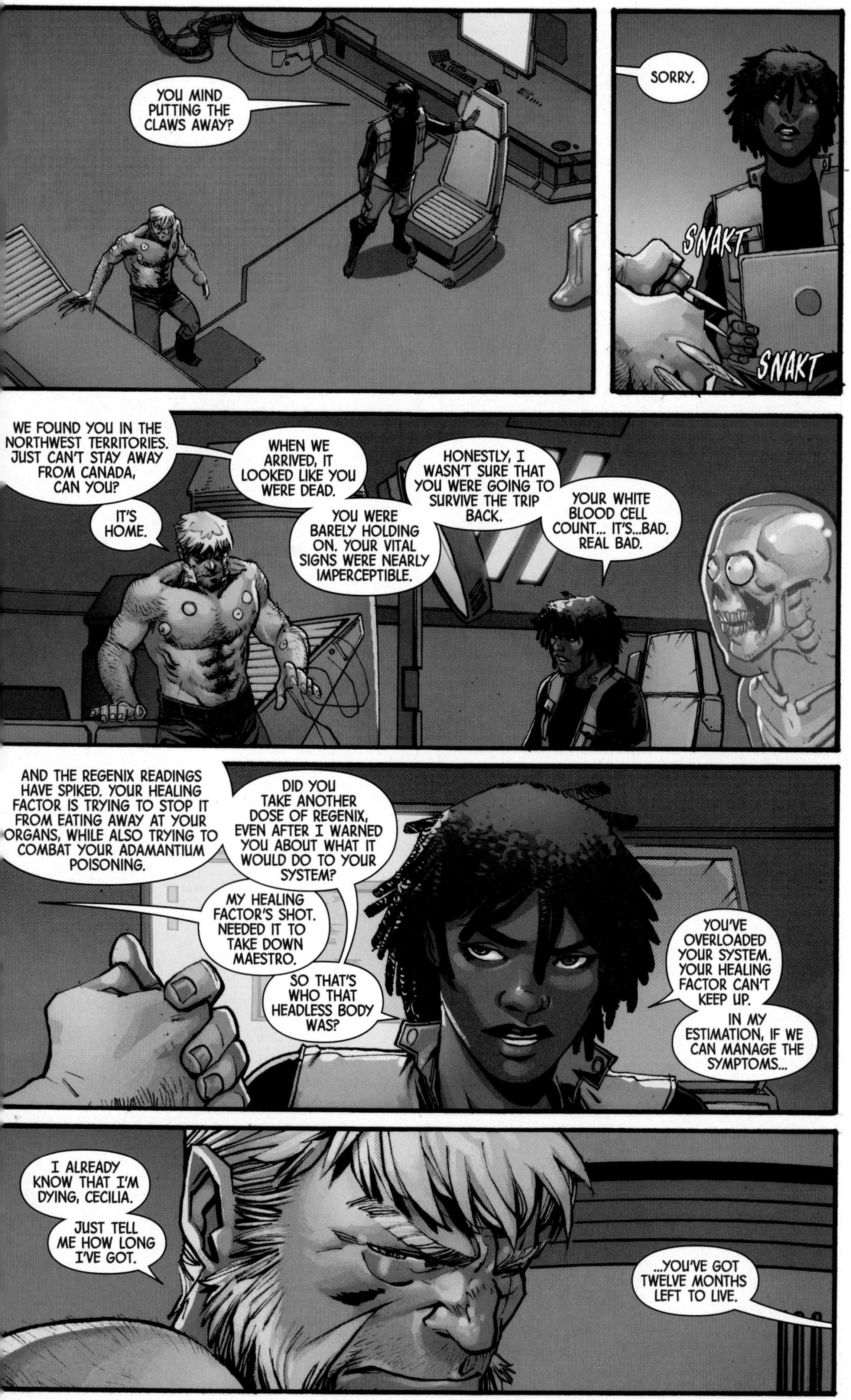
YOU MIND PUTTING THE CLAWS AWAY?
SORRY.
SNAKT
SNAKT
WE FOUND YOU IN THE NORTHWEST TERRITORIES. JUST CAN'T STAY AWAY FROM CANADA, CAN YOU?
IT'S HOME.
WHEN WE ARRIVED, IT LOOKED LIKE YOU WERE DEAD.
YOU WERE BARELY HOLDING ON. YOUR VITAL SIGNS WERE NEARLY IMPERCEPTIBLE.
HONESTLY, I WASN'T SURE THAT YOU WERE GOING TO SURVIVE THE TRIP BACK.
YOUR WHITE BLOOD CELL COUNT... IT'S...BAD. REAL BAD.
AND THE REGENIX READINGS HAVE SPIKED. YOUR HEALING FACTOR IS TRYING TO STOP IT FROM EATING AWAY AT YOUR ORGANS, WHILE ALSO TRYING TO COMBAT YOUR ADAMANTIUM POISONING.
DID YOU TAKE ANOTHER DOSE OF REGENIX, EVEN AFTER I WARNED YOU ABOUT WHAT IT WOULD DO TO YOUR SYSTEM?
MY HEALING FACTOR'S SHOT. NEEDED IT TO TAKE DOWN MAESTRO.
SO THAT'S WHO THAT HEADLESS BODY WAS?
YOU'VE OVERLOADED YOUR SYSTEM. YOUR HEALING FACTOR CAN'T KEEP UP.
IN MY ESTIMATION, IF WE CAN MANAGE THE SYMPTOMS...
I ALREADY KNOW THAT I'M DYING, CECILIA.
JUST TELL ME HOW LONG I'VE GOT.
...YOU'VE GOT TWELVE MONTHS LEFT TO LIVE.

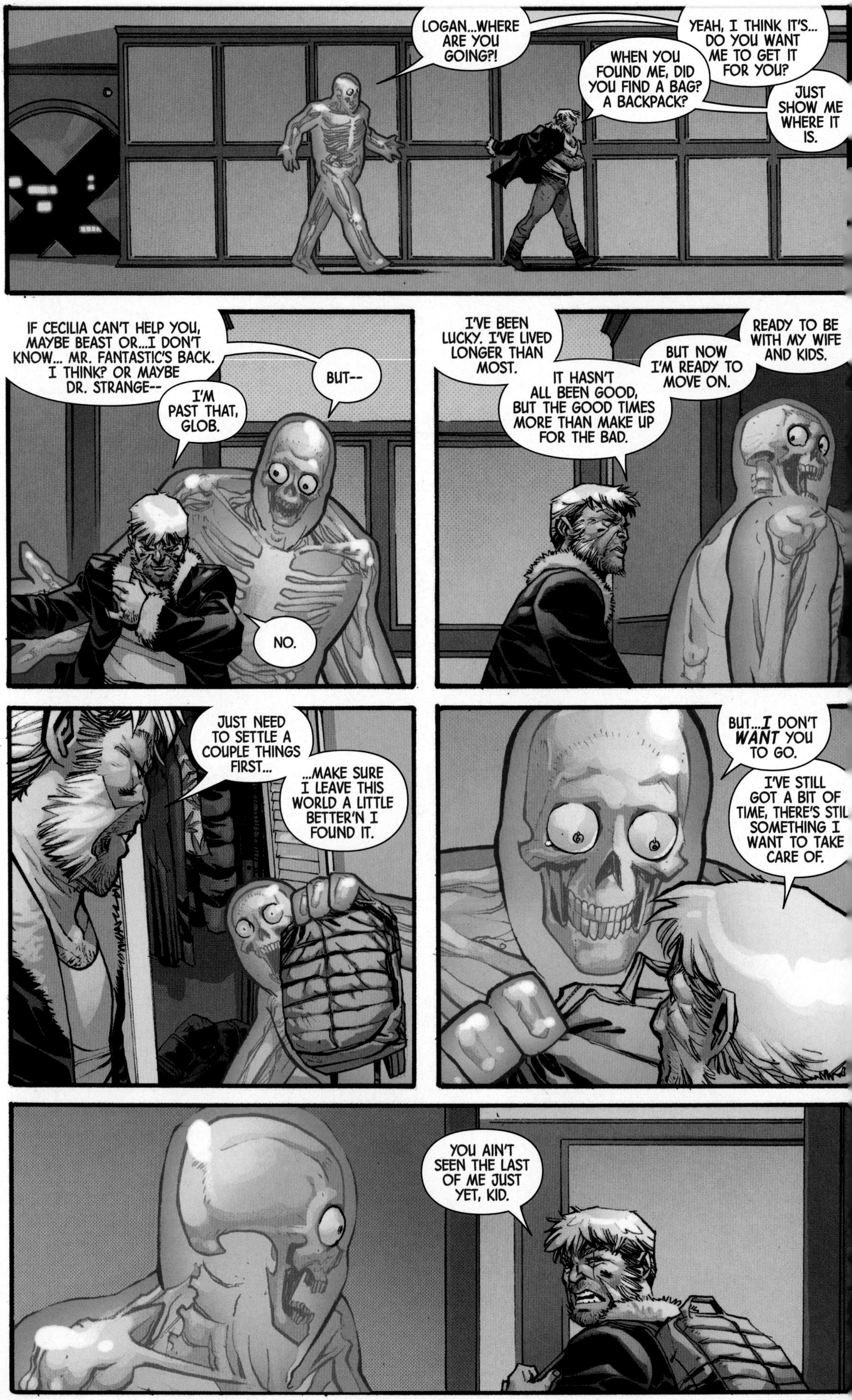

LOGAN...WHERE ARE YOU GOING?!
WHEN YOU FOUND ME, DID YOU FIND A BAG? A BACKPACK?
YEAH, I THINK IT'S... DO YOU WANT ME TO GET IT FOR YOU?
JUST SHOW ME WHERE IT IS.
IF CECILIA CAN'T HELP YOU, MAYBE BEAST OR...I DON'T KNOW... MR. FANTASTIC'S BACK. I THINK? OR MAYBE DR. STRANGE--
I'M PAST THAT, GLOB.
BUT--
NO.
I'VE BEEN LUCKY. I'VE LIVED LONGER THAN MOST.
IT HASN'T ALL BEEN GOOD, BUT THE GOOD TIMES MORE THAN MAKE UP FOR THE BAD.
BUT NOW I'M READY TO MOVE ON.
READY TO BE WITH MY WIFE AND KIDS.
JUST NEED TO SETTLE A COUPLE THINGS FIRST...
...MAKE SURE I LEAVE THIS WORLD A LITTLE BETTER'N I FOUND IT.
BUT...I DON'T WANT YOU TO GO.
I'VE STILL GOT A BIT OF TIME, THERE'S STILL SOMETHING I WANT TO TAKE CARE OF.
YOU AIN'T SEEN THE LAST OF ME JUST YET, KID.

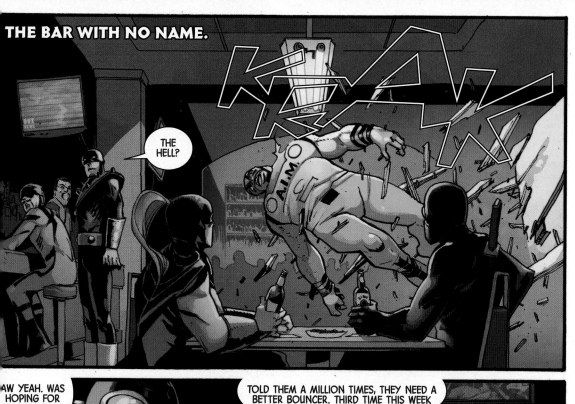

KRAK! KRAK!

THE HELL?

AW YEAH. WAS HOPING FOR A FIGHT TONIGHT.

TOLD THEM A MILLION TIMES, THEY NEED A BETTER BOUNCER. THIRD TIME THIS WEEK BRUISER'S BEEN KNOCKED OUT.

FIRST ONE OF YOU CLOWNS TO TELL ME WHERE CAN I FIND MYSTERIO GETS TO WALK OUTTA HERE IN ONE PIECE.

EVERYONE ELSE GETS THEIR ASSES KICKED.

NO DEAL.

WE AIN'T SNITCHES!

ALL RIGHT...

...DON'T SAY I DIDN'T WARN YOU.

SNIKT

SNIKT

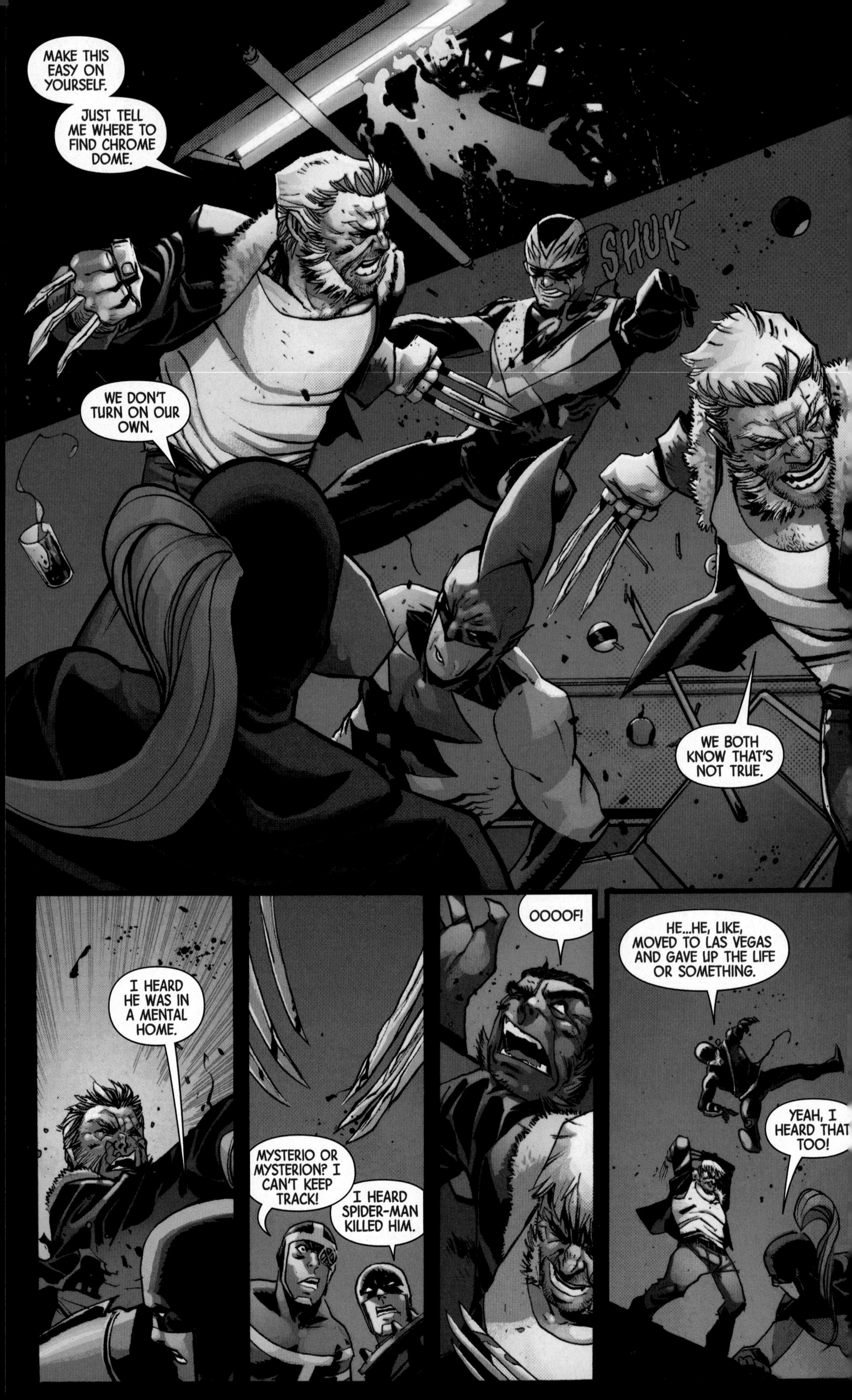
MAKE THIS EASY ON YOURSELF.
JUST TELL ME WHERE TO FIND CHROME DOME.
SHUK
WE DON'T TURN ON OUR OWN.
WE BOTH KNOW THAT'S NOT TRUE.
I HEARD HE WAS IN A MENTAL HOME.
MYSTERIO OR MYSTERION? I CAN'T KEEP TRACK!
I HEARD SPIDER-MAN KILLED HIM.
OOOOF!
HE...HE, LIKE, MOVED TO LAS VEGAS AND GAVE UP THE LIFE OR SOMETHING.
YEAH, I HEARD THAT TOO!

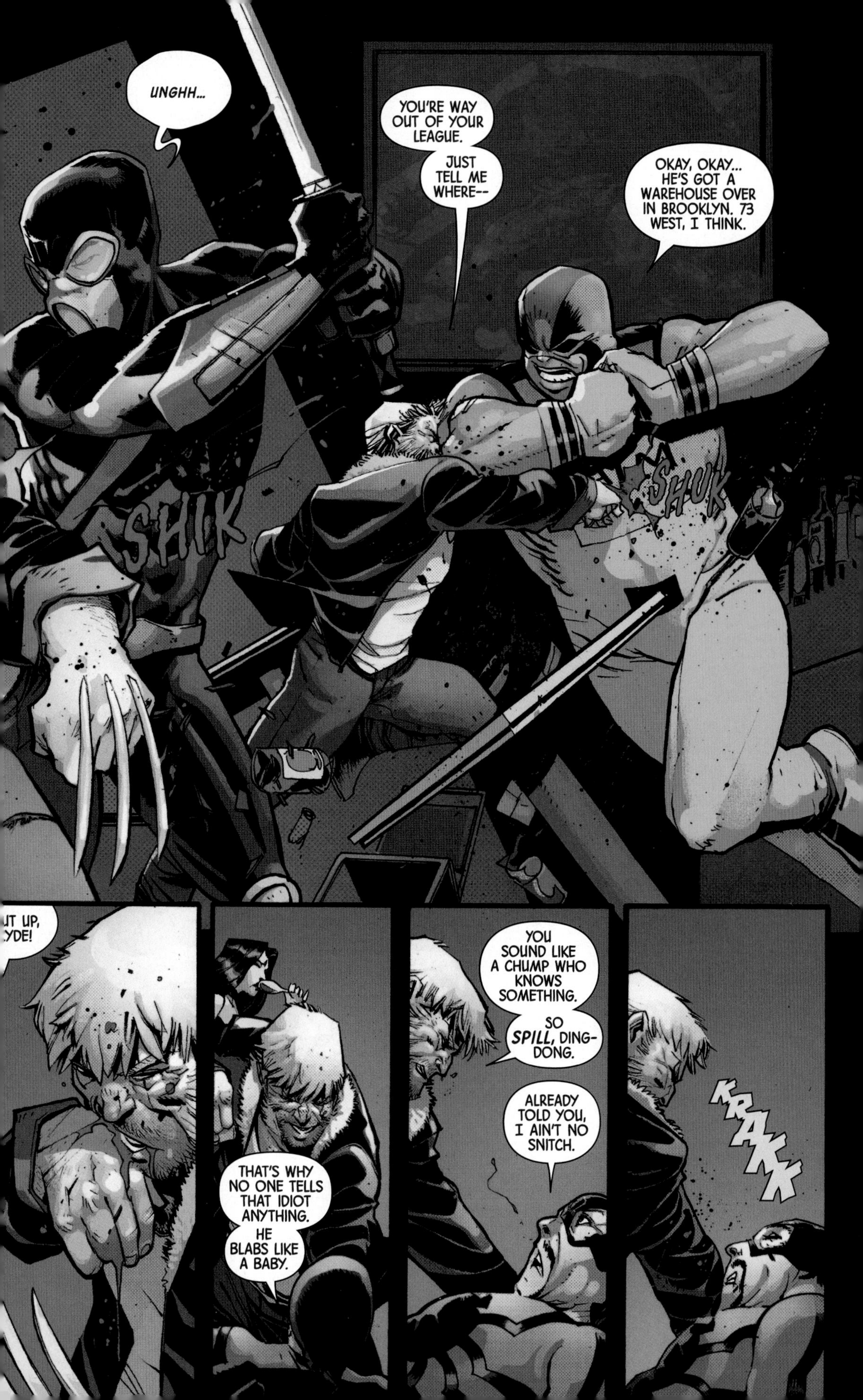
UNGHH...
YOU'RE WAY OUT OF YOUR LEAGUE.
JUST TELL ME WHERE--
OKAY, OKAY... HE'S GOT A WAREHOUSE OVER IN BROOKLYN. 73 WEST, I THINK.
SHIK
SHUK
THAT'S WHY NO ONE TELLS THAT IDIOT ANYTHING.
HE BLABS LIKE A BABY.
YOU SOUND LIKE A CHUMP WHO KNOWS SOMETHING.
SO SPILL, DING-DONG.
ALREADY TOLD YOU, I AIN'T NO SNITCH.
KRAKK

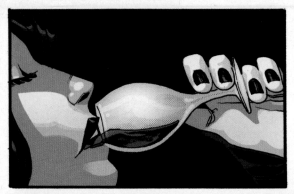

THE TESTOSTERONE IN THIS PLACE IS SO THICK YOU COULD CUT IT WITH A CHAINSAW.

TAK

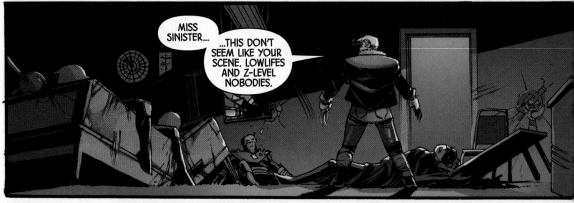

MISS SINISTER... ...THIS DON'T SEEM LIKE YOUR SCENE. LOWLIFES AND Z-LEVEL NOBODIES.

WELL, YOU KNOW...WHEN LOOKING FOR BAD BOYS, YOU GO WHERE THE BAD BOYS GO.

THOUGH, I MUST CONFESS, AFTER SEEING YOU WHIP THEM SO EASILY, I'M NOT SO SURE THAT THEY'RE QUITE *BAD* ENOUGH FOR MY TASTES.

YOU MIND FILLING ME UP?

ANYHOW, I WANT TO THANK YOU...

...THIS AFTERNOON HAS CERTAINLY BEEN A *LEARNING EXPERIENCE* FOR ME.

IF I THOUGHT FOR A SECOND YOU KNEW WHERE MYSTERIO WAS, YOU'D BE A PILE OF MEAT ON THE GROUND WITH THE REST OF THE MEAT.

GUESS I SHOULD BE THANKFUL.

HAPPY HUNTING.

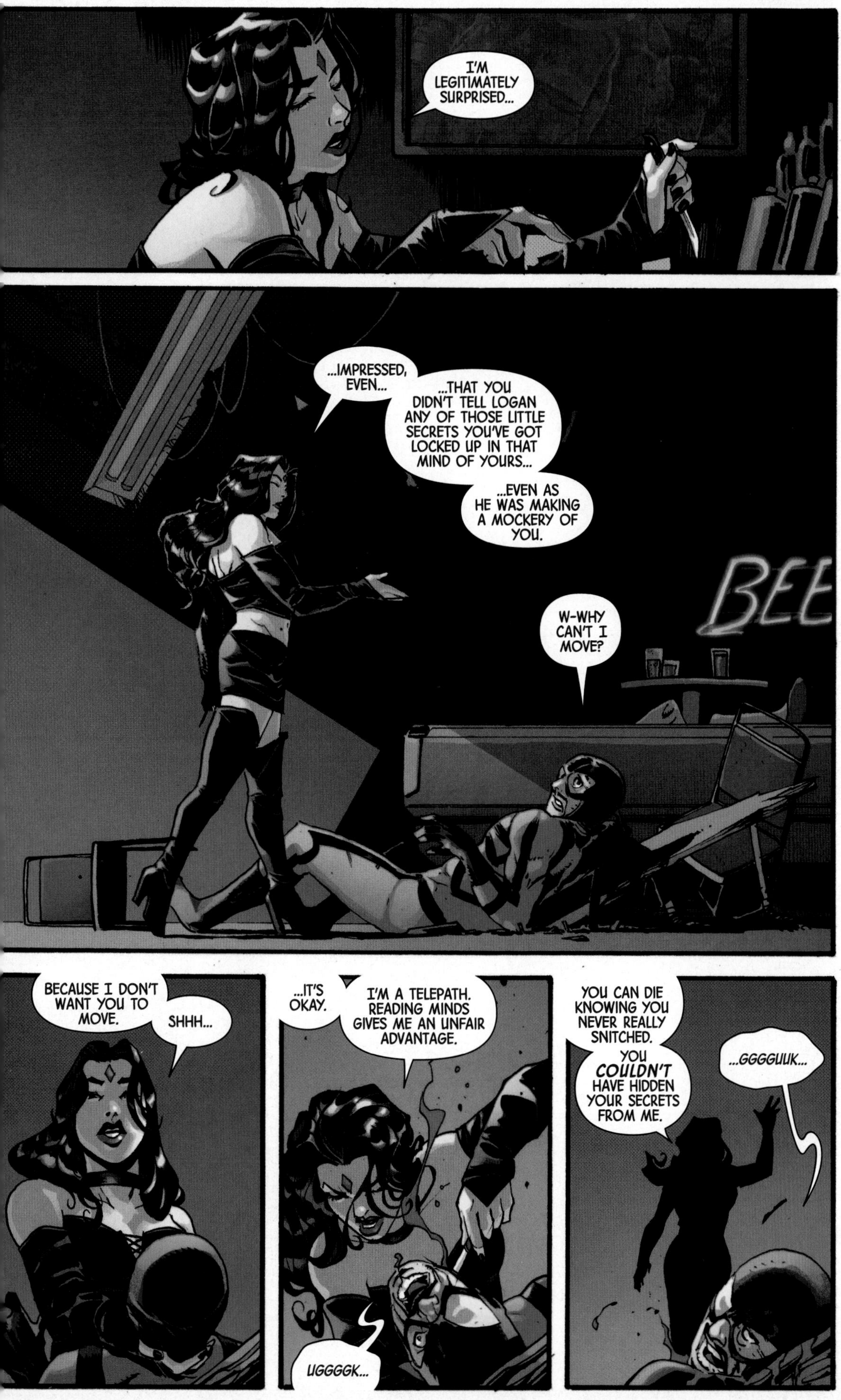
I'M LEGITIMATELY SURPRISED...
...IMPRESSED, EVEN...
...THAT YOU DIDN'T TELL LOGAN ANY OF THOSE LITTLE SECRETS YOU'VE GOT LOCKED UP IN THAT MIND OF YOURS...
...EVEN AS HE WAS MAKING A MOCKERY OF YOU.
BEE
W-WHY CAN'T I MOVE?
BECAUSE I DON'T WANT YOU TO MOVE.
SHHH...
...IT'S OKAY.
I'M A TELEPATH. READING MINDS GIVES ME AN UNFAIR ADVANTAGE.
UGGGGK...
YOU CAN DIE KNOWING YOU NEVER REALLY SNITCHED.
YOU *COULDN'T* HAVE HIDDEN YOUR SECRETS FROM ME.
...GGGGUUK...

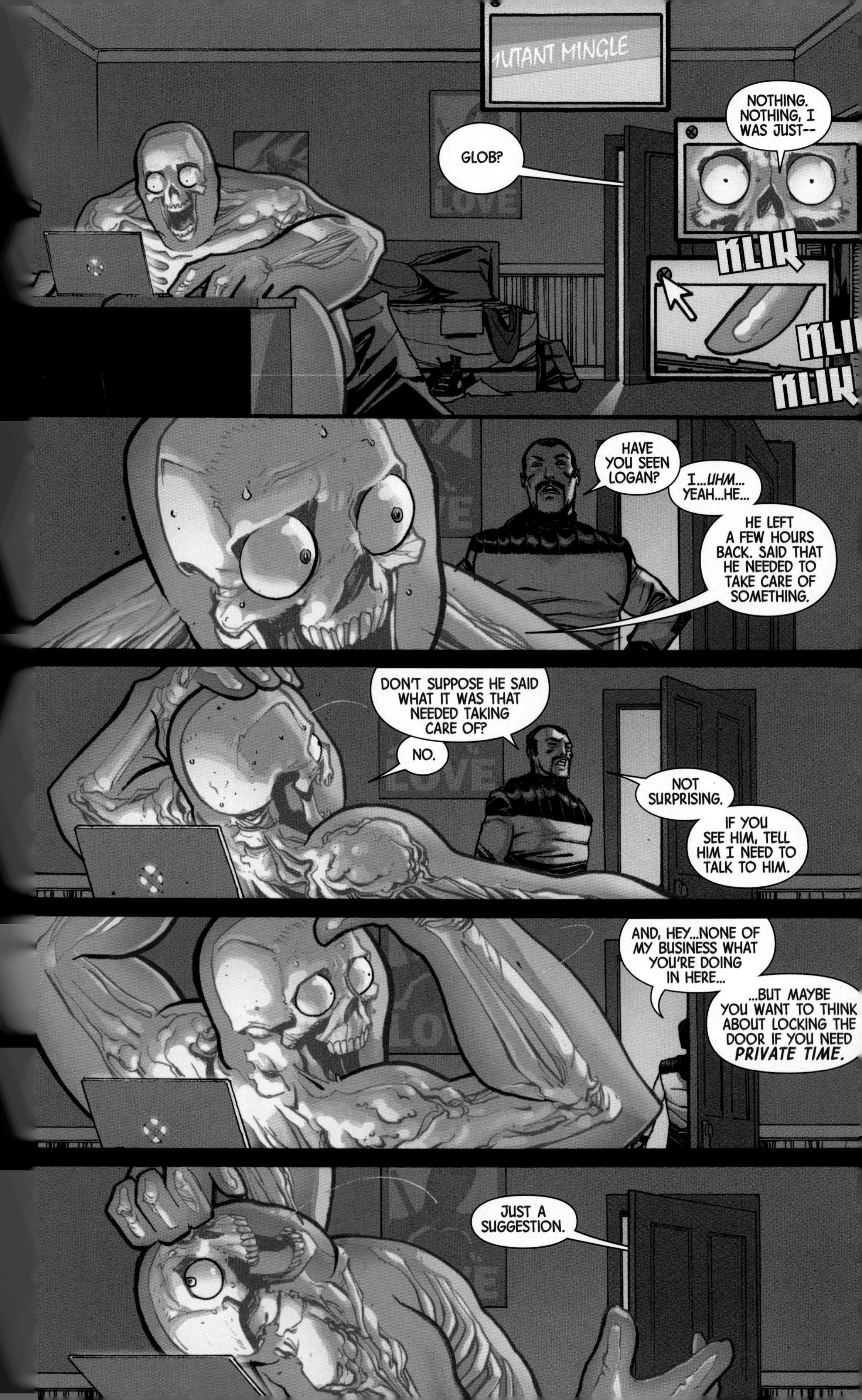
MUTANT MINGLE
GLOB?
NOTHING. NOTHING, I WAS JUST--
KLIK
KLIK
KLIK
HAVE YOU SEEN LOGAN?
I...UHM... YEAH...HE...
HE LEFT A FEW HOURS BACK. SAID THAT HE NEEDED TO TAKE CARE OF SOMETHING.
DON'T SUPPOSE HE SAID WHAT IT WAS THAT NEEDED TAKING CARE OF?
NO.
NOT SURPRISING.
IF YOU SEE HIM, TELL HIM I NEED TO TALK TO HIM.
AND, HEY...NONE OF MY BUSINESS WHAT YOU'RE DOING IN HERE...
...BUT MAYBE YOU WANT TO THINK ABOUT LOCKING THE DOOR IF YOU NEED PRIVATE TIME.
JUST A SUGGESTION.

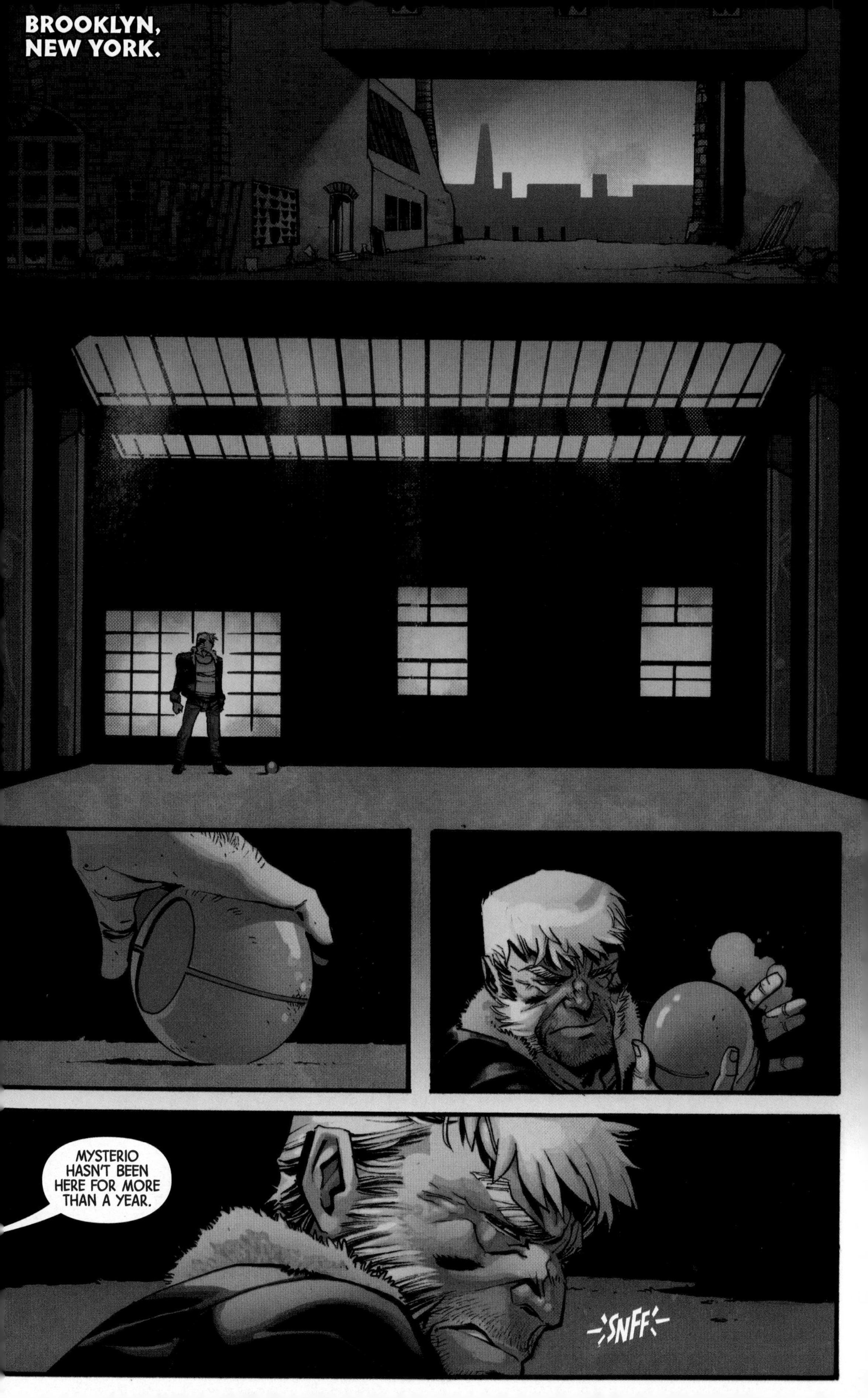
BROOKLYN, NEW YORK.
MYSTERIO HASN'T BEEN HERE FOR MORE THAN A YEAR.
SNFF

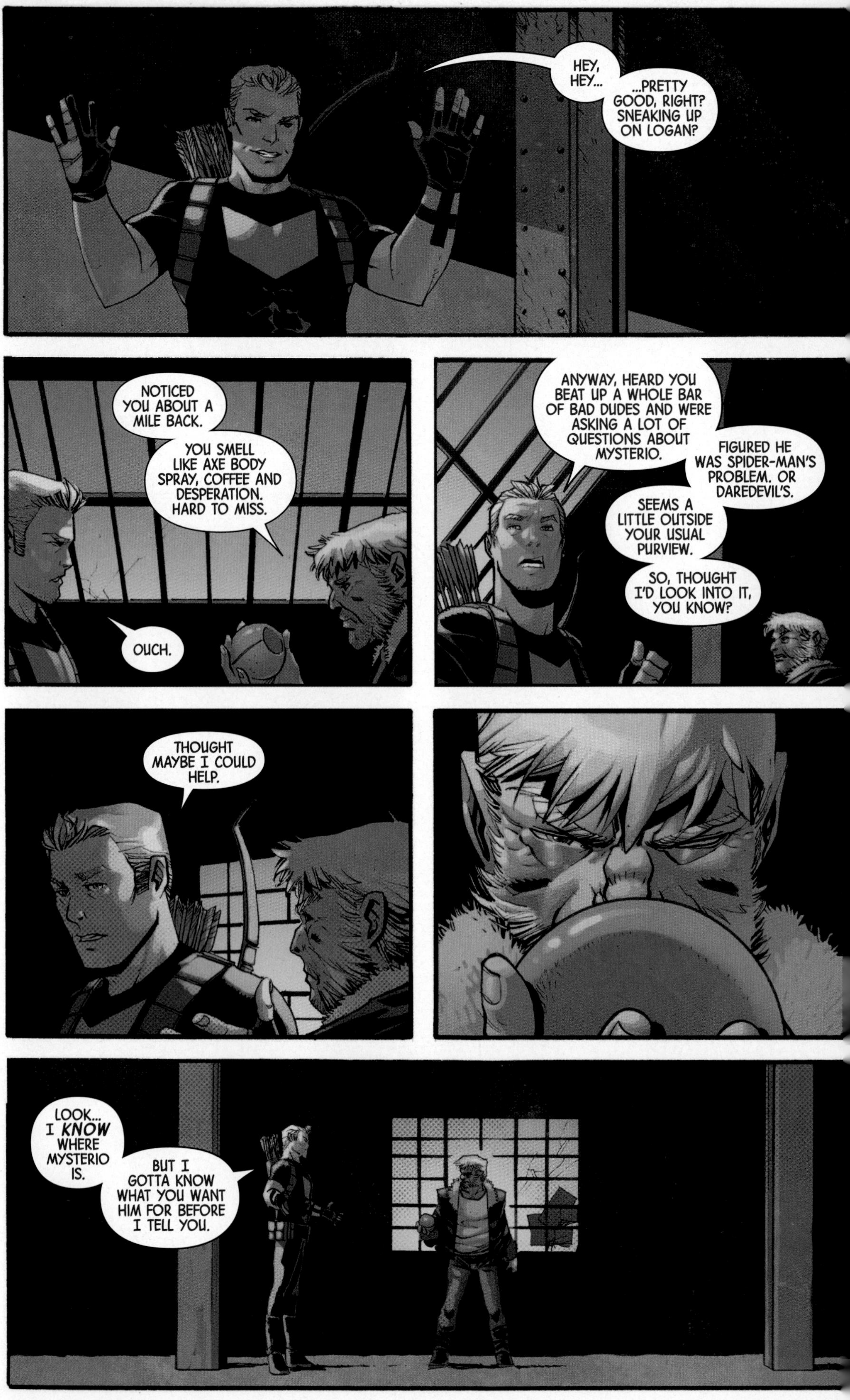
HEY, HEY...
...PRETTY GOOD, RIGHT? SNEAKING UP ON LOGAN?
NOTICED YOU ABOUT A MILE BACK.
YOU SMELL LIKE AXE BODY SPRAY, COFFEE AND DESPERATION. HARD TO MISS.
OUCH.
ANYWAY, HEARD YOU BEAT UP A WHOLE BAR OF BAD DUDES AND WERE ASKING A LOT OF QUESTIONS ABOUT MYSTERIO.
FIGURED HE WAS SPIDER-MAN'S PROBLEM. OR DAREDEVIL'S.
SEEMS A LITTLE OUTSIDE YOUR USUAL PURVIEW.
SO, THOUGHT I'D LOOK INTO IT, YOU KNOW?
THOUGHT MAYBE I COULD HELP.
LOOK... I *KNOW* WHERE MYSTERIO IS.
BUT I GOTTA KNOW WHAT YOU WANT HIM FOR BEFORE I TELL YOU.

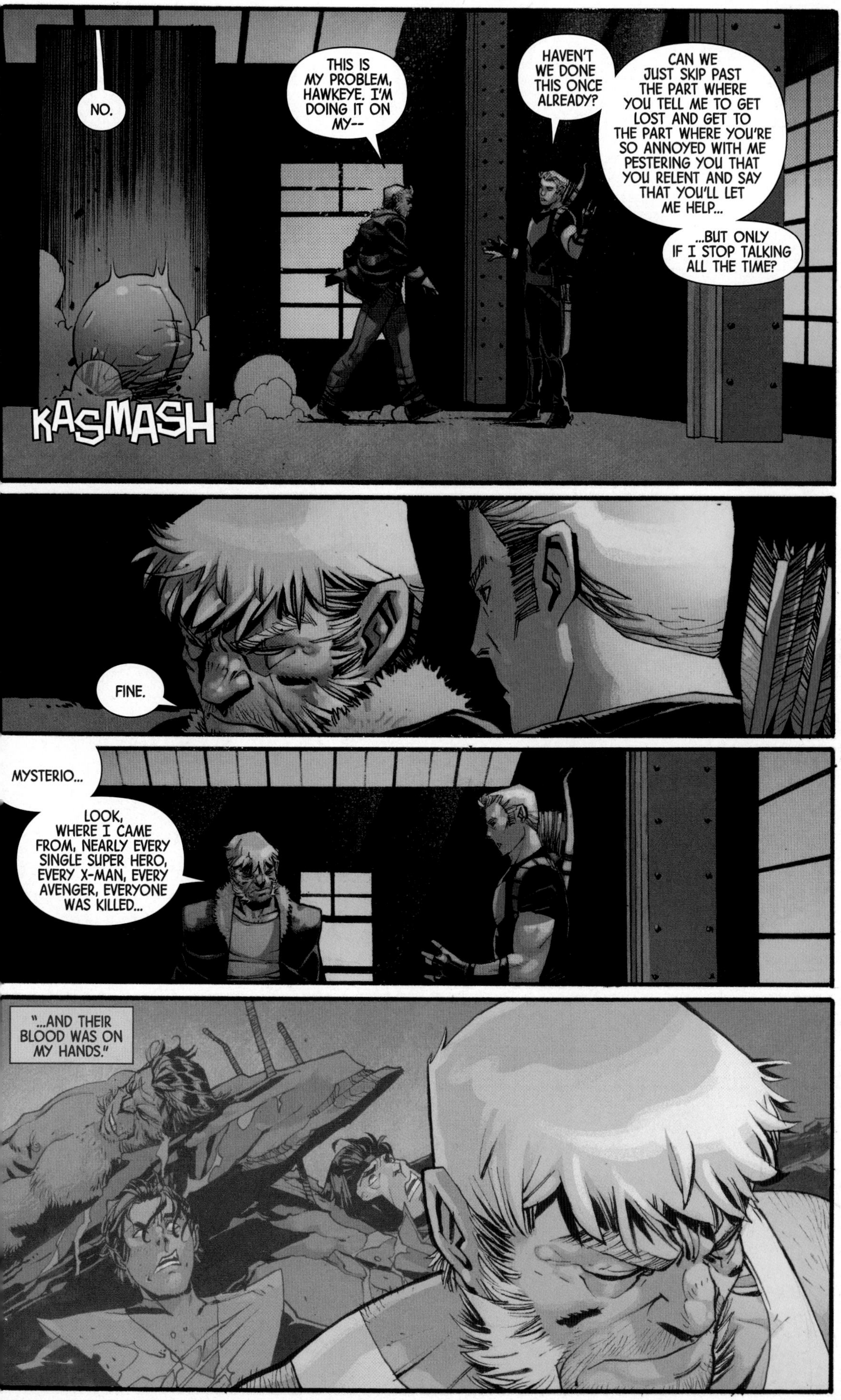

NO.
THIS IS MY PROBLEM, HAWKEYE. I'M DOING IT ON MY--
KASMASH
HAVEN'T WE DONE THIS ONCE ALREADY?
CAN WE JUST SKIP PAST THE PART WHERE YOU TELL ME TO GET LOST AND GET TO THE PART WHERE YOU'RE SO ANNOYED WITH ME PESTERING YOU THAT YOU RELENT AND SAY THAT YOU'LL LET ME HELP...
...BUT ONLY IF I STOP TALKING ALL THE TIME?
FINE.
MYSTERIO...
LOOK, WHERE I CAME FROM, NEARLY EVERY SINGLE SUPER HERO, EVERY X-MAN, EVERY AVENGER, EVERYONE WAS KILLED...
"...AND THEIR BLOOD WAS ON MY HANDS."

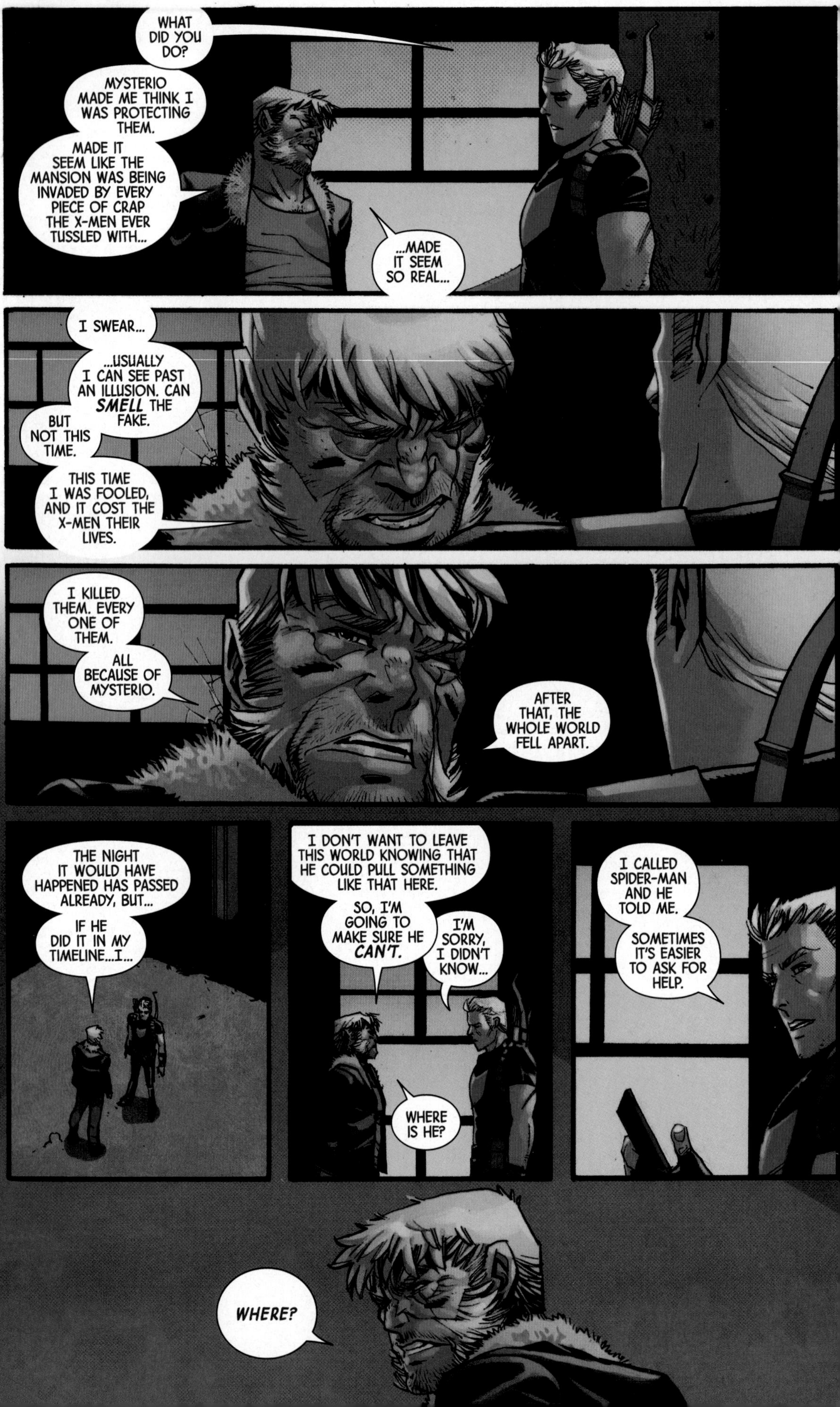
WHAT DID YOU DO?
MYSTERIO MADE ME THINK I WAS PROTECTING THEM.
MADE IT SEEM LIKE THE MANSION WAS BEING INVADED BY EVERY PIECE OF CRAP THE X-MEN EVER TUSSLED WITH...
...MADE IT SEEM SO REAL...
I SWEAR...
...USUALLY I CAN SEE PAST AN ILLUSION. CAN *SMELL* THE FAKE.
BUT NOT THIS TIME.
THIS TIME I WAS FOOLED, AND IT COST THE X-MEN THEIR LIVES.
I KILLED THEM. EVERY ONE OF THEM.
ALL BECAUSE OF MYSTERIO.
AFTER THAT, THE WHOLE WORLD FELL APART.
THE NIGHT IT WOULD HAVE HAPPENED HAS PASSED ALREADY, BUT...
IF HE DID IT IN MY TIMELINE...I...
I DON'T WANT TO LEAVE THIS WORLD KNOWING THAT HE COULD PULL SOMETHING LIKE THAT HERE.
SO, I'M GOING TO MAKE SURE HE *CAN'T.*
I'M SORRY, I DIDN'T KNOW...
WHERE IS HE?
I CALLED SPIDER-MAN AND HE TOLD ME.
SOMETIMES IT'S EASIER TO ASK FOR HELP.
WHERE?

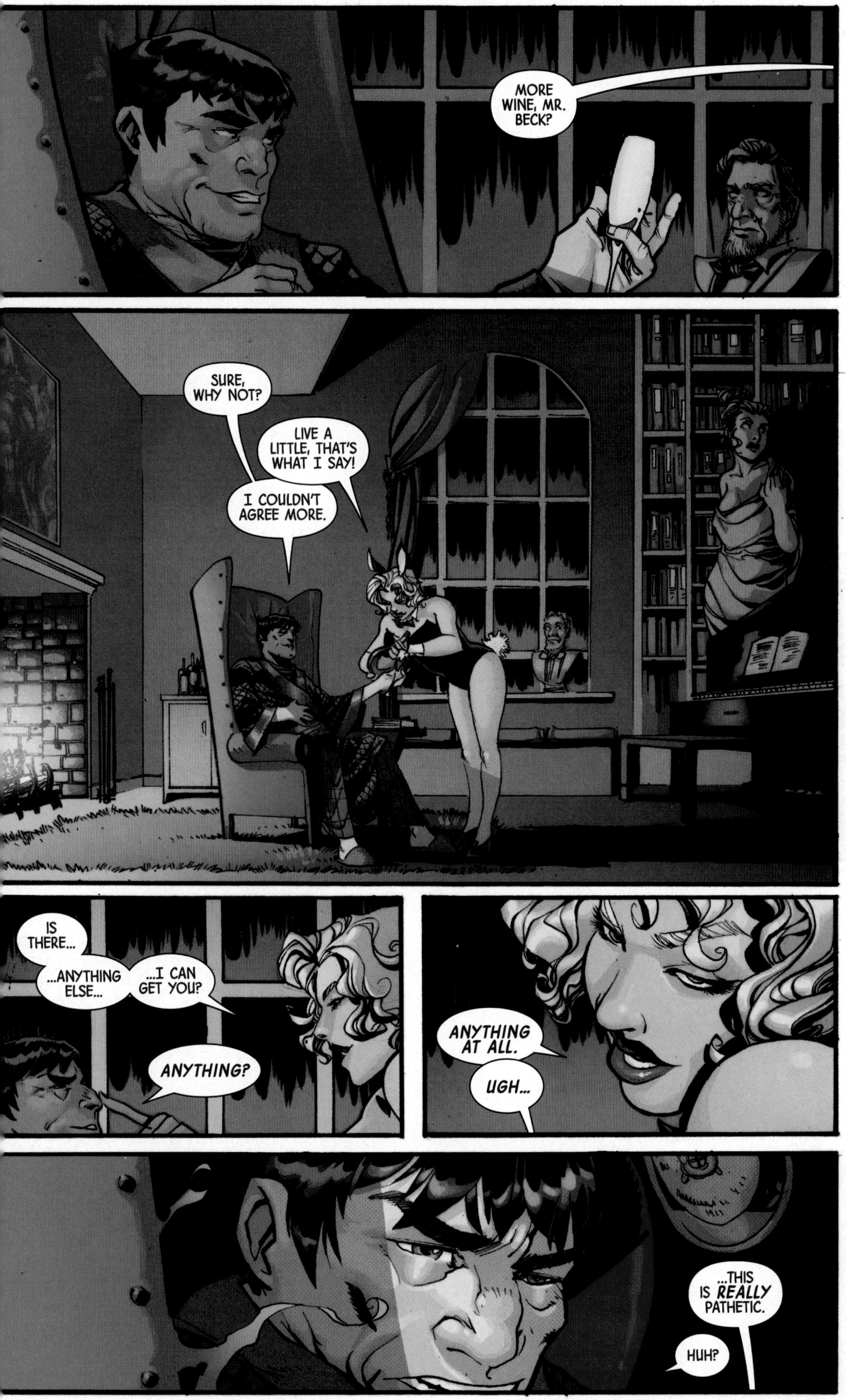
MORE WINE, MR. BECK?
SURE, WHY NOT?
LIVE A LITTLE, THAT'S WHAT I SAY!
I COULDN'T AGREE MORE.
IS THERE...
...ANYTHING ELSE...
...I CAN GET YOU?
ANYTHING?
ANYTHING AT ALL.
UGH...
...THIS IS REALLY PATHETIC.
HUH?

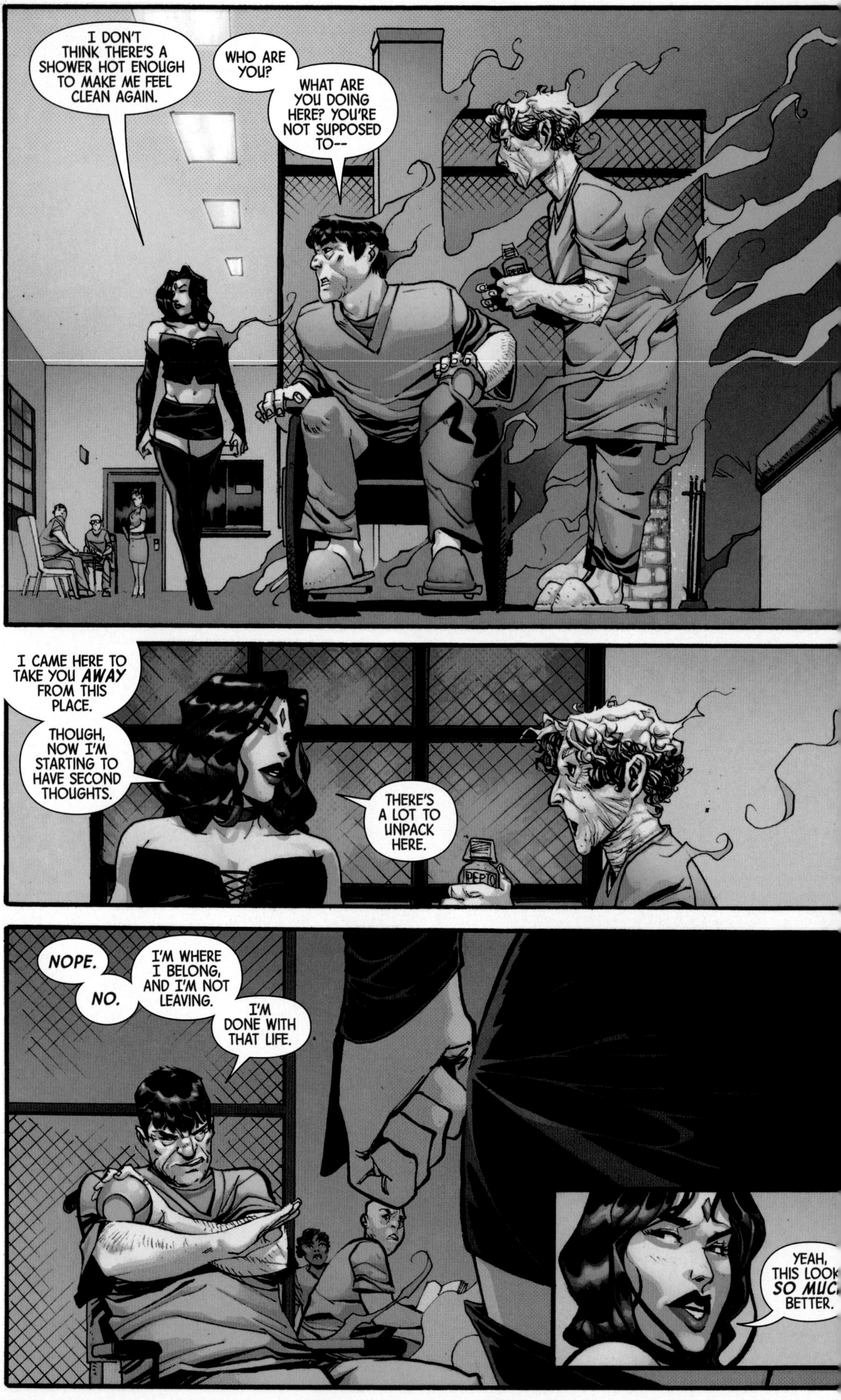
I DON'T THINK THERE'S A SHOWER HOT ENOUGH TO MAKE ME FEEL CLEAN AGAIN.
WHO ARE YOU?
WHAT ARE YOU DOING HERE? YOU'RE NOT SUPPOSED TO--
I CAME HERE TO TAKE YOU AWAY FROM THIS PLACE.
THOUGH, NOW I'M STARTING TO HAVE SECOND THOUGHTS.
THERE'S A LOT TO UNPACK HERE.
PEPTO
NOPE.
NO.
I'M WHERE I BELONG, AND I'M NOT LEAVING.
I'M DONE WITH THAT LIFE.
YEAH, THIS LOOK SO MUC BETTER.

LOOK, LADY, I DON'T KNOW WHO YOU ARE--

--AND I DON'T CARE.

MISS SINISTER.

I'M TIRED OF GETTING MY ASS KICKED OUT THERE.

TIRED OF SPIDER-MAN AND DAREDEVIL TAKING TURNS BEATING ON ME.

DEADPOOL HUMILIATED ME. DROVE OVER ME WITH A DUNE BUGGY!

EVEN THOSE LAME SPIDER-MAN KNOCKOFFS IN LAS VEGAS BESTED ME.

I CAN'T TAKE IT ANYMORE.

ALL I WANT IS TO BE LEFT ALONE.

IN HERE, I'M SAFE.

IN HERE, I HAVE ROUTINE.

IN HERE, THERE ARE NO SPIDER-MEN OR DAREDEVILS OR DEADPOOLS.

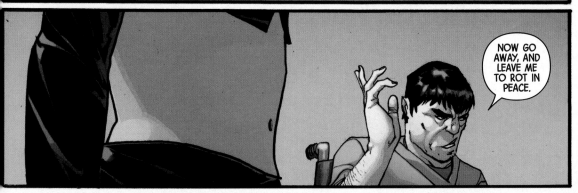

NOW GO AWAY, AND LEAVE ME TO ROT IN PEACE.

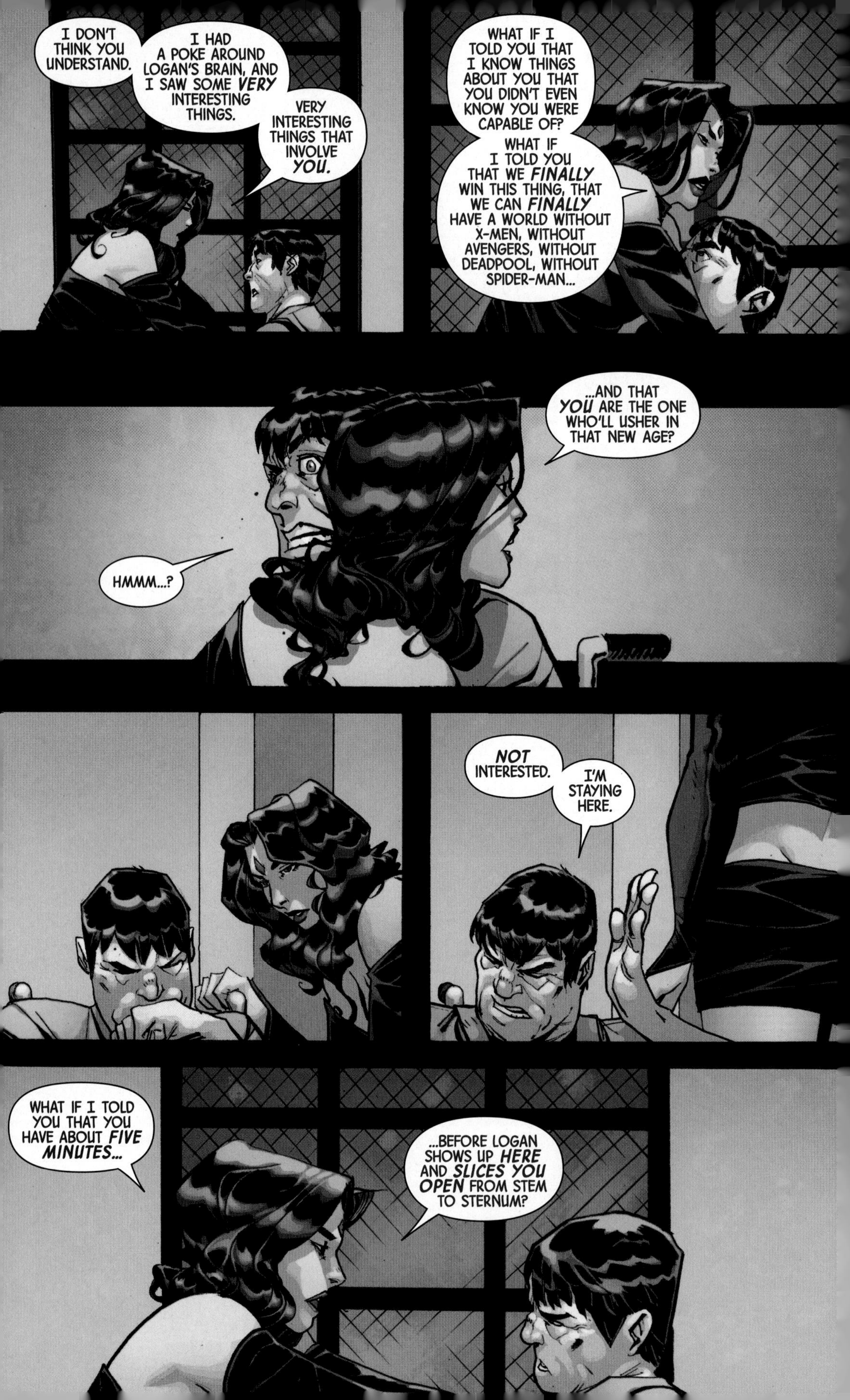
I DON'T THINK YOU UNDERSTAND.
I HAD A POKE AROUND LOGAN'S BRAIN, AND I SAW SOME VERY INTERESTING THINGS.
VERY INTERESTING THINGS THAT INVOLVE YOU.
WHAT IF I TOLD YOU THAT I KNOW THINGS ABOUT YOU THAT YOU DIDN'T EVEN KNOW YOU WERE CAPABLE OF?
WHAT IF I TOLD YOU THAT WE FINALLY WIN THIS THING, THAT WE CAN FINALLY HAVE A WORLD WITHOUT X-MEN, WITHOUT AVENGERS, WITHOUT DEADPOOL, WITHOUT SPIDER-MAN...
...AND THAT YOU ARE THE ONE WHO'LL USHER IN THAT NEW AGE?
HMMM...?
NOT INTERESTED.
I'M STAYING HERE.
WHAT IF I TOLD YOU THAT YOU HAVE ABOUT FIVE MINUTES...
...BEFORE LOGAN SHOWS UP HERE AND SLICES YOU OPEN FROM STEM TO STERNUM?

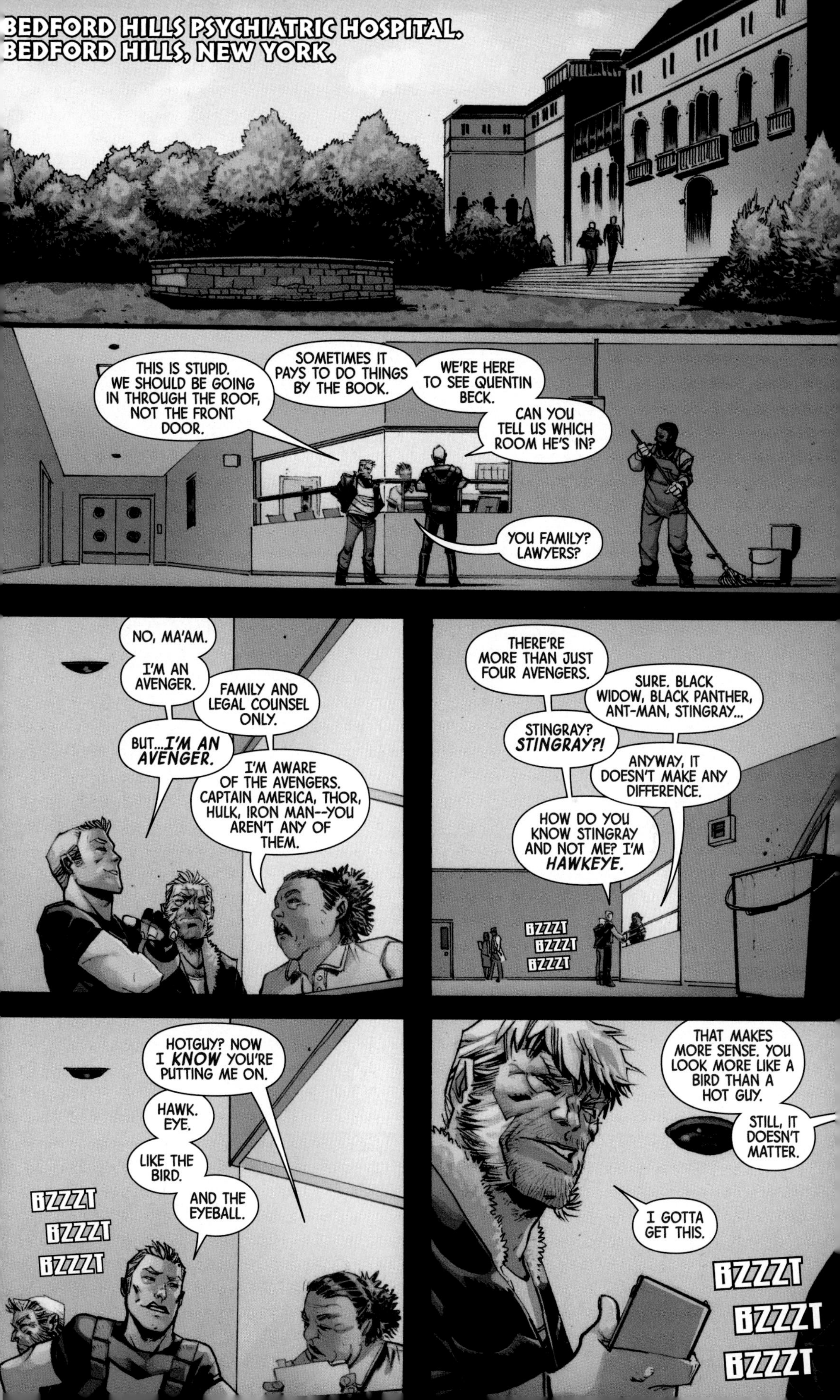
BEDFORD HILLS PSYCHIATRIC HOSPITAL. BEDFORD HILLS, NEW YORK.
THIS IS STUPID. WE SHOULD BE GOING IN THROUGH THE ROOF, NOT THE FRONT DOOR.
SOMETIMES IT PAYS TO DO THINGS BY THE BOOK.
WE'RE HERE TO SEE QUENTIN BECK.
CAN YOU TELL US WHICH ROOM HE'S IN?
YOU FAMILY? LAWYERS?
NO, MA'AM.
I'M AN AVENGER.
FAMILY AND LEGAL COUNSEL ONLY.
BUT...*I'M AN AVENGER.*
I'M AWARE OF THE AVENGERS. CAPTAIN AMERICA, THOR, HULK, IRON MAN--YOU AREN'T ANY OF THEM.
THERE'RE MORE THAN JUST FOUR AVENGERS.
SURE. BLACK WIDOW, BLACK PANTHER, ANT-MAN, STINGRAY...
STINGRAY? *STINGRAY?!*
ANYWAY, IT DOESN'T MAKE ANY DIFFERENCE.
HOW DO YOU KNOW STINGRAY AND NOT ME? I'M *HAWKEYE.*
BZZZT BZZZT BZZZT
HOTGUY? NOW I *KNOW* YOU'RE PUTTING ME ON.
HAWK. EYE.
LIKE THE BIRD.
AND THE EYEBALL.
BZZZT BZZZT BZZZT
THAT MAKES MORE SENSE. YOU LOOK MORE LIKE A BIRD THAN A HOT GUY.
STILL, IT DOESN'T MATTER.
I GOTTA GET THIS.
BZZZT BZZZT BZZZT

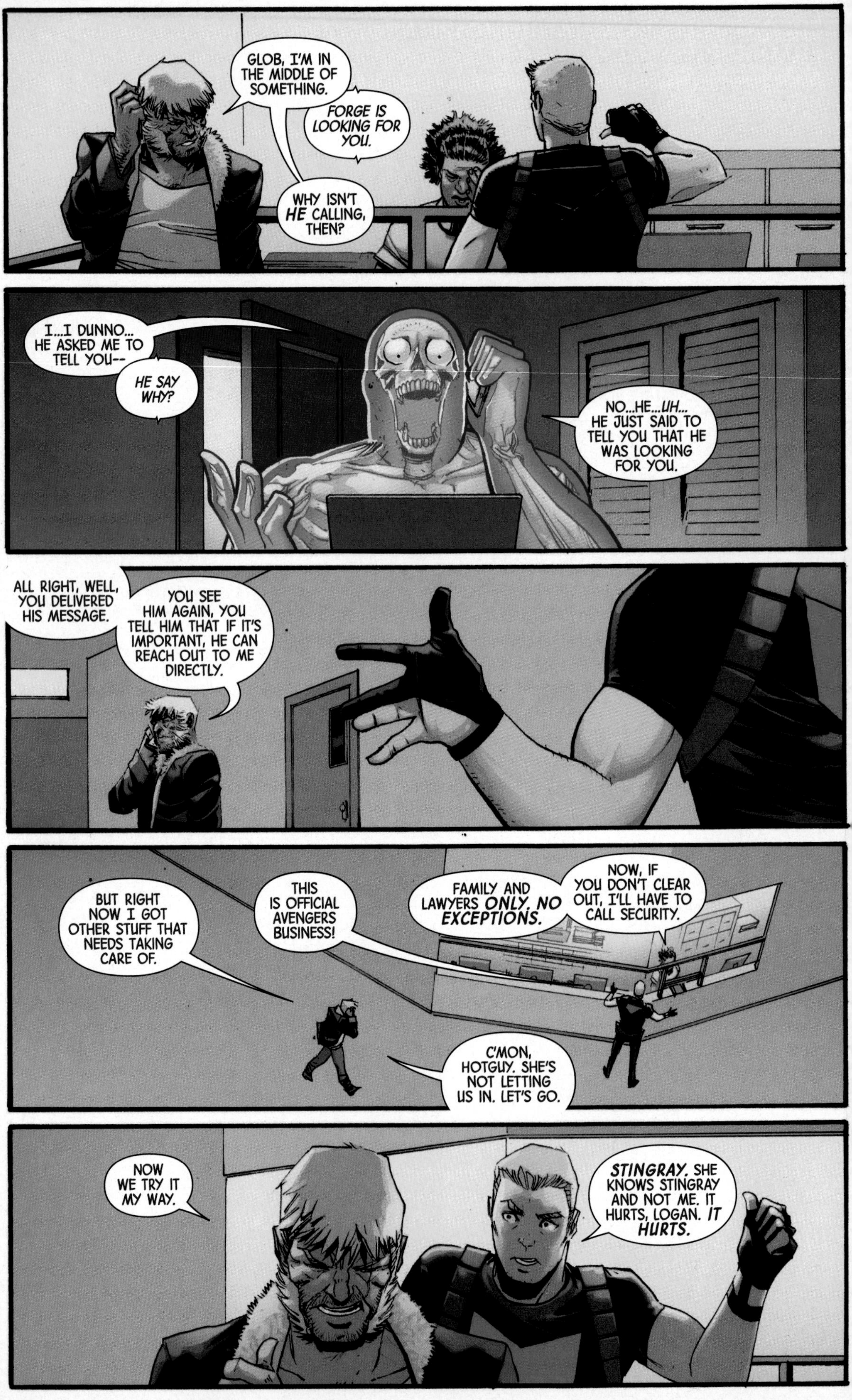
GLOB, I'M IN THE MIDDLE OF SOMETHING.
FORGE IS LOOKING FOR YOU.
WHY ISN'T HE CALLING, THEN?
I...I DUNNO... HE ASKED ME TO TELL YOU--
HE SAY WHY?
NO...HE...UH... HE JUST SAID TO TELL YOU THAT HE WAS LOOKING FOR YOU.
ALL RIGHT, WELL, YOU DELIVERED HIS MESSAGE.
YOU SEE HIM AGAIN, YOU TELL HIM THAT IF IT'S IMPORTANT, HE CAN REACH OUT TO ME DIRECTLY.
BUT RIGHT NOW I GOT OTHER STUFF THAT NEEDS TAKING CARE OF.
THIS IS OFFICIAL AVENGERS BUSINESS!
FAMILY AND LAWYERS ONLY. NO EXCEPTIONS.
NOW, IF YOU DON'T CLEAR OUT, I'LL HAVE TO CALL SECURITY.
C'MON, HOTGUY. SHE'S NOT LETTING US IN. LET'S GO.
NOW WE TRY IT MY WAY.
STINGRAY. SHE KNOWS STINGRAY AND NOT ME. IT HURTS, LOGAN. IT HURTS.

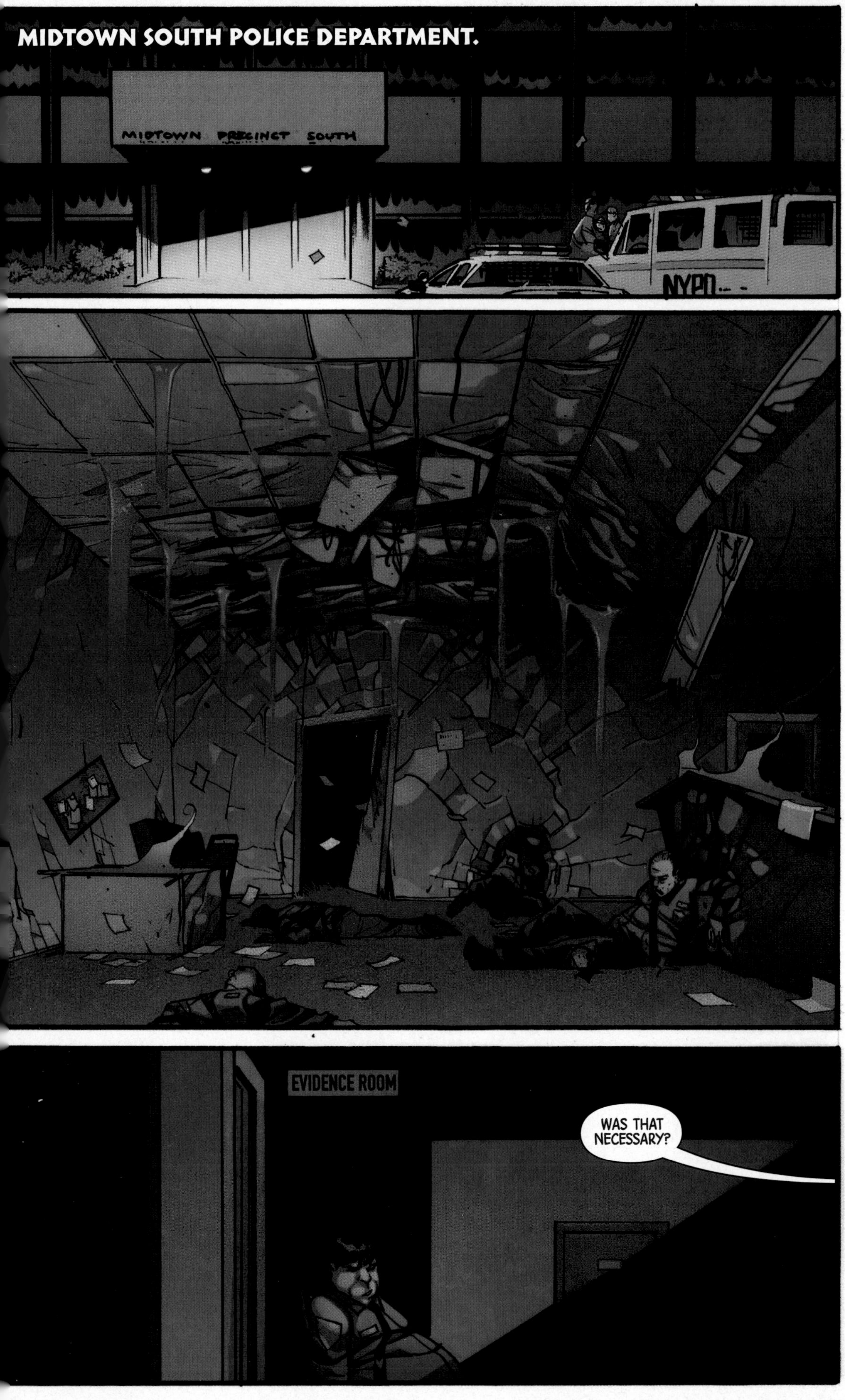
MIDTOWN SOUTH POLICE DEPARTMENT.
MIDTOWN PRECINCT SOUTH
NYPD
EVIDENCE ROOM
WAS THAT NECESSARY?

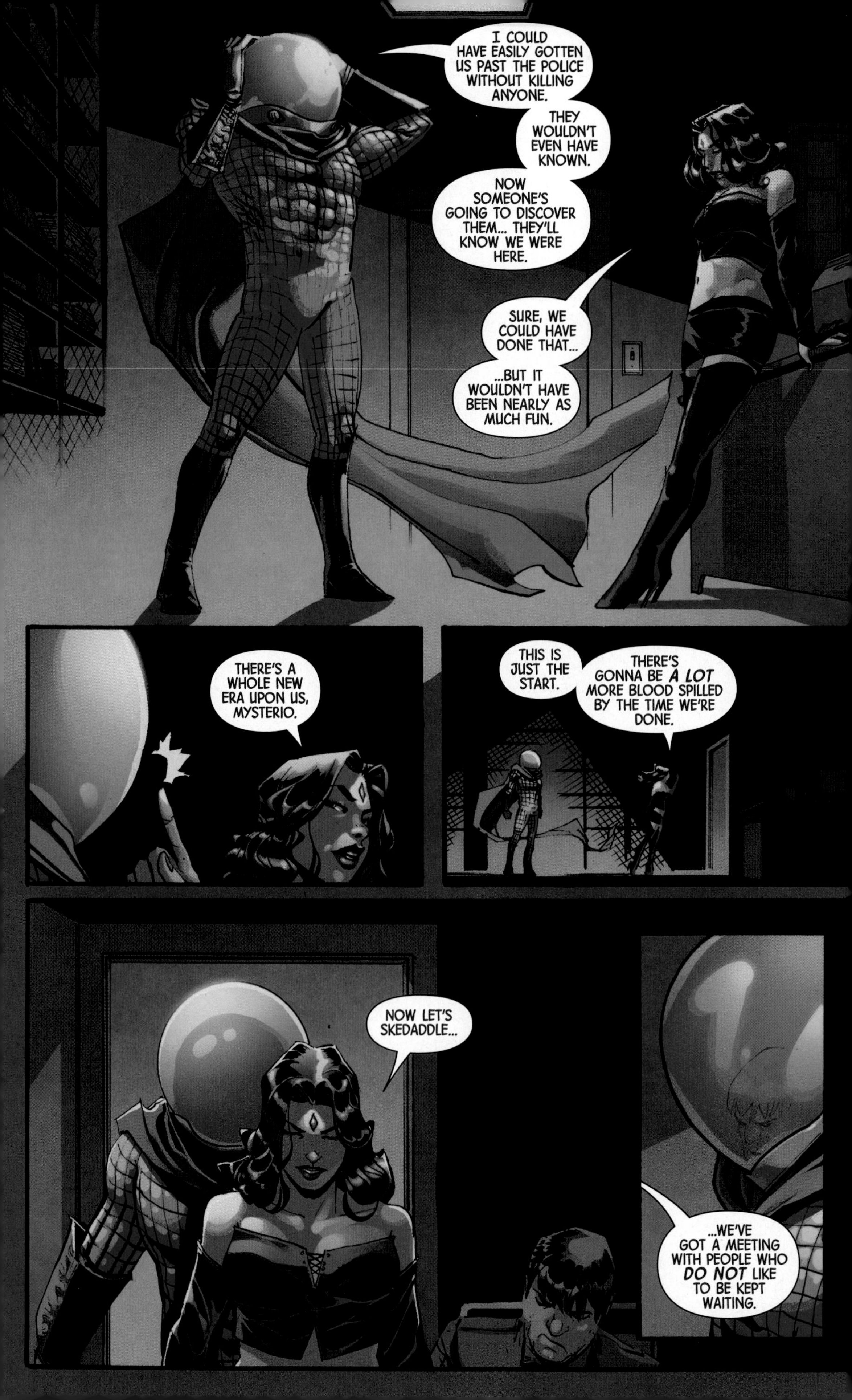
I COULD HAVE EASILY GOTTEN US PAST THE POLICE WITHOUT KILLING ANYONE.
THEY WOULDN'T EVEN HAVE KNOWN.
NOW SOMEONE'S GOING TO DISCOVER THEM... THEY'LL KNOW WE WERE HERE.
SURE, WE COULD HAVE DONE THAT...
...BUT IT WOULDN'T HAVE BEEN NEARLY AS MUCH FUN.
THERE'S A WHOLE NEW ERA UPON US, MYSTERIO.
THIS IS JUST THE START.
THERE'S GONNA BE *A LOT* MORE BLOOD SPILLED BY THE TIME WE'RE DONE.
NOW LET'S SKEDADDLE...
...WE'VE GOT A MEETING WITH PEOPLE WHO **DO NOT** LIKE TO BE KEPT WAITING.

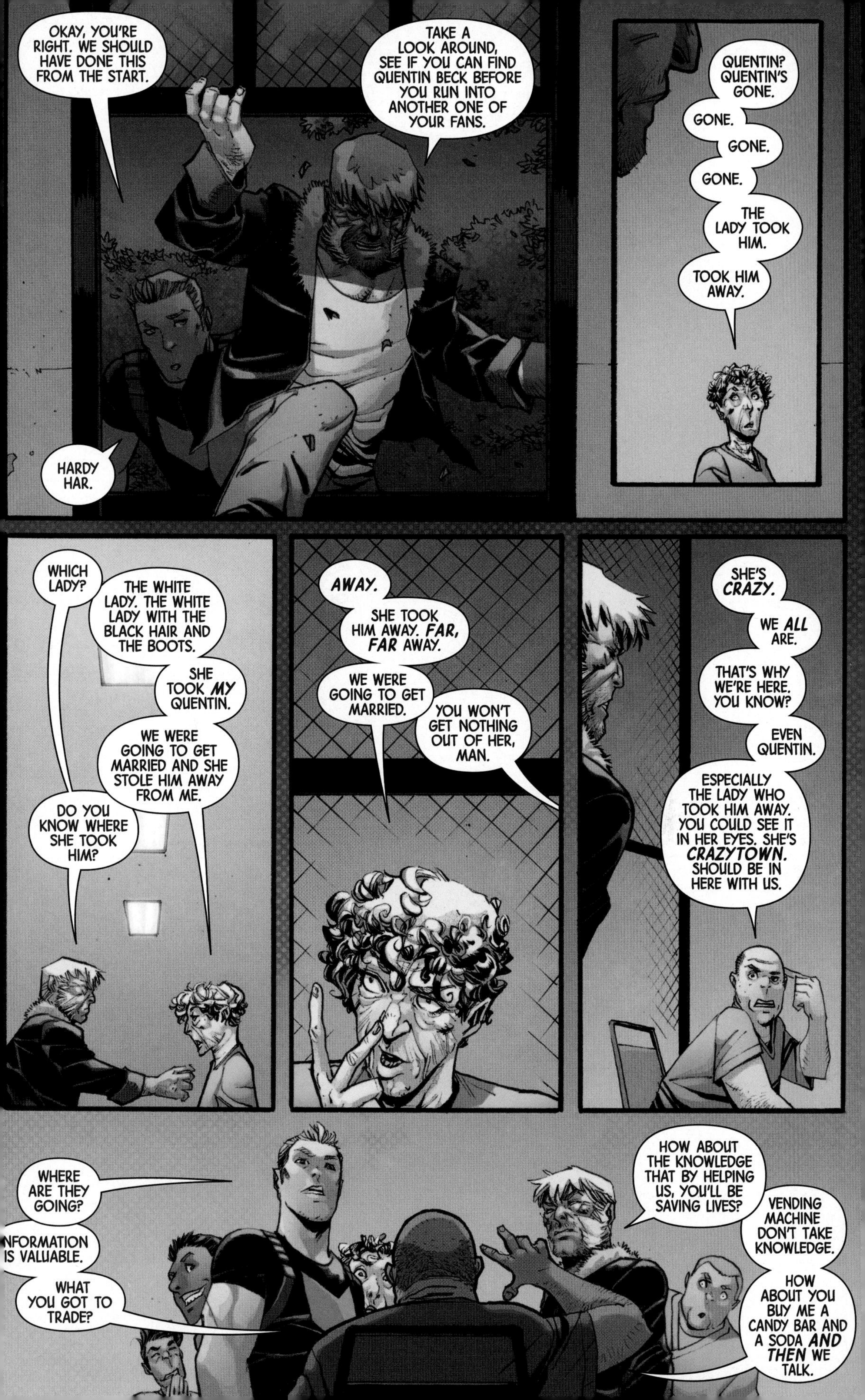
OKAY, YOU'RE RIGHT. WE SHOULD HAVE DONE THIS FROM THE START.
TAKE A LOOK AROUND, SEE IF YOU CAN FIND QUENTIN BECK BEFORE YOU RUN INTO ANOTHER ONE OF YOUR FANS.
HARDY HAR.
QUENTIN? QUENTIN'S GONE.
GONE.
GONE.
GONE.
THE LADY TOOK HIM.
TOOK HIM AWAY.
WHICH LADY?
THE WHITE LADY. THE WHITE LADY WITH THE BLACK HAIR AND THE BOOTS.
SHE TOOK MY QUENTIN.
WE WERE GOING TO GET MARRIED AND SHE STOLE HIM AWAY FROM ME.
DO YOU KNOW WHERE SHE TOOK HIM?
AWAY.
SHE TOOK HIM AWAY. FAR, FAR AWAY.
WE WERE GOING TO GET MARRIED.
YOU WON'T GET NOTHING OUT OF HER, MAN.
SHE'S CRAZY.
WE ALL ARE.
THAT'S WHY WE'RE HERE. YOU KNOW?
EVEN QUENTIN.
ESPECIALLY THE LADY WHO TOOK HIM AWAY. YOU COULD SEE IT IN HER EYES. SHE'S CRAZYTOWN. SHOULD BE IN HERE WITH US.
WHERE ARE THEY GOING?
NFORMATION IS VALUABLE.
WHAT YOU GOT TO TRADE?
HOW ABOUT THE KNOWLEDGE THAT BY HELPING US, YOU'LL BE SAVING LIVES?
VENDING MACHINE DON'T TAKE KNOWLEDGE.
HOW ABOUT YOU BUY ME A CANDY BAR AND A SODA AND THEN WE TALK.

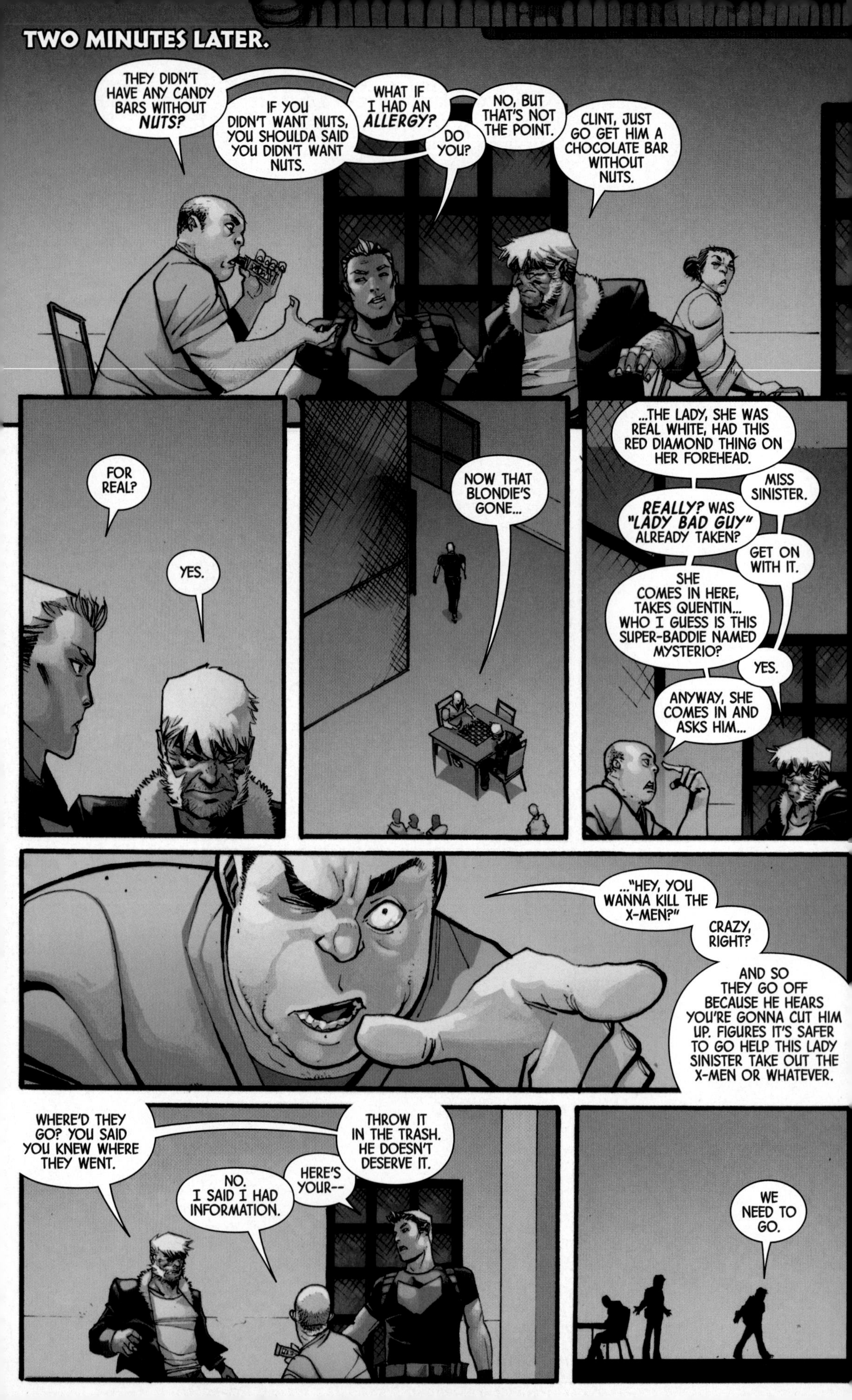
TWO MINUTES LATER.
THEY DIDN'T HAVE ANY CANDY BARS WITHOUT NUTS?
IF YOU DIDN'T WANT NUTS, YOU SHOULDA SAID YOU DIDN'T WANT NUTS.
WHAT IF I HAD AN ALLERGY?
DO YOU?
NO, BUT THAT'S NOT THE POINT.
CLINT, JUST GO GET HIM A CHOCOLATE BAR WITHOUT NUTS.
FOR REAL?
YES.
NOW THAT BLONDIE'S GONE...
...THE LADY, SHE WAS REAL WHITE, HAD THIS RED DIAMOND THING ON HER FOREHEAD.
MISS SINISTER.
REALLY? WAS "LADY BAD GUY" ALREADY TAKEN?
GET ON WITH IT.
SHE COMES IN HERE, TAKES QUENTIN... WHO I GUESS IS THIS SUPER-BADDIE NAMED MYSTERIO?
YES.
ANYWAY, SHE COMES IN AND ASKS HIM...
..."HEY, YOU WANNA KILL THE X-MEN?"
CRAZY, RIGHT?
AND SO THEY GO OFF BECAUSE HE HEARS YOU'RE GONNA CUT HIM UP. FIGURES IT'S SAFER TO GO HELP THIS LADY SINISTER TAKE OUT THE X-MEN OR WHATEVER.
WHERE'D THEY GO? YOU SAID YOU KNEW WHERE THEY WENT.
NO. I SAID I HAD INFORMATION.
HERE'S YOUR--
THROW IT IN THE TRASH. HE DOESN'T DESERVE IT.
WE NEED TO GO.

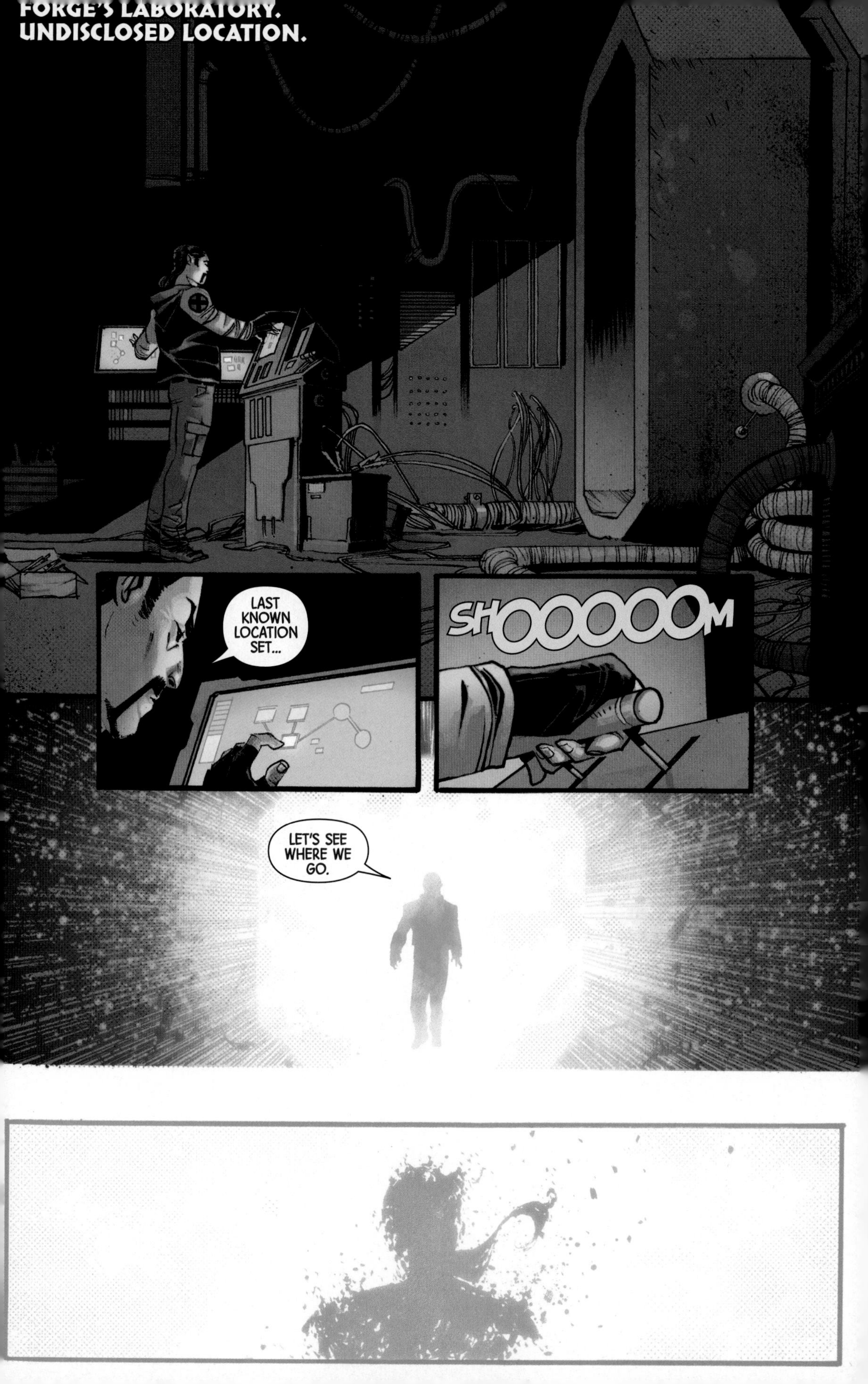
FORGE'S LABORATORY. UNDISCLOSED LOCATION.
LAST KNOWN LOCATION SET...
SHOOOOOOM
LET'S SEE WHERE WE GO.

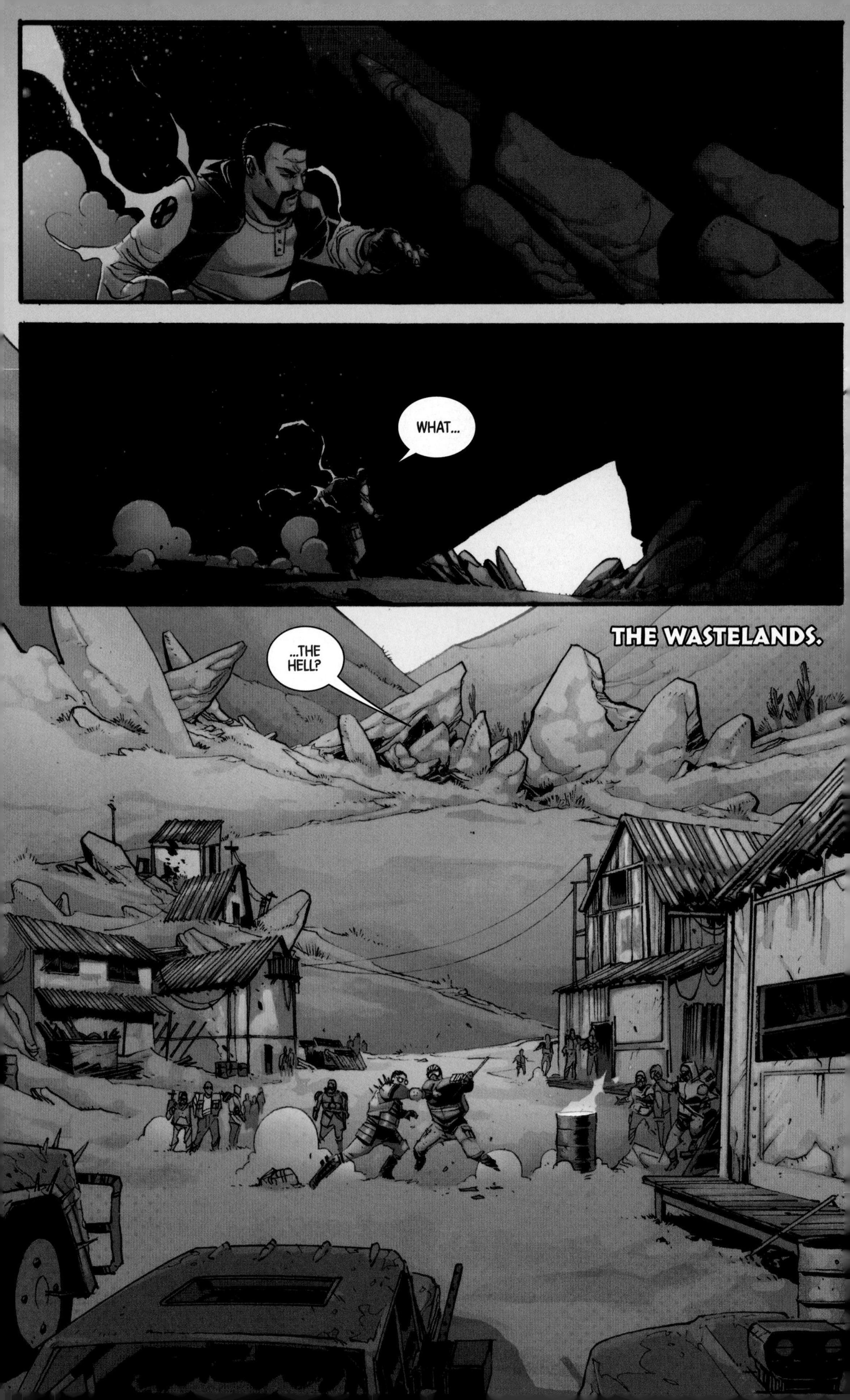
WHAT...
THE WASTELANDS.
...THE HELL?

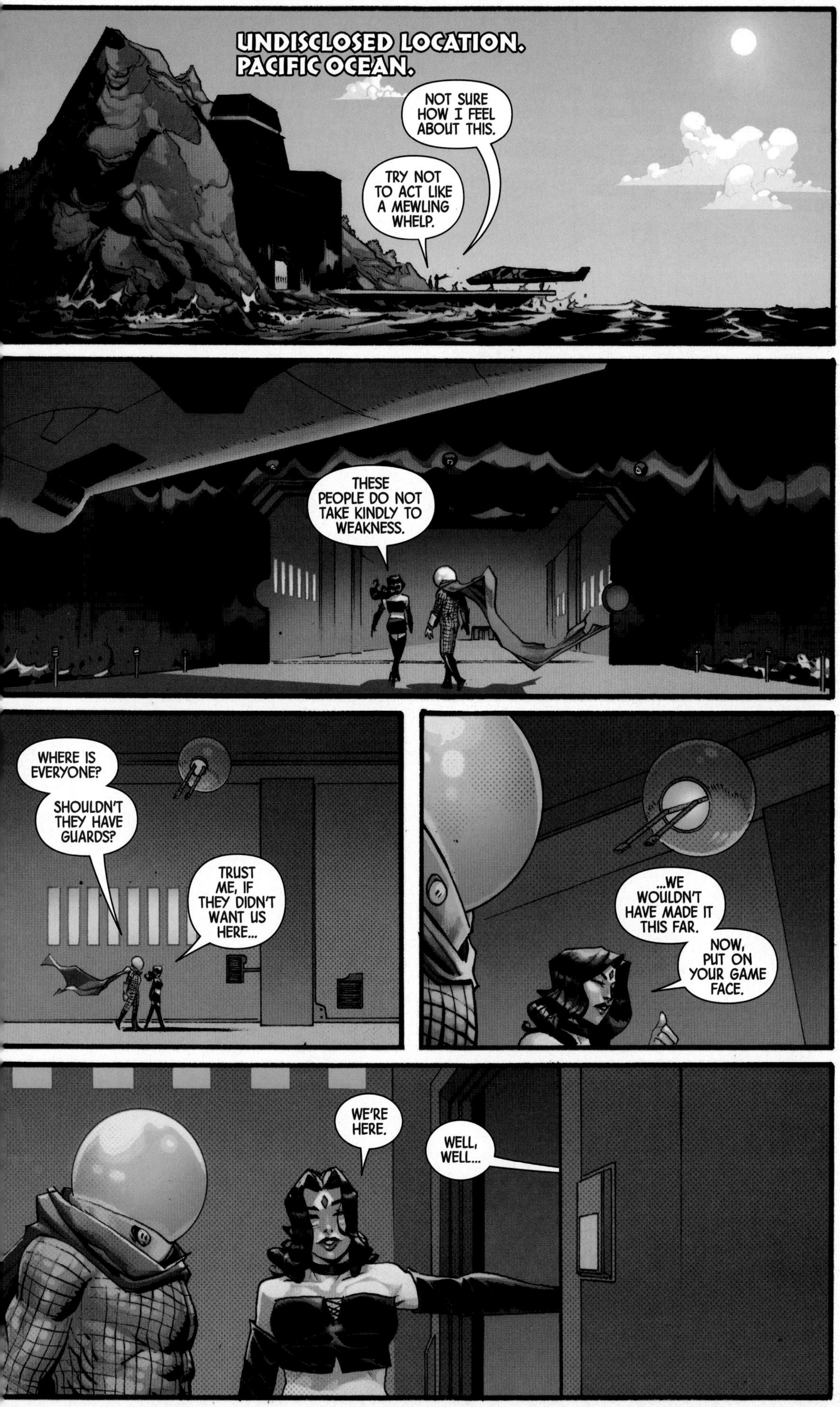
UNDISCLOSED LOCATION. PACIFIC OCEAN.
NOT SURE HOW I FEEL ABOUT THIS.
TRY NOT TO ACT LIKE A MEWLING WHELP.
THESE PEOPLE DO NOT TAKE KINDLY TO WEAKNESS.
WHERE IS EVERYONE?
SHOULDN'T THEY HAVE GUARDS?
TRUST ME, IF THEY DIDN'T WANT US HERE...
...WE WOULDN'T HAVE MADE IT THIS FAR.
NOW, PUT ON YOUR GAME FACE.
WE'RE HERE.
WELL, WELL...

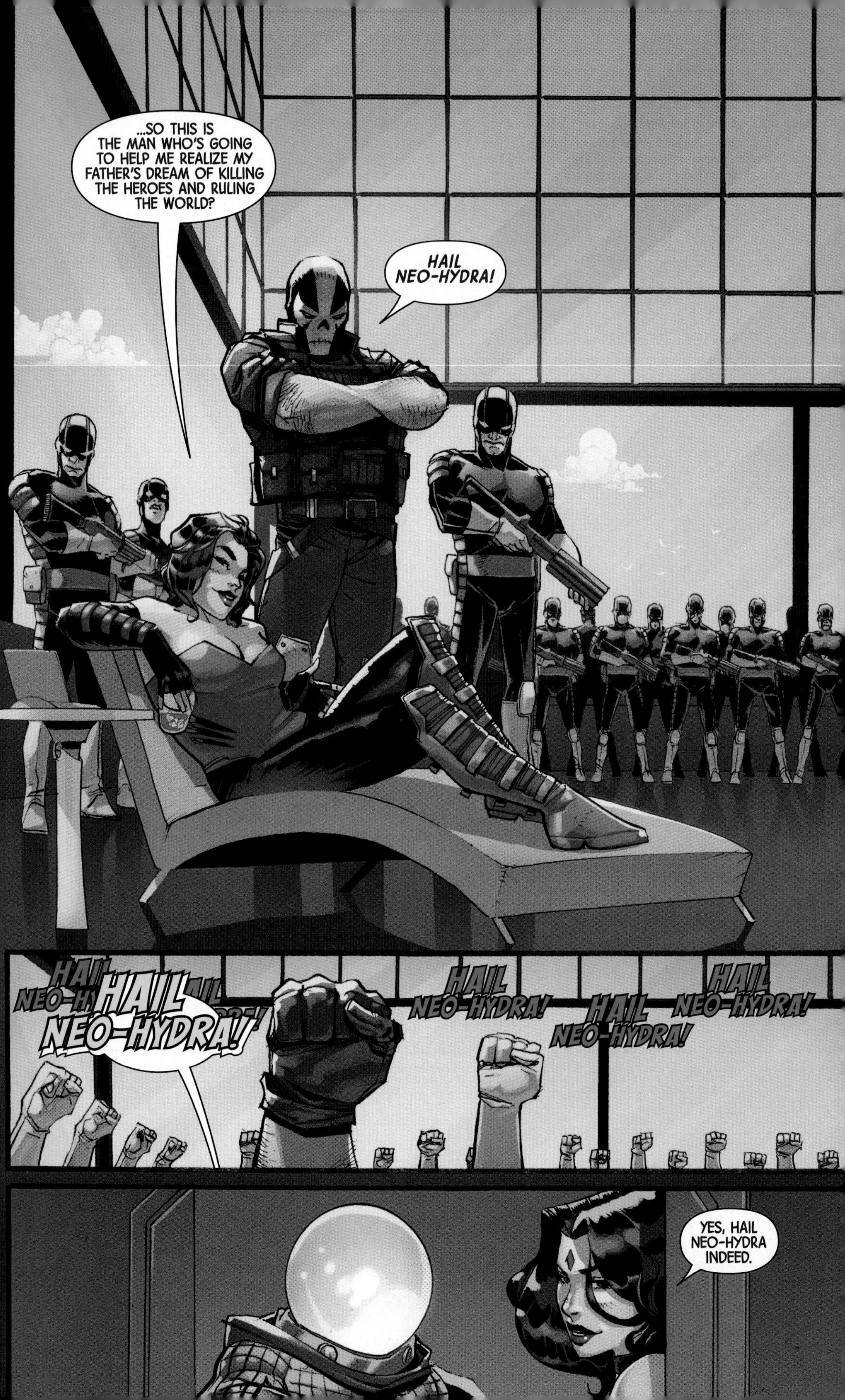
...SO THIS IS THE MAN WHO'S GOING TO HELP ME REALIZE MY FATHER'S DREAM OF KILLING THE HEROES AND RULING THE WORLD?
HAIL NEO-HYDRA!
HAIL NEO-HYDRA!
HAIL NEO-HYDRA!
HAIL NEO-HYDRA!
HAIL NEO-HYDRA!
YES, HAIL NEO-HYDRA INDEED.

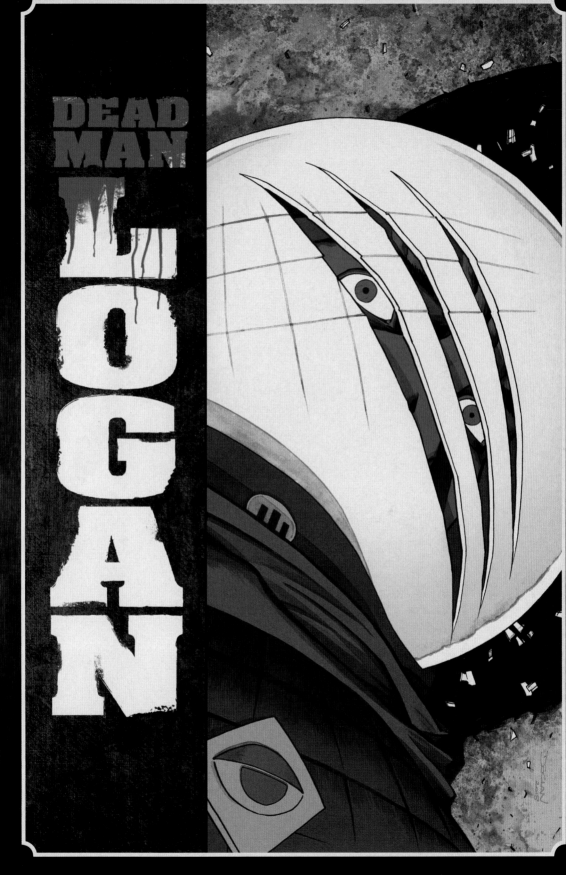

DEAD MAN LOGAN

2

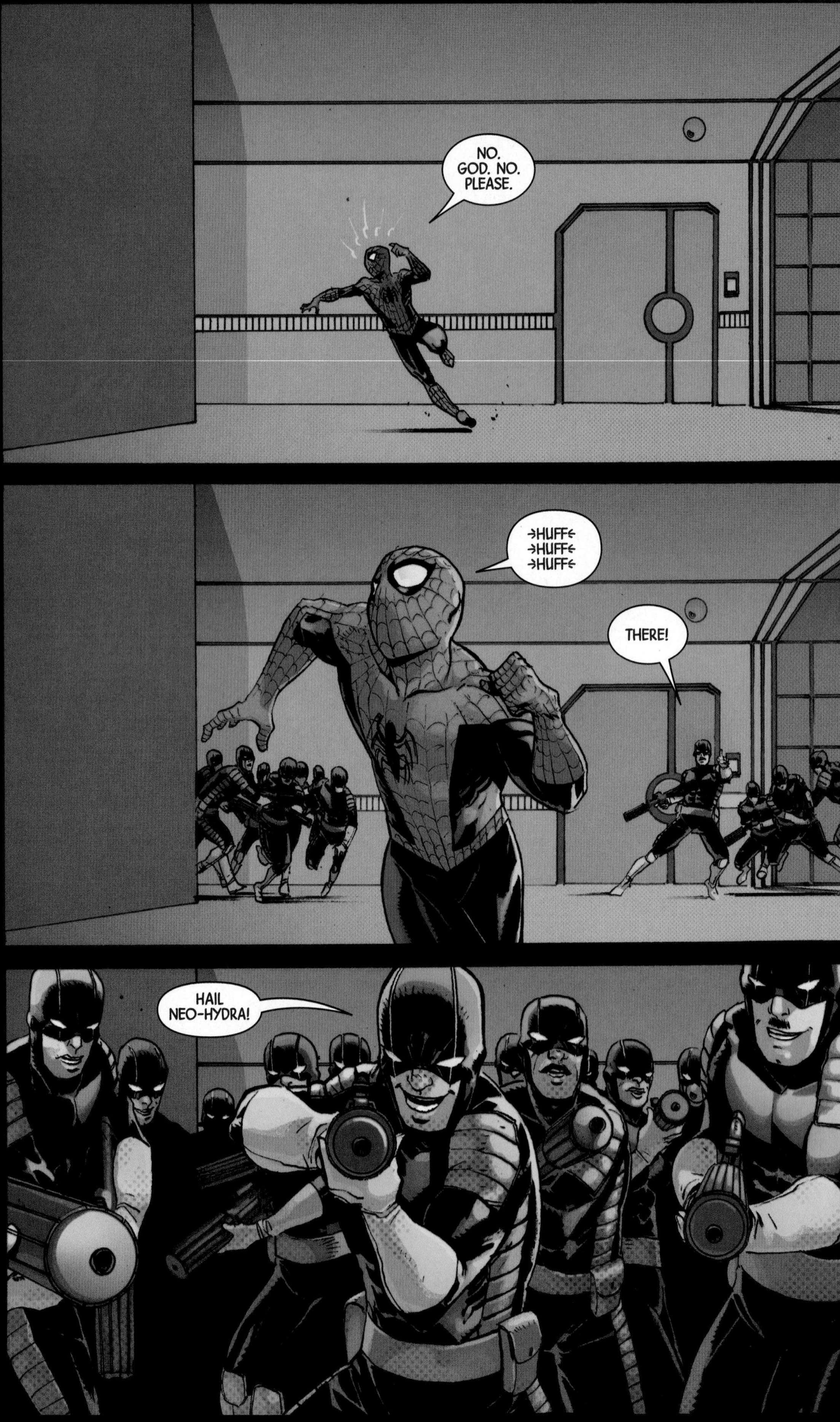
NO.
GOD. NO.
PLEASE.
HUFF
HUFF
HUFF
THERE!
HAIL
NEO-HYDRA!

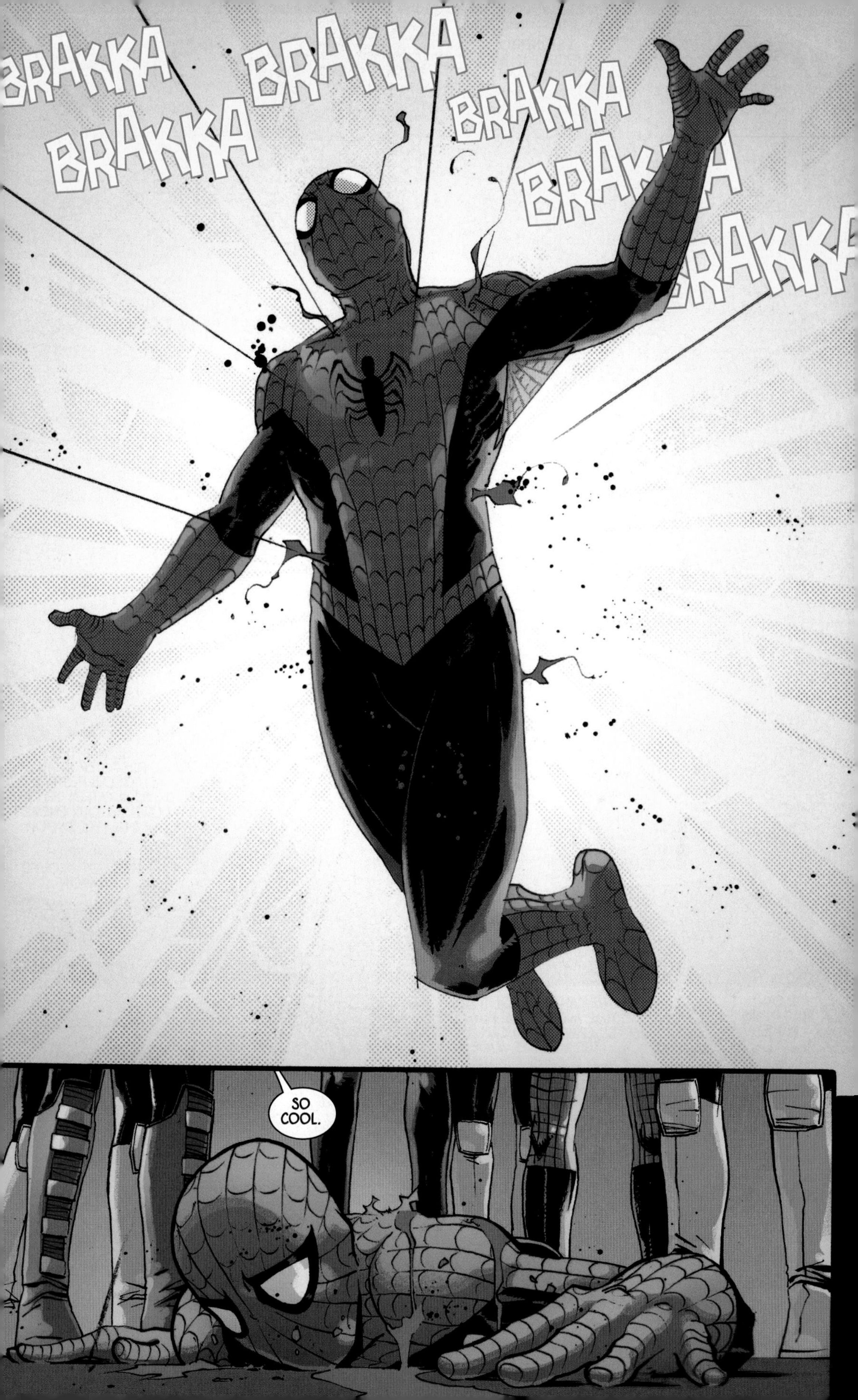
BRAKKA
BRAKKA
BRAKKA
BRAKKA
BRAKKA
BRAKKA
BRAKKA
SO COOL.

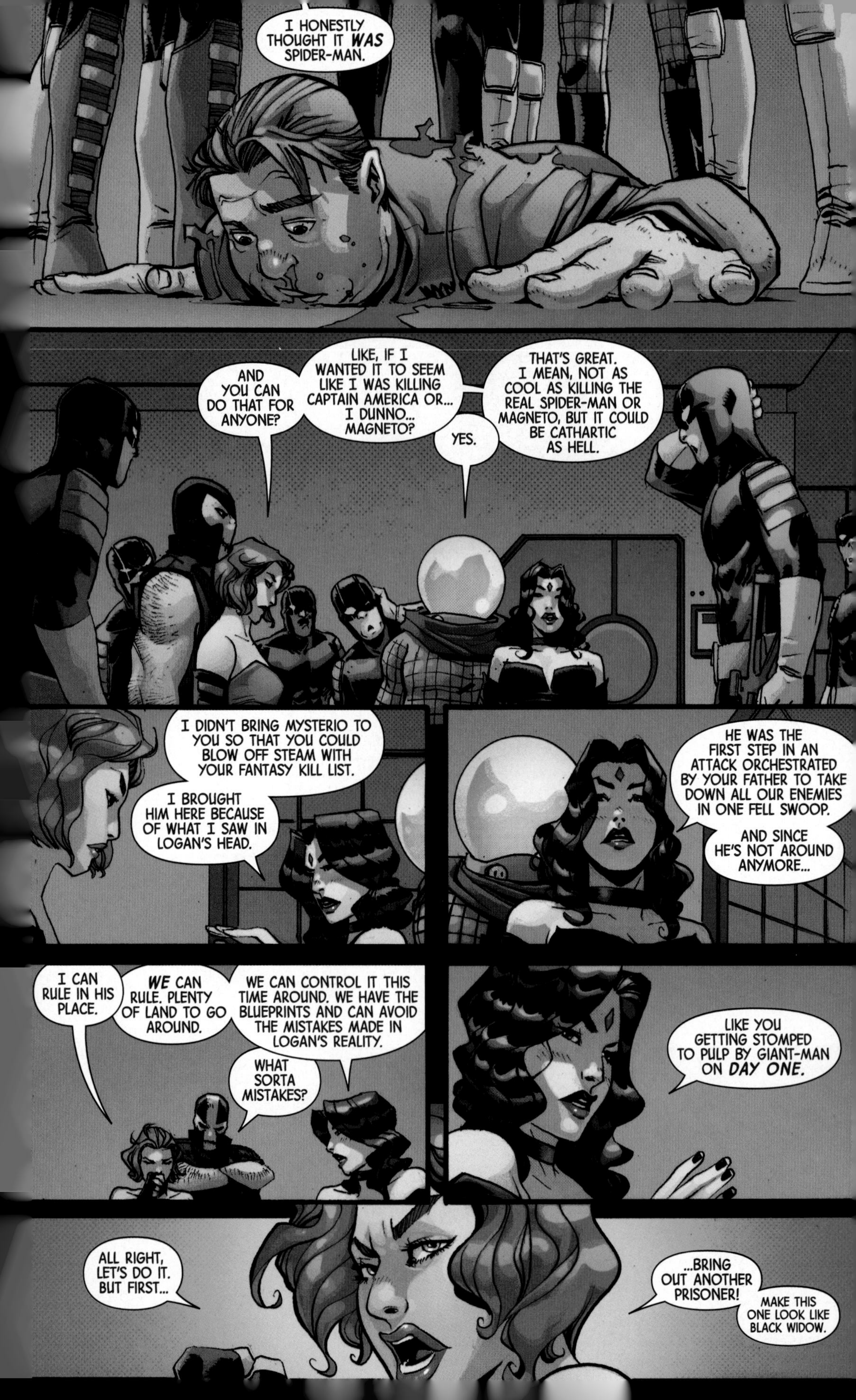
I HONESTLY THOUGHT IT WAS SPIDER-MAN.
AND YOU CAN DO THAT FOR ANYONE?
LIKE, IF I WANTED IT TO SEEM LIKE I WAS KILLING CAPTAIN AMERICA OR... I DUNNO... MAGNETO?
YES.
THAT'S GREAT. I MEAN, NOT AS COOL AS KILLING THE REAL SPIDER-MAN OR MAGNETO, BUT IT COULD BE CATHARTIC AS HELL.
I DIDN'T BRING MYSTERIO TO YOU SO THAT YOU COULD BLOW OFF STEAM WITH YOUR FANTASY KILL LIST.
I BROUGHT HIM HERE BECAUSE OF WHAT I SAW IN LOGAN'S HEAD.
HE WAS THE FIRST STEP IN AN ATTACK ORCHESTRATED BY YOUR FATHER TO TAKE DOWN ALL OUR ENEMIES IN ONE FELL SWOOP.
AND SINCE HE'S NOT AROUND ANYMORE...
I CAN RULE IN HIS PLACE.
WE CAN RULE. PLENTY OF LAND TO GO AROUND.
WE CAN CONTROL IT THIS TIME AROUND. WE HAVE THE BLUEPRINTS AND CAN AVOID THE MISTAKES MADE IN LOGAN'S REALITY.
WHAT SORTA MISTAKES?
LIKE YOU GETTING STOMPED TO PULP BY GIANT-MAN ON DAY ONE.
ALL RIGHT, LET'S DO IT. BUT FIRST...
...BRING OUT ANOTHER PRISONER!
MAKE THIS ONE LOOK LIKE BLACK WIDOW.

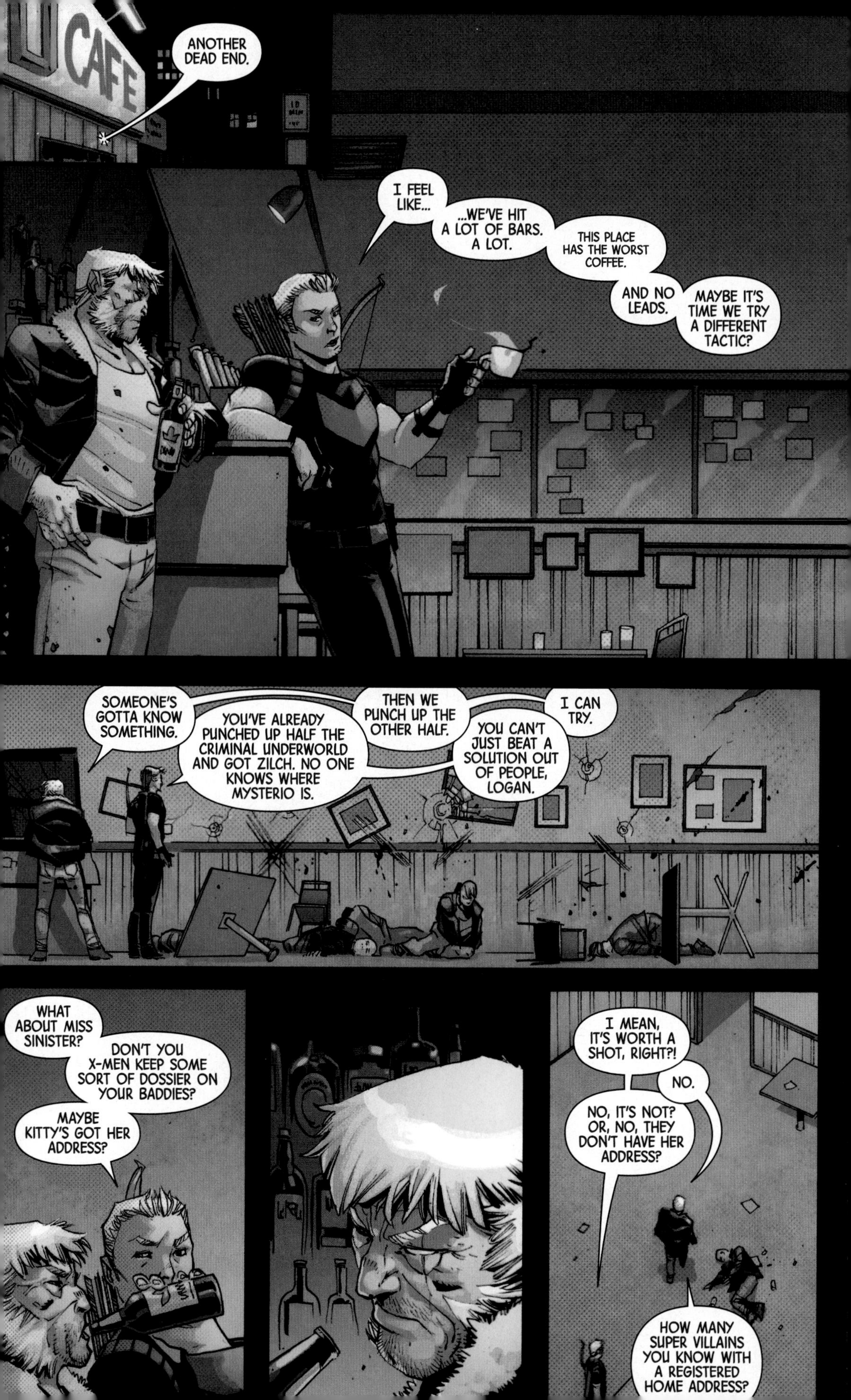
CAFE
ANOTHER DEAD END.
I FEEL LIKE...
...WE'VE HIT A LOT OF BARS. A LOT.
THIS PLACE HAS THE WORST COFFEE.
AND NO LEADS.
MAYBE IT'S TIME WE TRY A DIFFERENT TACTIC?
SOMEONE'S GOTTA KNOW SOMETHING.
YOU'VE ALREADY PUNCHED UP HALF THE CRIMINAL UNDERWORLD AND GOT ZILCH. NO ONE KNOWS WHERE MYSTERIO IS.
THEN WE PUNCH UP THE OTHER HALF.
YOU CAN'T JUST BEAT A SOLUTION OUT OF PEOPLE, LOGAN.
I CAN TRY.
WHAT ABOUT MISS SINISTER?
DON'T YOU X-MEN KEEP SOME SORT OF DOSSIER ON YOUR BADDIES?
MAYBE KITTY'S GOT HER ADDRESS?
I MEAN, IT'S WORTH A SHOT, RIGHT?!
NO.
NO, IT'S NOT? OR, NO, THEY DON'T HAVE HER ADDRESS?
HOW MANY SUPER VILLAINS YOU KNOW WITH A REGISTERED HOME ADDRESS?

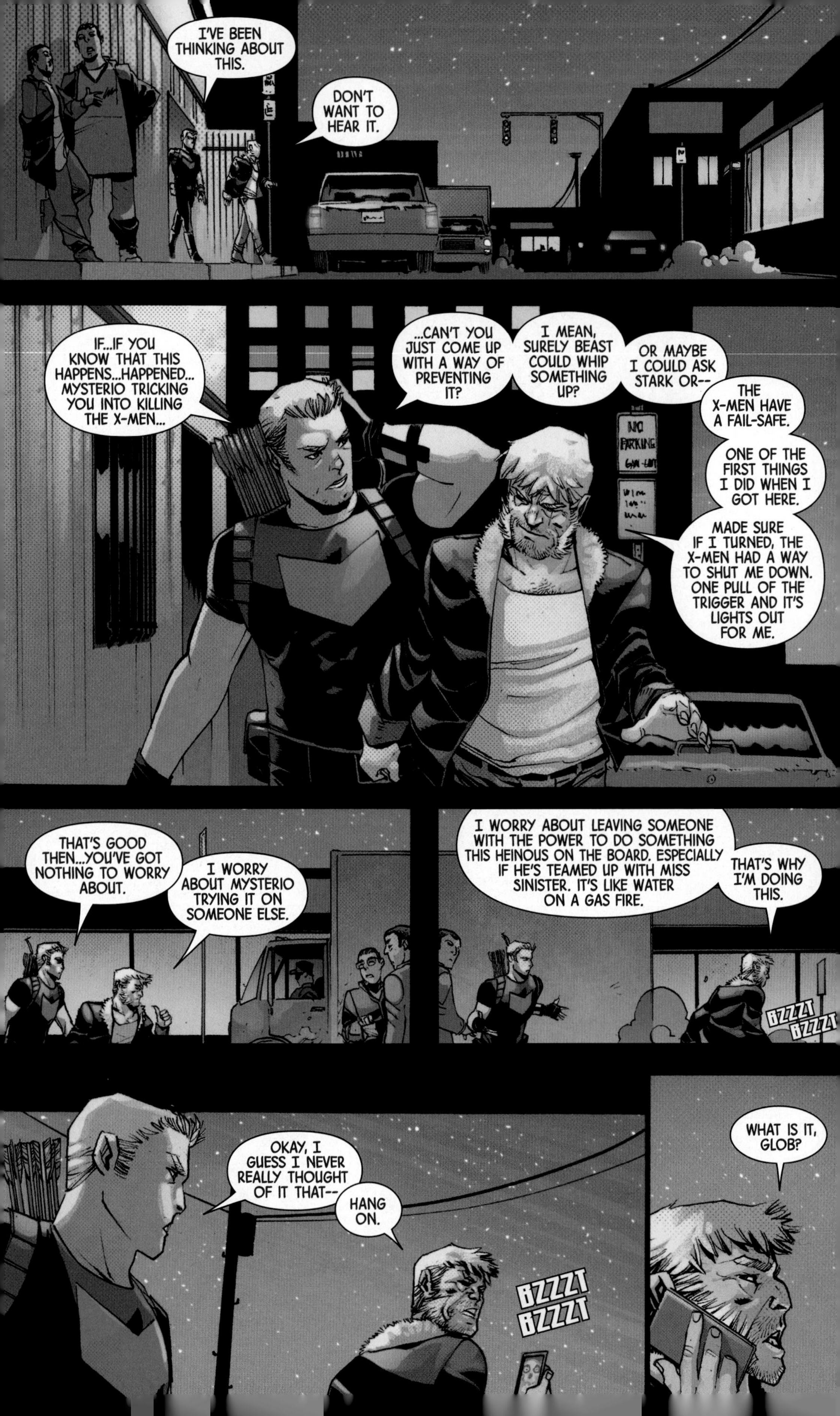
I'VE BEEN THINKING ABOUT THIS.
DON'T WANT TO HEAR IT.
IF...IF YOU KNOW THAT THIS HAPPENS...HAPPENED... MYSTERIO TRICKING YOU INTO KILLING THE X-MEN...
...CAN'T YOU JUST COME UP WITH A WAY OF PREVENTING IT?
I MEAN, SURELY BEAST COULD WHIP SOMETHING UP?
OR MAYBE I COULD ASK STARK OR--
THE X-MEN HAVE A FAIL-SAFE.
ONE OF THE FIRST THINGS I DID WHEN I GOT HERE.
MADE SURE IF I TURNED, THE X-MEN HAD A WAY TO SHUT ME DOWN. ONE PULL OF THE TRIGGER AND IT'S LIGHTS OUT FOR ME.
THAT'S GOOD THEN...YOU'VE GOT NOTHING TO WORRY ABOUT.
I WORRY ABOUT MYSTERIO TRYING IT ON SOMEONE ELSE.
I WORRY ABOUT LEAVING SOMEONE WITH THE POWER TO DO SOMETHING THIS HEINOUS ON THE BOARD. ESPECIALLY IF HE'S TEAMED UP WITH MISS SINISTER. IT'S LIKE WATER ON A GAS FIRE.
THAT'S WHY I'M DOING THIS.
BZZZT BZZZT
OKAY, I GUESS I NEVER REALLY THOUGHT OF IT THAT--
HANG ON.
BZZZT BZZZT
WHAT IS IT, GLOB?

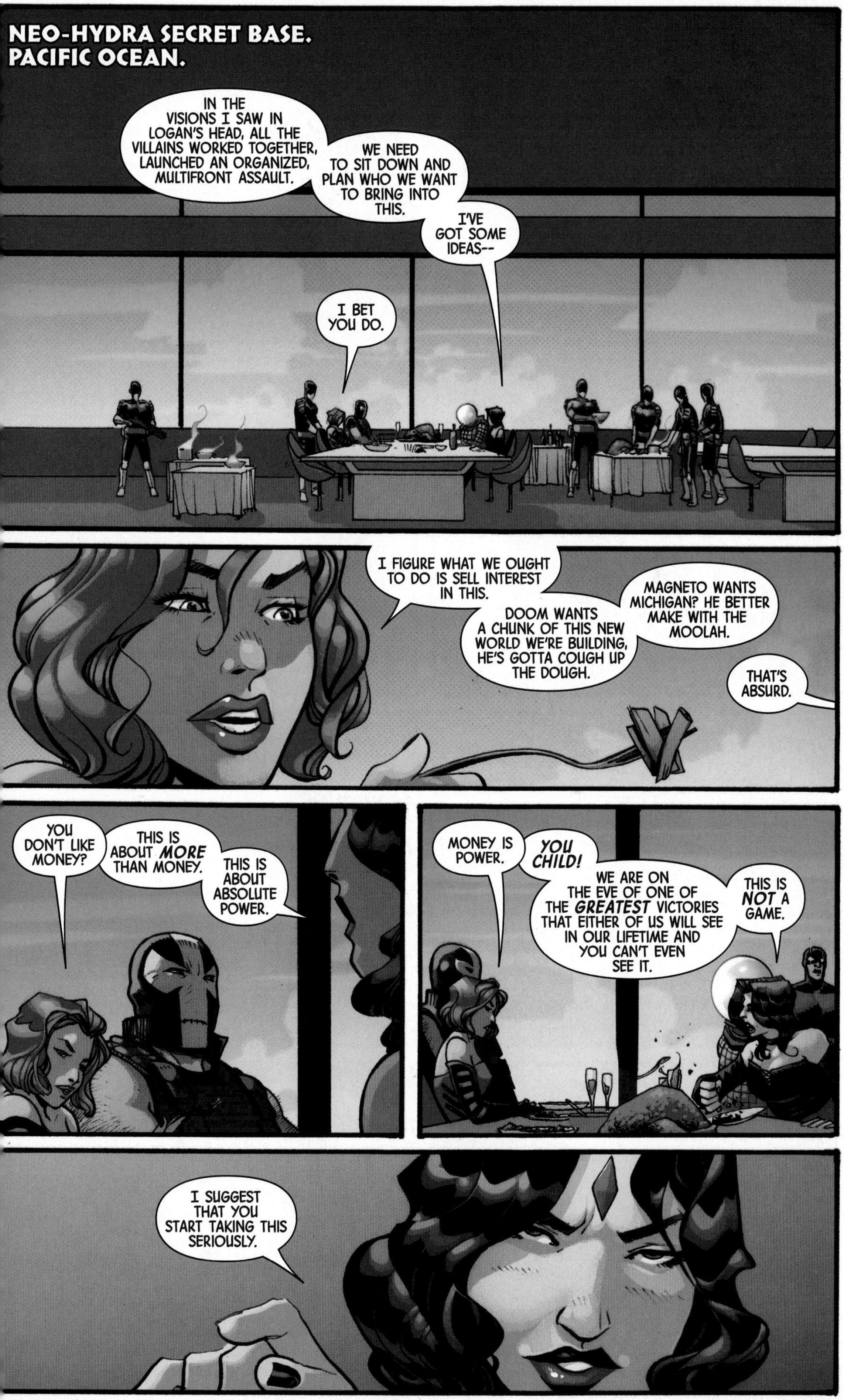
NEO-HYDRA SECRET BASE. PACIFIC OCEAN.
IN THE VISIONS I SAW IN LOGAN'S HEAD, ALL THE VILLAINS WORKED TOGETHER, LAUNCHED AN ORGANIZED, MULTIFRONT ASSAULT.
WE NEED TO SIT DOWN AND PLAN WHO WE WANT TO BRING INTO THIS.
I'VE GOT SOME IDEAS--
I BET YOU DO.
I FIGURE WHAT WE OUGHT TO DO IS SELL INTEREST IN THIS.
DOOM WANTS A CHUNK OF THIS NEW WORLD WE'RE BUILDING, HE'S GOTTA COUGH UP THE DOUGH.
MAGNETO WANTS MICHIGAN? HE BETTER MAKE WITH THE MOOLAH.
THAT'S ABSURD.
YOU DON'T LIKE MONEY?
THIS IS ABOUT MORE THAN MONEY.
THIS IS ABOUT ABSOLUTE POWER.
MONEY IS POWER.
YOU CHILD!
WE ARE ON THE EVE OF ONE OF THE GREATEST VICTORIES THAT EITHER OF US WILL SEE IN OUR LIFETIME AND YOU CAN'T EVEN SEE IT.
THIS IS NOT A GAME.
I SUGGEST THAT YOU START TAKING THIS SERIOUSLY.

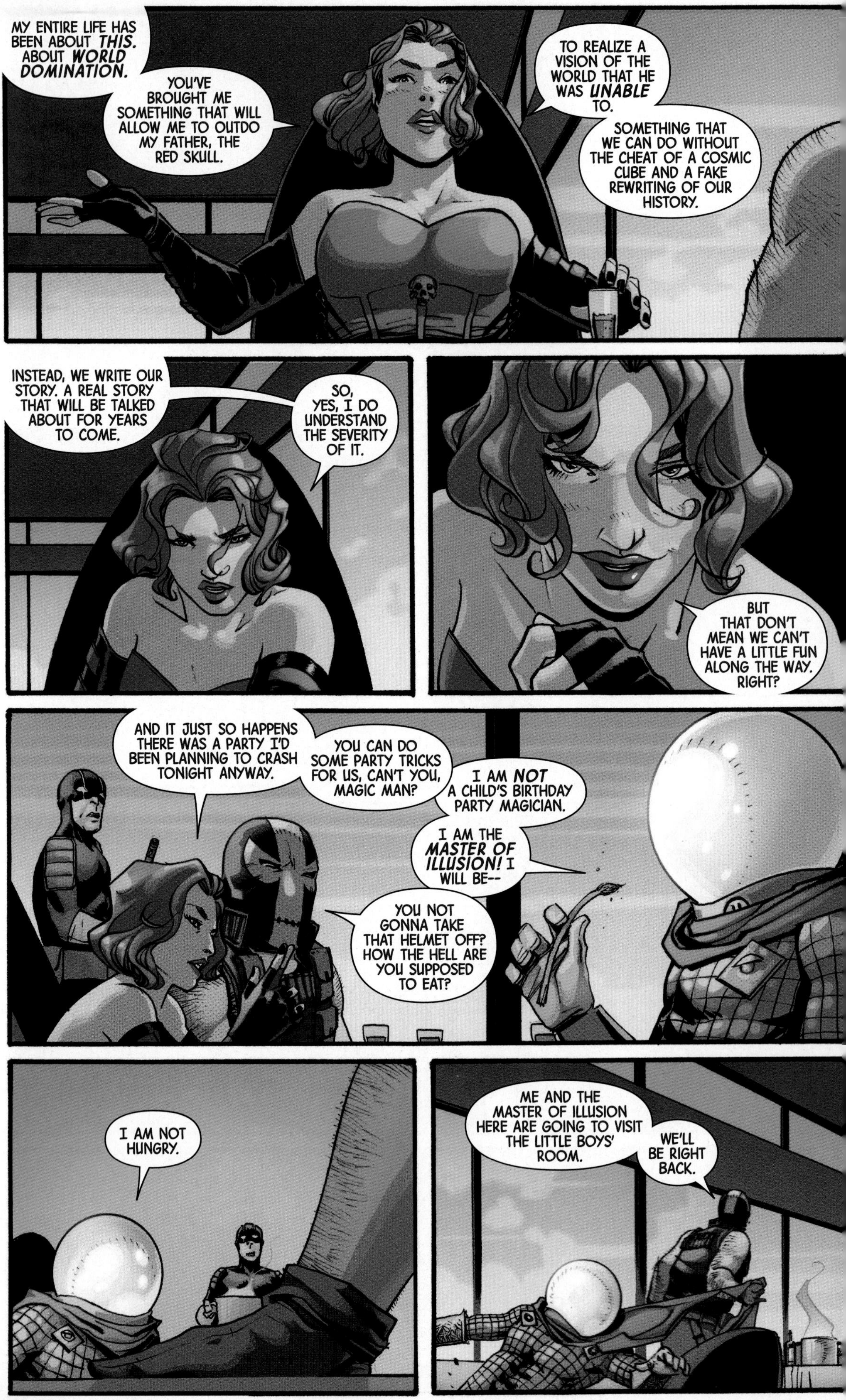
MY ENTIRE LIFE HAS BEEN ABOUT *THIS.* ABOUT *WORLD DOMINATION.*
YOU'VE BROUGHT ME SOMETHING THAT WILL ALLOW ME TO OUTDO MY FATHER, THE RED SKULL.
TO REALIZE A VISION OF THE WORLD THAT HE WAS *UNABLE* TO.
SOMETHING THAT WE CAN DO WITHOUT THE CHEAT OF A COSMIC CUBE AND A FAKE REWRITING OF OUR HISTORY.
INSTEAD, WE WRITE OUR STORY. A REAL STORY THAT WILL BE TALKED ABOUT FOR YEARS TO COME.
SO, YES, I DO UNDERSTAND THE SEVERITY OF IT.
BUT THAT DON'T MEAN WE CAN'T HAVE A LITTLE FUN ALONG THE WAY. RIGHT?
AND IT JUST SO HAPPENS THERE WAS A PARTY I'D BEEN PLANNING TO CRASH TONIGHT ANYWAY.
YOU CAN DO SOME PARTY TRICKS FOR US, CAN'T YOU, MAGIC MAN?
I AM *NOT* A CHILD'S BIRTHDAY PARTY MAGICIAN.
I AM THE *MASTER OF ILLUSION!* I WILL BE--
YOU NOT GONNA TAKE THAT HELMET OFF? HOW THE HELL ARE YOU SUPPOSED TO EAT?
I AM NOT HUNGRY.
ME AND THE MASTER OF ILLUSION HERE ARE GOING TO VISIT THE LITTLE BOYS' ROOM.
WE'LL BE RIGHT BACK.

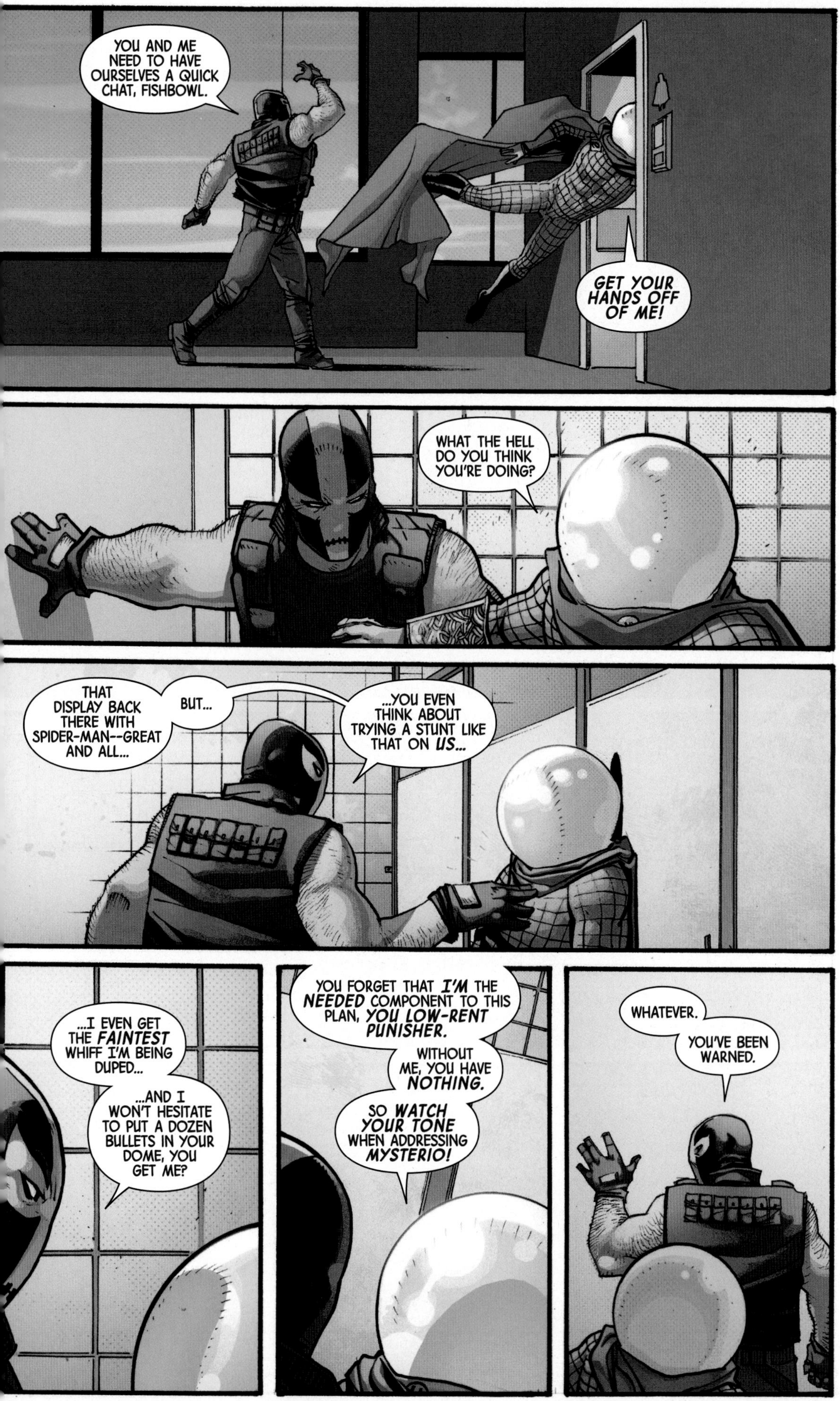
YOU AND ME NEED TO HAVE OURSELVES A QUICK CHAT, FISHBOWL.
GET YOUR HANDS OFF OF ME!
WHAT THE HELL DO YOU THINK YOU'RE DOING?
THAT DISPLAY BACK THERE WITH SPIDER-MAN--GREAT AND ALL...
BUT...
...YOU EVEN THINK ABOUT TRYING A STUNT LIKE THAT ON US...
...I EVEN GET THE FAINTEST WHIFF I'M BEING DUPED...
...AND I WON'T HESITATE TO PUT A DOZEN BULLETS IN YOUR DOME, YOU GET ME?
YOU FORGET THAT I'M THE NEEDED COMPONENT TO THIS PLAN, YOU LOW-RENT PUNISHER.
WITHOUT ME, YOU HAVE NOTHING.
SO WATCH YOUR TONE WHEN ADDRESSING MYSTERIO!
WHATEVER.
YOU'VE BEEN WARNED.

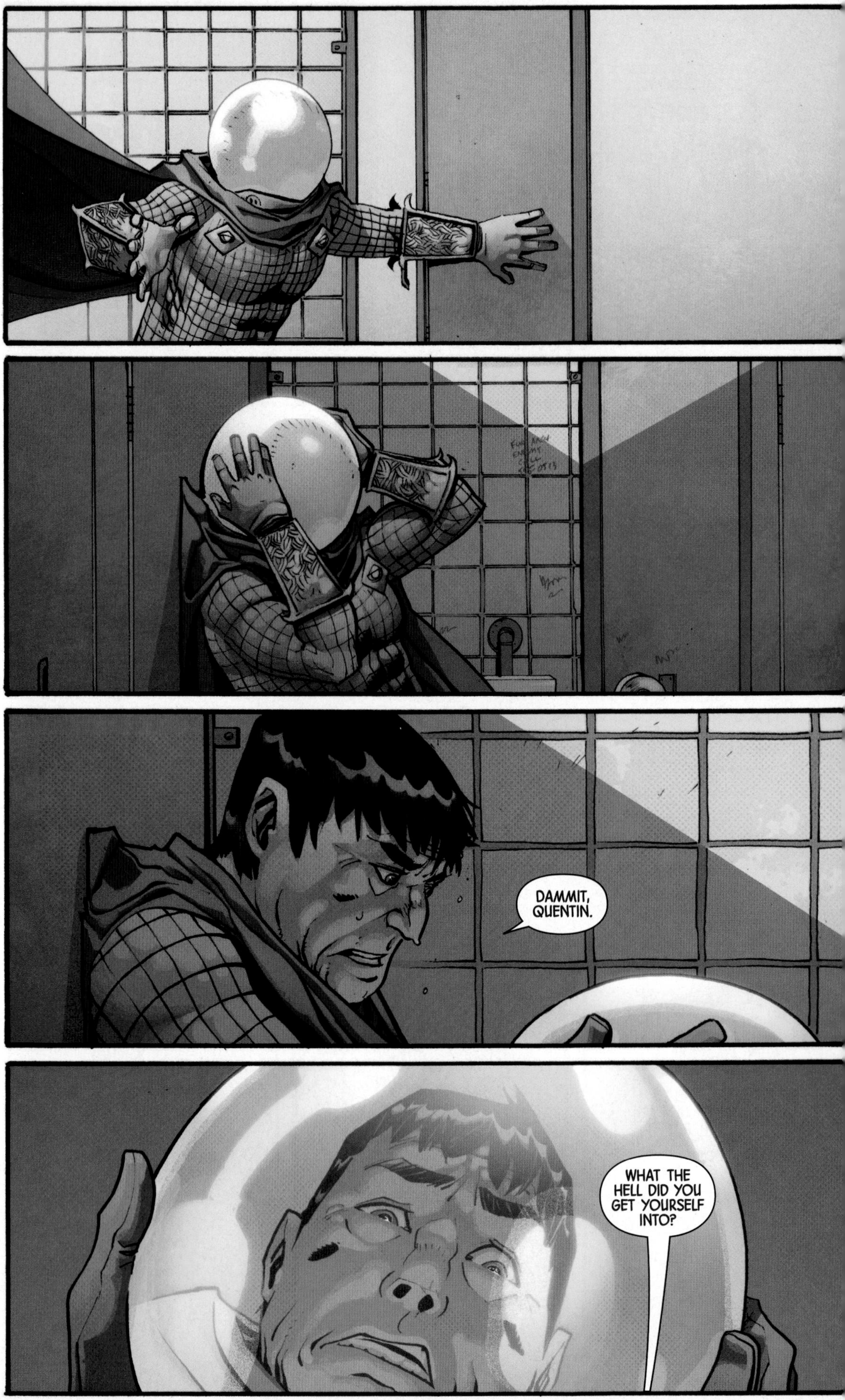
DAMMIT, QUENTIN.
WHAT THE HELL DID YOU GET YOURSELF INTO?

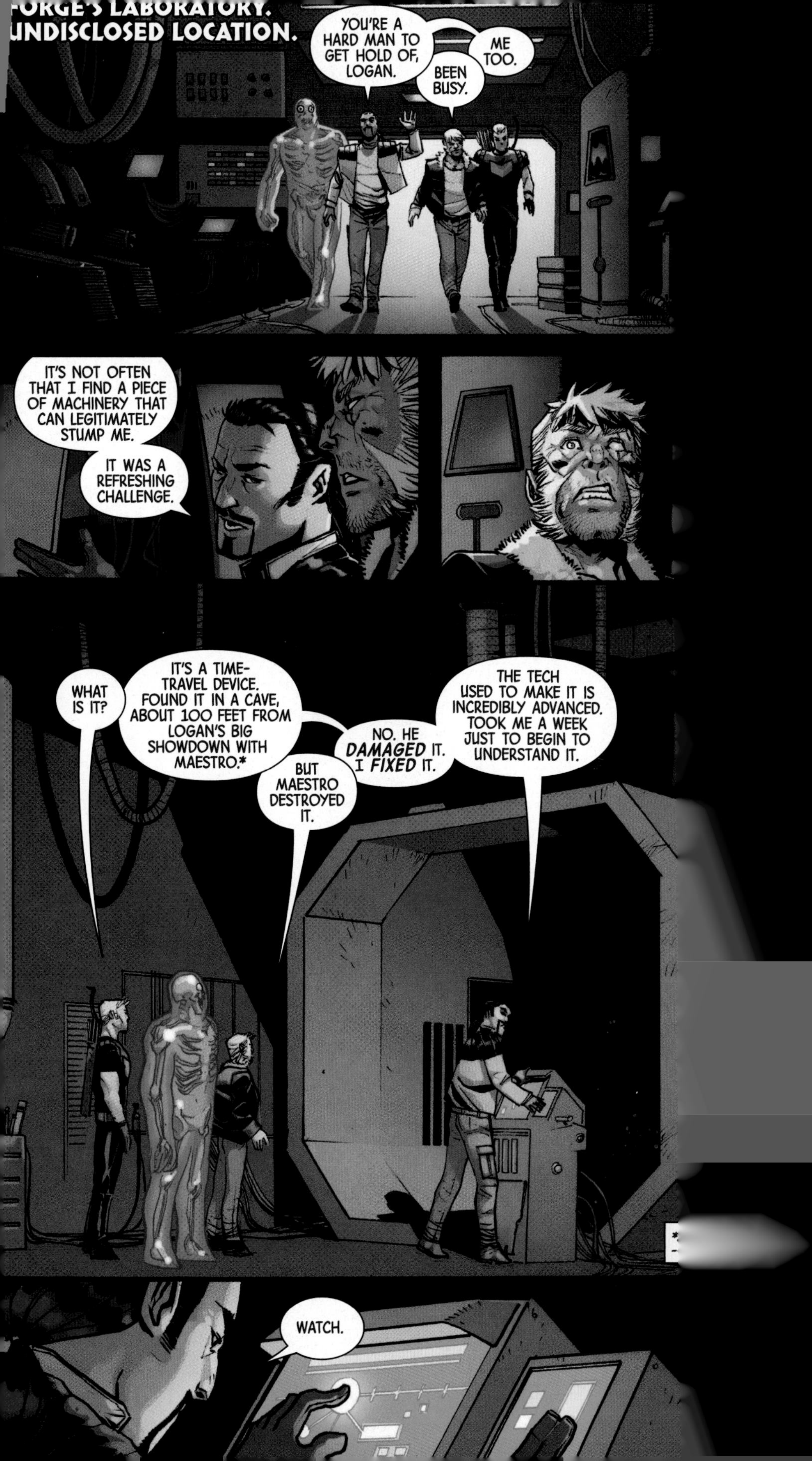
FORGE'S LABORATORY.
UNDISCLOSED LOCATION.
YOU'RE A HARD MAN TO GET HOLD OF, LOGAN.
BEEN BUSY.
ME TOO.
IT'S NOT OFTEN THAT I FIND A PIECE OF MACHINERY THAT CAN LEGITIMATELY STUMP ME.
IT WAS A REFRESHING CHALLENGE.
WHAT IS IT?
IT'S A TIME-TRAVEL DEVICE. FOUND IT IN A CAVE, ABOUT 100 FEET FROM LOGAN'S BIG SHOWDOWN WITH MAESTRO.*
BUT MAESTRO DESTROYED IT.
NO. HE DAMAGED IT. I FIXED IT.
THE TECH USED TO MAKE IT IS INCREDIBLY ADVANCED. TOOK ME A WEEK JUST TO BEGIN TO UNDERSTAND IT.
WATCH.

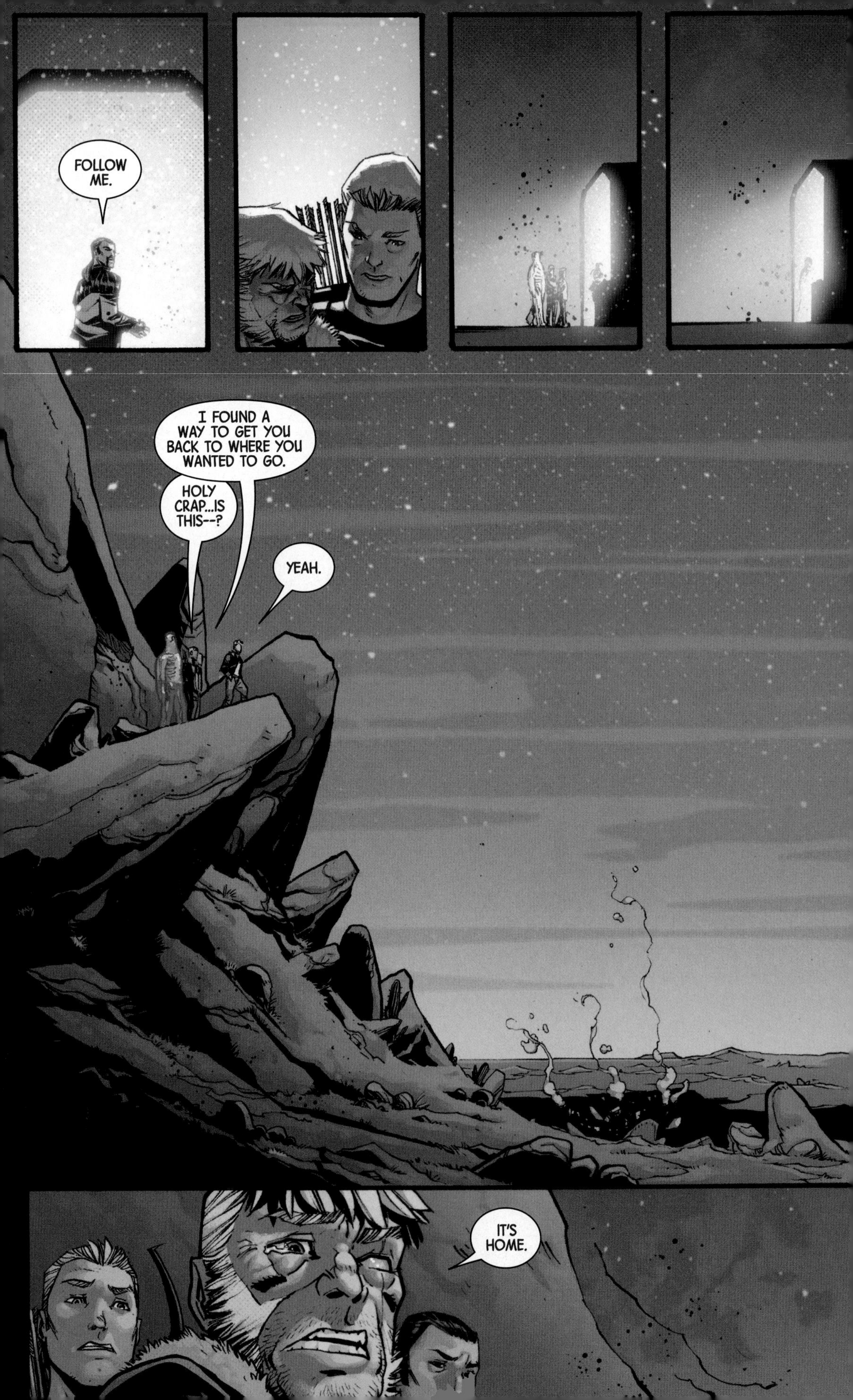
FOLLOW ME.
I FOUND A WAY TO GET YOU BACK TO WHERE YOU WANTED TO GO.
HOLY CRAP...IS THIS--?
YEAH.
IT'S HOME.

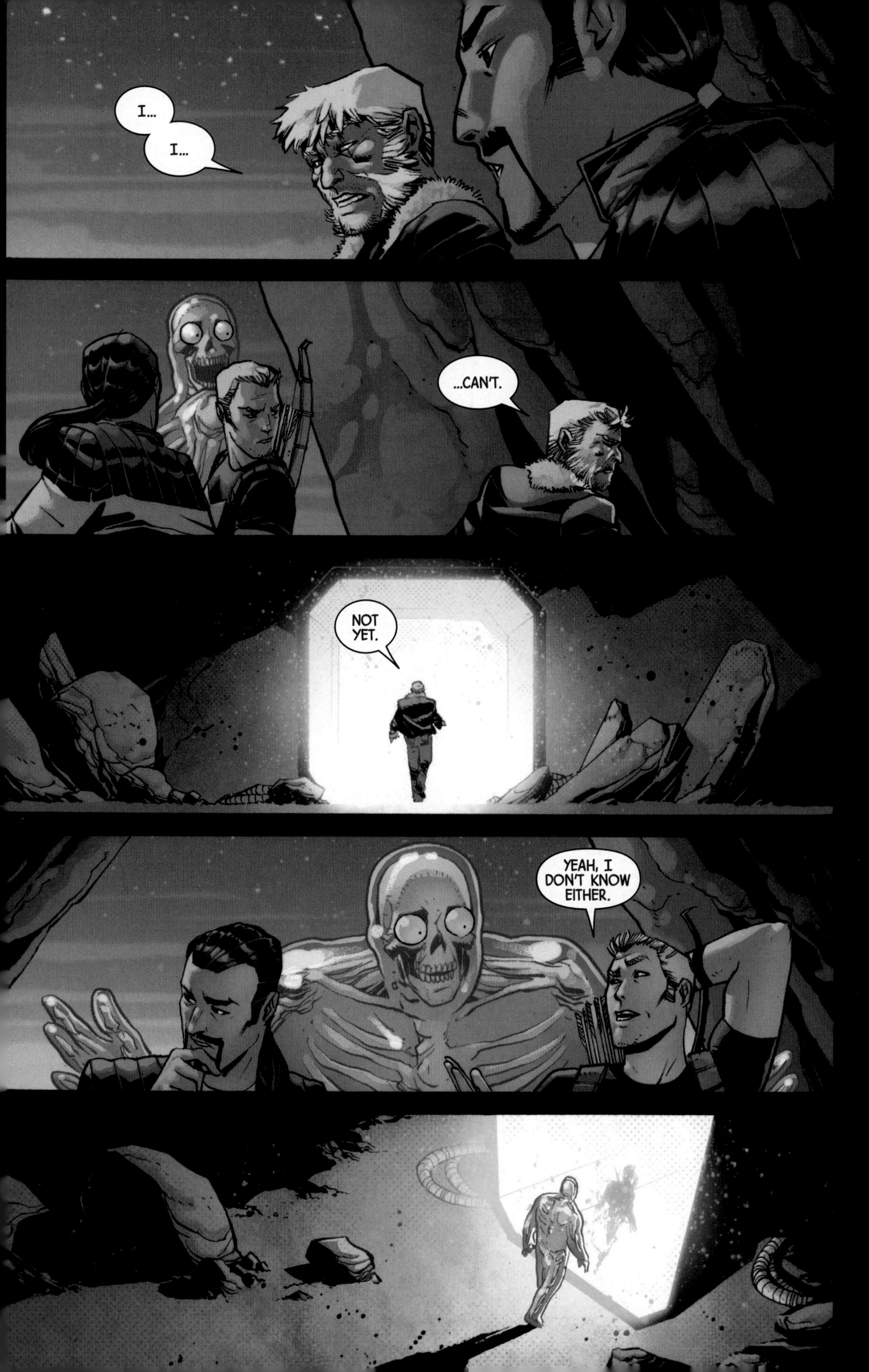
I...
I...
...CAN'T.
NOT YET.
YEAH, I DON'T KNOW EITHER.

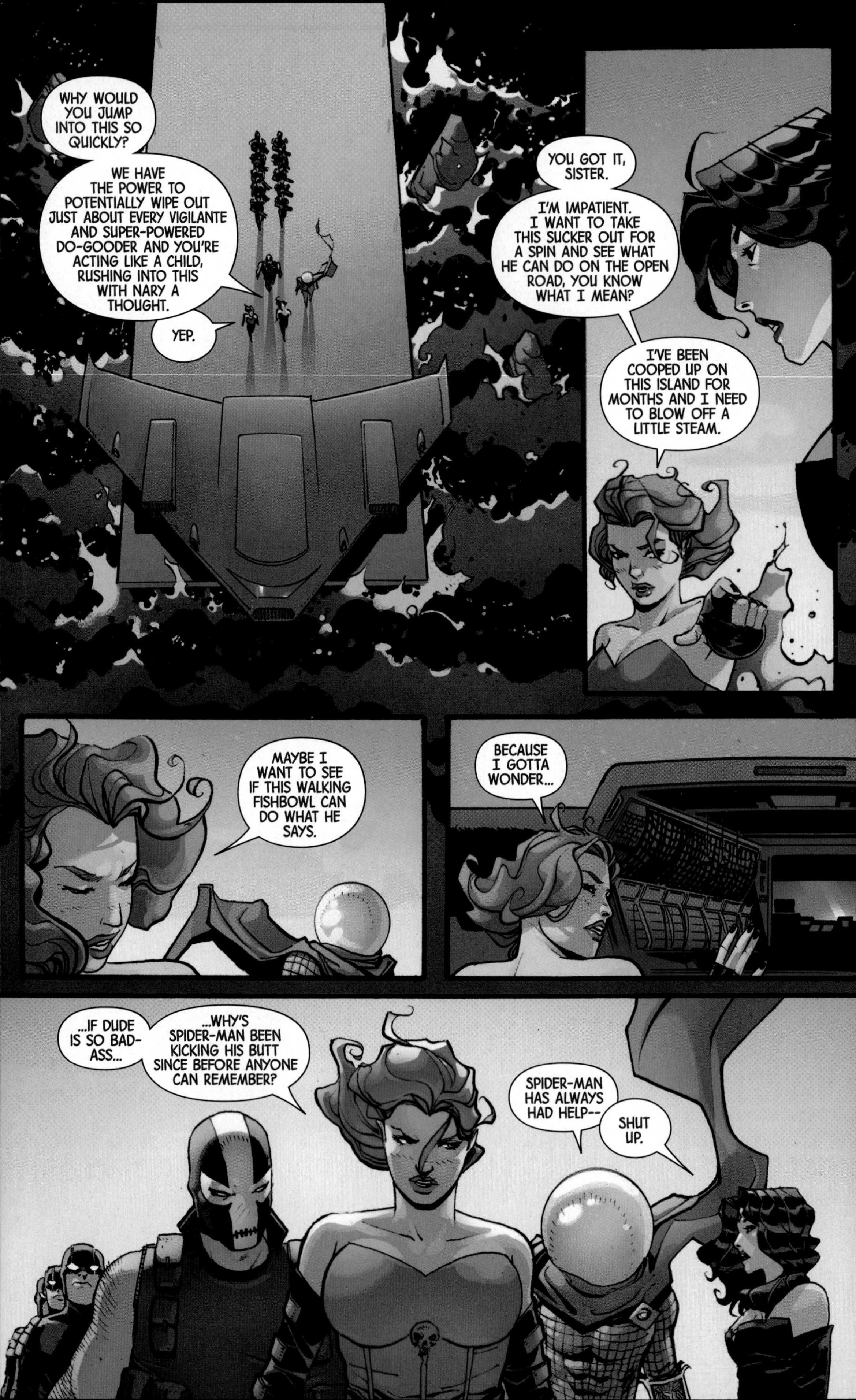
WHY WOULD YOU JUMP INTO THIS SO QUICKLY?
WE HAVE THE POWER TO POTENTIALLY WIPE OUT JUST ABOUT EVERY VIGILANTE AND SUPER-POWERED DO-GOODER AND YOU'RE ACTING LIKE A CHILD, RUSHING INTO THIS WITH NARY A THOUGHT.
YEP.
YOU GOT IT, SISTER.
I'M IMPATIENT. I WANT TO TAKE THIS SUCKER OUT FOR A SPIN AND SEE WHAT HE CAN DO ON THE OPEN ROAD, YOU KNOW WHAT I MEAN?
I'VE BEEN COOPED UP ON THIS ISLAND FOR MONTHS AND I NEED TO BLOW OFF A LITTLE STEAM.
MAYBE I WANT TO SEE IF THIS WALKING FISHBOWL CAN DO WHAT HE SAYS.
BECAUSE I GOTTA WONDER...
...IF DUDE IS SO BAD-ASS...
...WHY'S SPIDER-MAN BEEN KICKING HIS BUTT SINCE BEFORE ANYONE CAN REMEMBER?
SPIDER-MAN HAS ALWAYS HAD HELP--
SHUT UP.

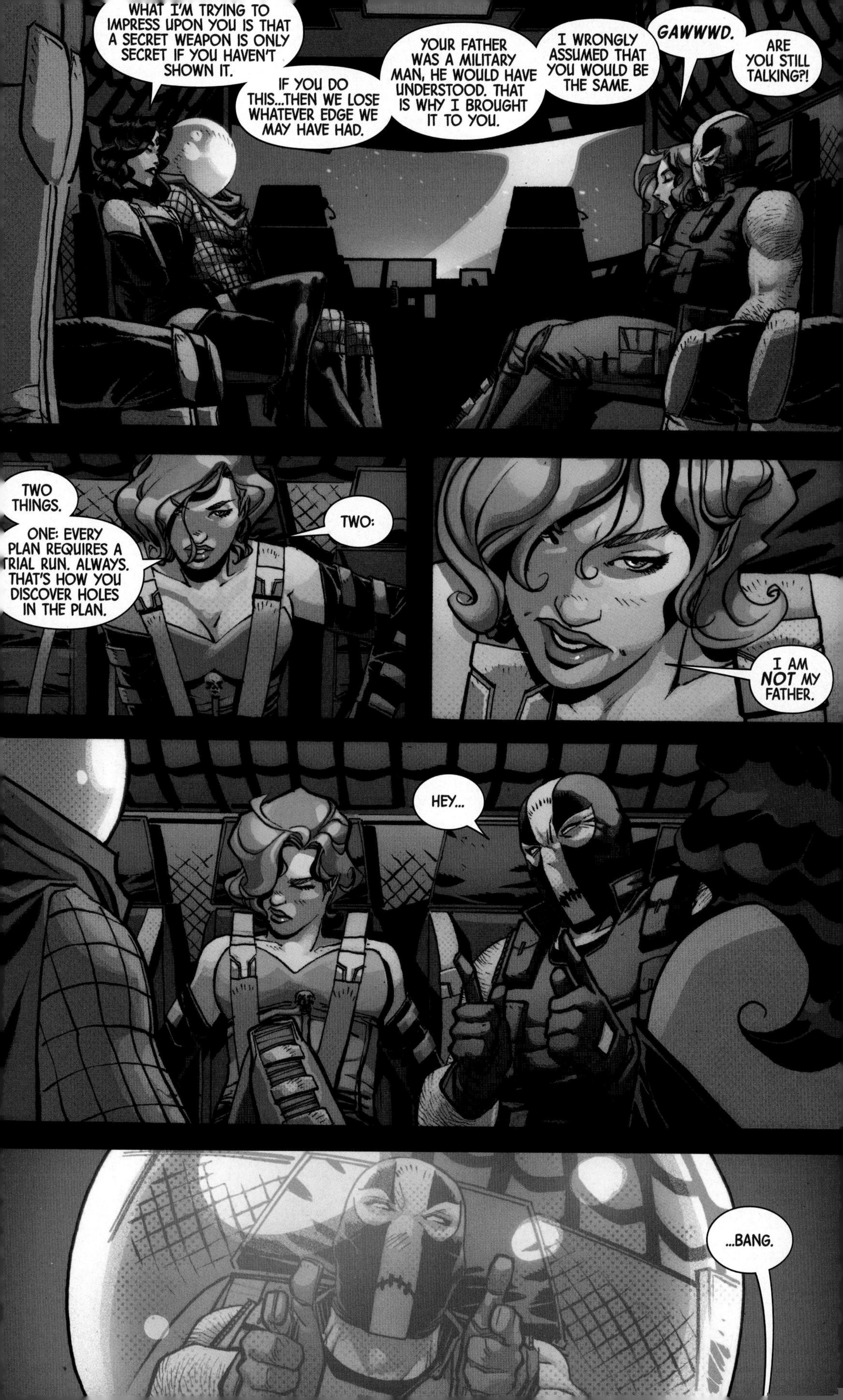
WHAT I'M TRYING TO IMPRESS UPON YOU IS THAT A SECRET WEAPON IS ONLY SECRET IF YOU HAVEN'T SHOWN IT.
IF YOU DO THIS...THEN WE LOSE WHATEVER EDGE WE MAY HAVE HAD.
YOUR FATHER WAS A MILITARY MAN, HE WOULD HAVE UNDERSTOOD. THAT IS WHY I BROUGHT IT TO YOU.
I WRONGLY ASSUMED THAT YOU WOULD BE THE SAME.
GAWWWD.
ARE YOU STILL TALKING?!
TWO THINGS.
ONE: EVERY PLAN REQUIRES A TRIAL RUN. ALWAYS. THAT'S HOW YOU DISCOVER HOLES IN THE PLAN.
TWO:
I AM *NOT* MY FATHER.
HEY...
...BANG.

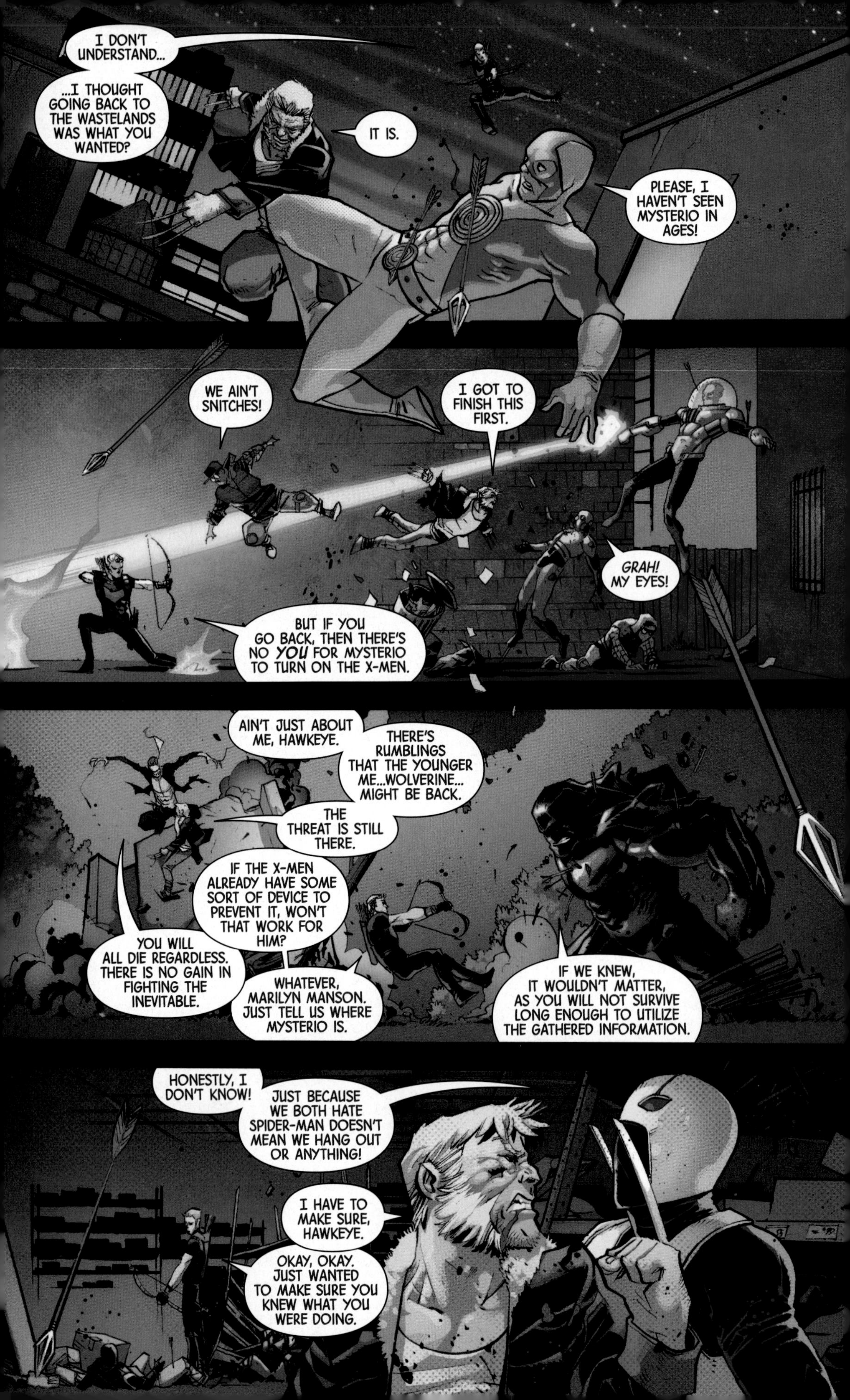
I DON'T UNDERSTAND...
...I THOUGHT GOING BACK TO THE WASTELANDS WAS WHAT YOU WANTED?
IT IS.
PLEASE, I HAVEN'T SEEN MYSTERIO IN AGES!
WE AIN'T SNITCHES!
I GOT TO FINISH THIS FIRST.
GRAH! MY EYES!
BUT IF YOU GO BACK, THEN THERE'S NO *YOU* FOR MYSTERIO TO TURN ON THE X-MEN.
AIN'T JUST ABOUT ME, HAWKEYE.
THERE'S RUMBLINGS THAT THE YOUNGER ME...WOLVERINE... MIGHT BE BACK.
THE THREAT IS STILL THERE.
IF THE X-MEN ALREADY HAVE SOME SORT OF DEVICE TO PREVENT IT, WON'T THAT WORK FOR HIM?
YOU WILL ALL DIE REGARDLESS. THERE IS NO GAIN IN FIGHTING THE INEVITABLE.
WHATEVER, MARILYN MANSON. JUST TELL US WHERE MYSTERIO IS.
IF WE KNEW, IT WOULDN'T MATTER, AS YOU WILL NOT SURVIVE LONG ENOUGH TO UTILIZE THE GATHERED INFORMATION.
HONESTLY, I DON'T KNOW!
JUST BECAUSE WE BOTH HATE SPIDER-MAN DOESN'T MEAN WE HANG OUT OR ANYTHING!
I HAVE TO MAKE SURE, HAWKEYE.
OKAY, OKAY. JUST WANTED TO MAKE SURE YOU KNEW WHAT YOU WERE DOING.

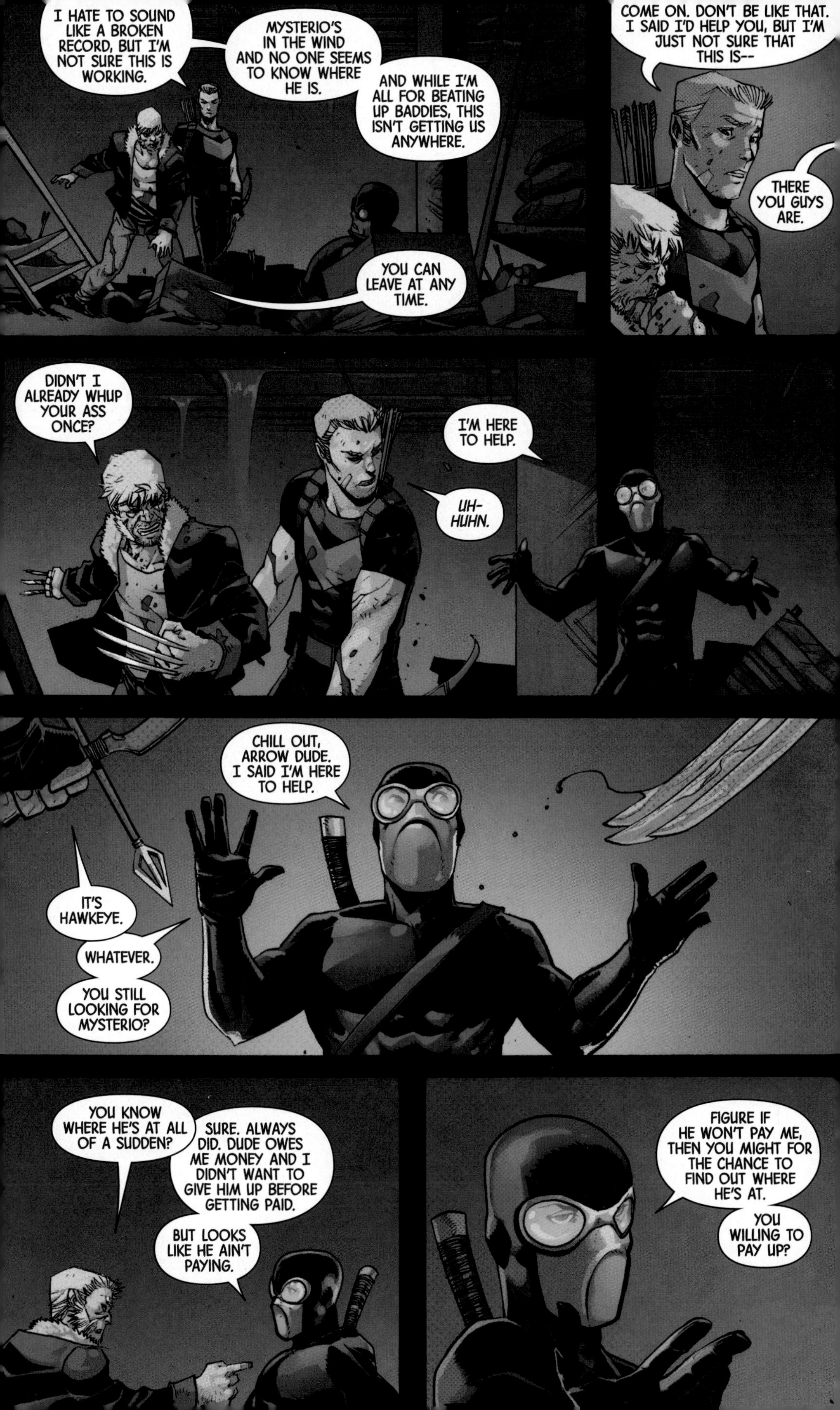
I HATE TO SOUND LIKE A BROKEN RECORD, BUT I'M NOT SURE THIS IS WORKING.
MYSTERIO'S IN THE WIND AND NO ONE SEEMS TO KNOW WHERE HE IS.
AND WHILE I'M ALL FOR BEATING UP BADDIES, THIS ISN'T GETTING US ANYWHERE.
YOU CAN LEAVE AT ANY TIME.
COME ON. DON'T BE LIKE THAT. I SAID I'D HELP YOU, BUT I'M JUST NOT SURE THAT THIS IS--
THERE YOU GUYS ARE.
DIDN'T I ALREADY WHUP YOUR ASS ONCE?
I'M HERE TO HELP.
UH-HUHN.
CHILL OUT, ARROW DUDE. I SAID I'M HERE TO HELP.
IT'S HAWKEYE.
WHATEVER.
YOU STILL LOOKING FOR MYSTERIO?
YOU KNOW WHERE HE'S AT ALL OF A SUDDEN?
SURE. ALWAYS DID. DUDE OWES ME MONEY AND I DIDN'T WANT TO GIVE HIM UP BEFORE GETTING PAID.
BUT LOOKS LIKE HE AIN'T PAYING.
FIGURE IF HE WON'T PAY ME, THEN YOU MIGHT FOR THE CHANCE TO FIND OUT WHERE HE'S AT.
YOU WILLING TO PAY UP?

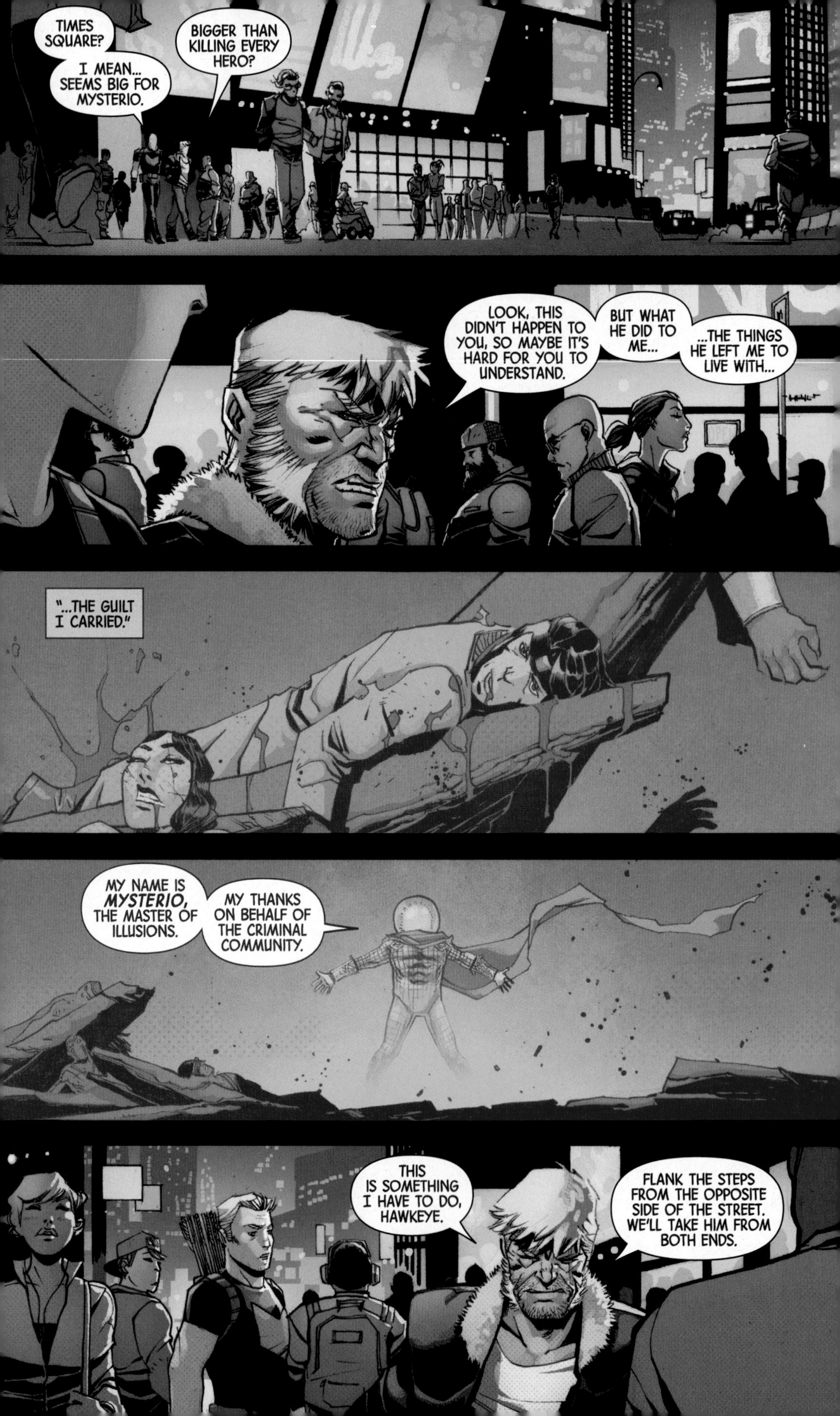
TIMES SQUARE?
I MEAN... SEEMS BIG FOR MYSTERIO.
BIGGER THAN KILLING EVERY HERO?
LOOK, THIS DIDN'T HAPPEN TO YOU, SO MAYBE IT'S HARD FOR YOU TO UNDERSTAND.
BUT WHAT HE DID TO ME...
...THE THINGS HE LEFT ME TO LIVE WITH...
"...THE GUILT I CARRIED."
MY NAME IS MYSTERIO, THE MASTER OF ILLUSIONS.
MY THANKS ON BEHALF OF THE CRIMINAL COMMUNITY.
THIS IS SOMETHING I HAVE TO DO, HAWKEYE.
FLANK THE STEPS FROM THE OPPOSITE SIDE OF THE STREET. WE'LL TAKE HIM FROM BOTH ENDS.

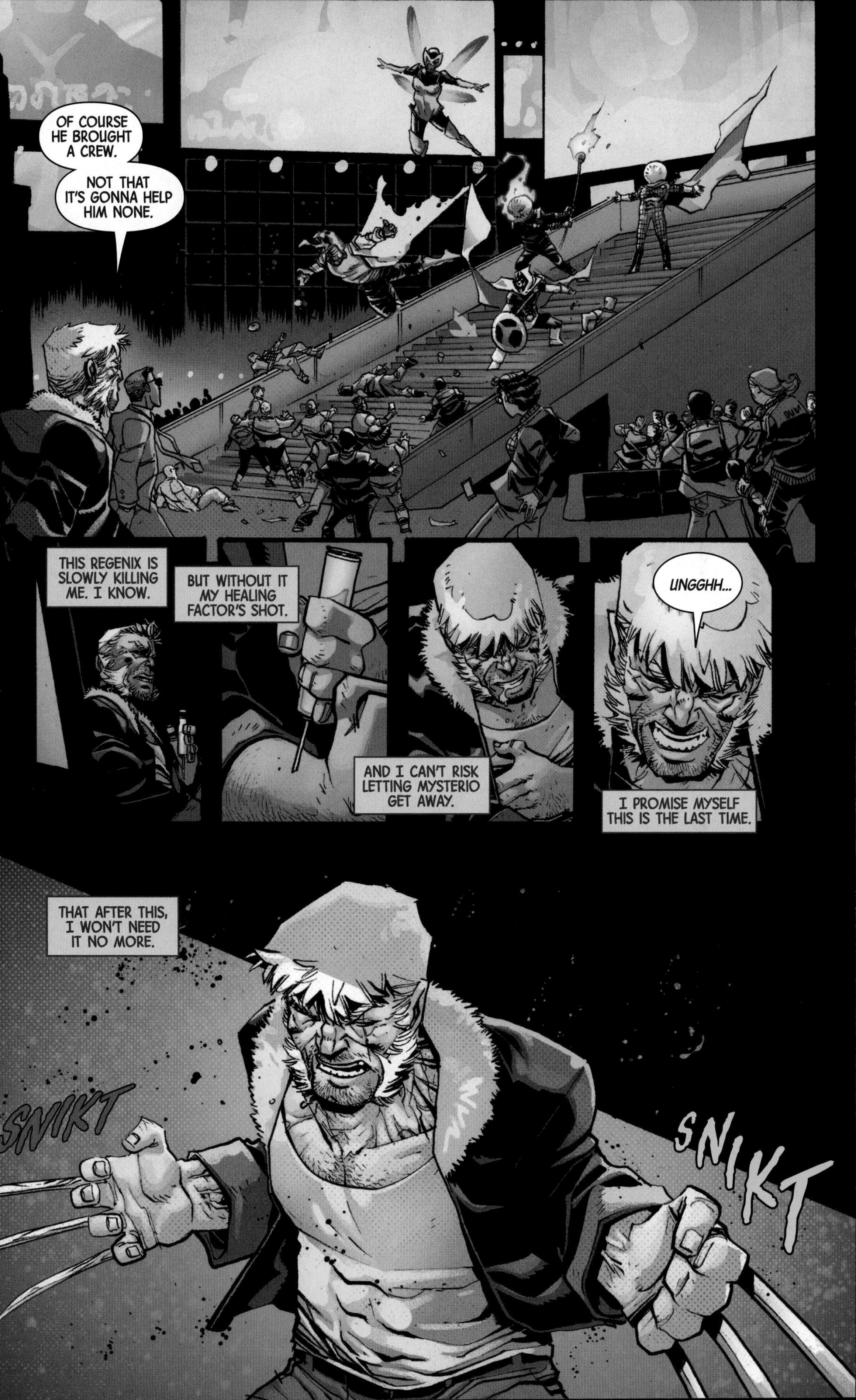

OF COURSE HE BROUGHT A CREW.
NOT THAT IT'S GONNA HELP HIM NONE.
THIS REGENIX IS SLOWLY KILLING ME. I KNOW.
BUT WITHOUT IT MY HEALING FACTOR'S SHOT.
AND I CAN'T RISK LETTING MYSTERIO GET AWAY.
UNGGHH...
I PROMISE MYSELF THIS IS THE LAST TIME.
THAT AFTER THIS, I WON'T NEED IT NO MORE.
SNIKT
SNIKT

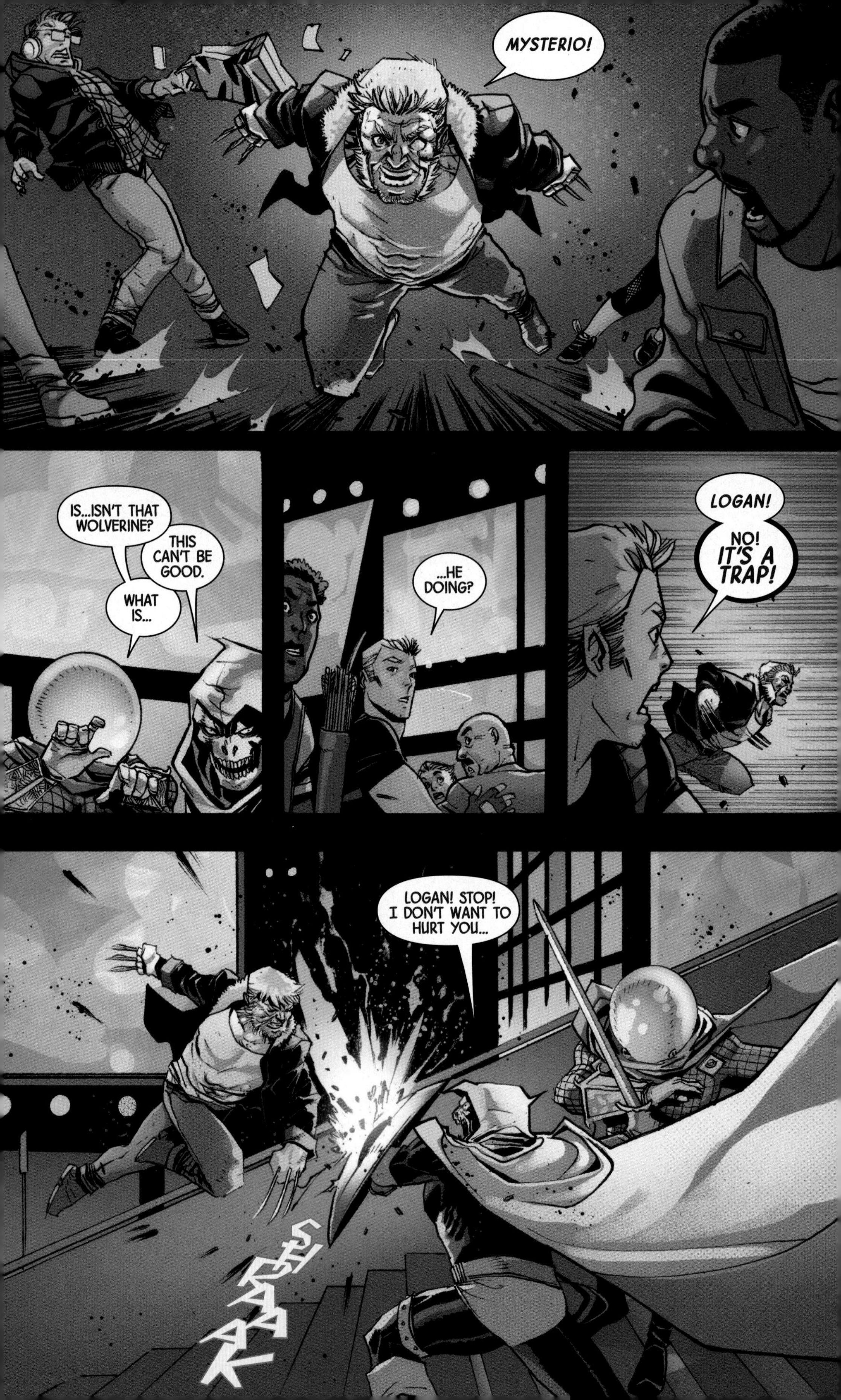
MYSTERIO!
IS...ISN'T THAT WOLVERINE?
THIS CAN'T BE GOOD.
WHAT IS...
...HE DOING?
LOGAN!
NO! IT'S A TRAP!
LOGAN! STOP! I DON'T WANT TO HURT YOU...
SHRAAAK

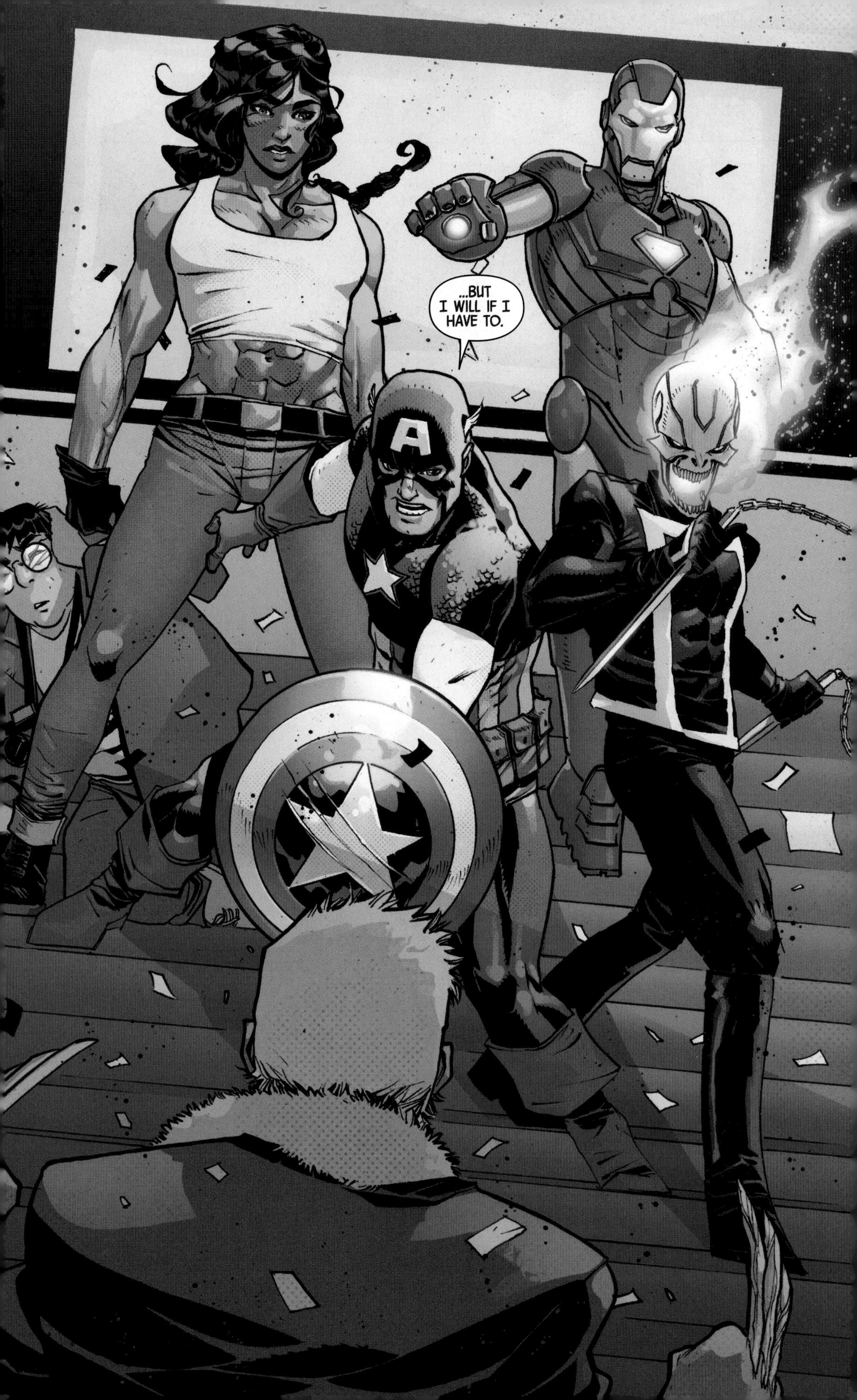
...BUT
I WILL IF I
HAVE TO.

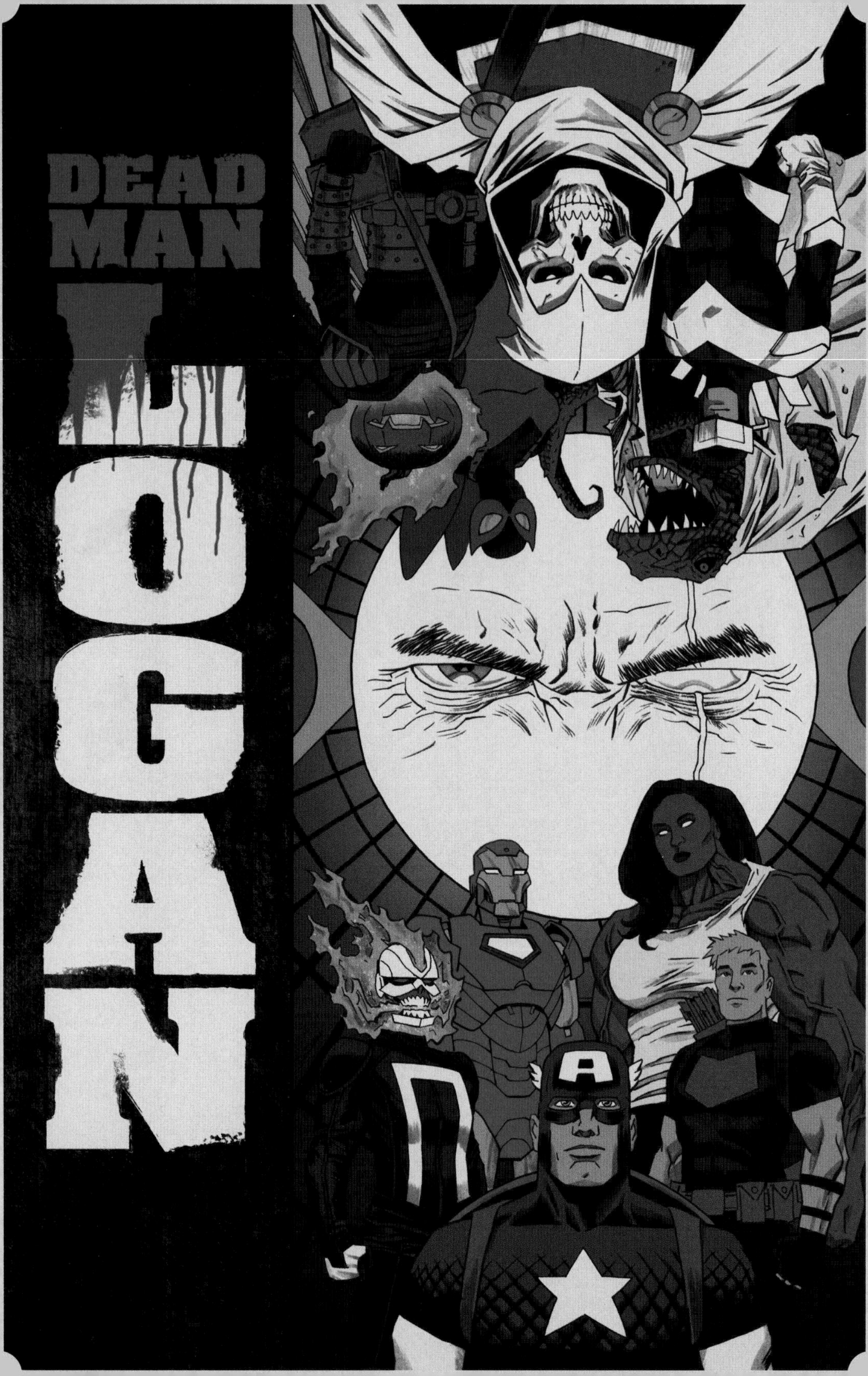
DEAD MAN
LOGAN

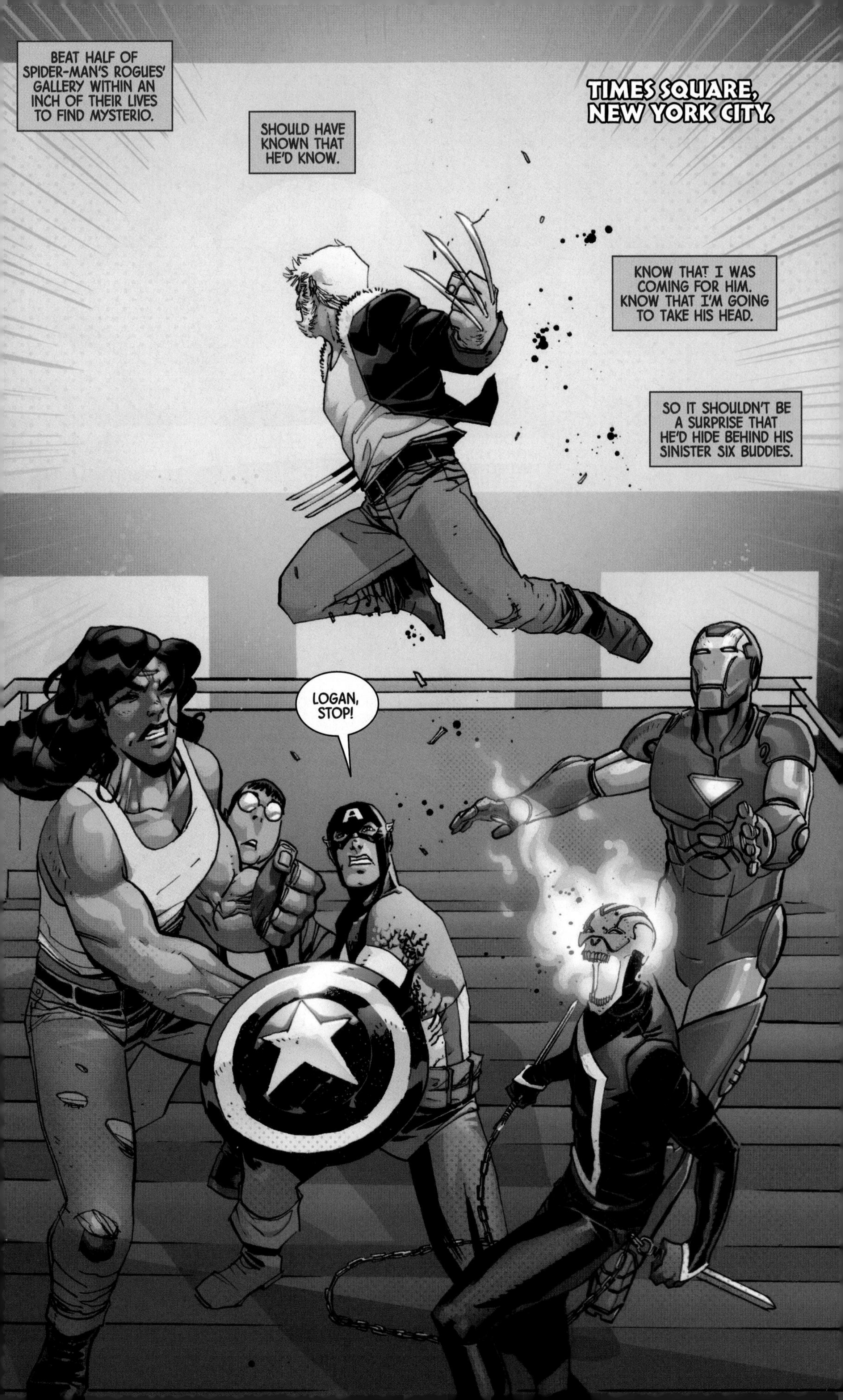
BEAT HALF OF SPIDER-MAN'S ROGUES' GALLERY WITHIN AN INCH OF THEIR LIVES TO FIND MYSTERIO.
SHOULD HAVE KNOWN THAT HE'D KNOW.
TIMES SQUARE, NEW YORK CITY.
KNOW THAT I WAS COMING FOR HIM. KNOW THAT I'M GOING TO TAKE HIS HEAD.
SO IT SHOULDN'T BE A SURPRISE THAT HE'D HIDE BEHIND HIS SINISTER SIX BUDDIES.
LOGAN, STOP!

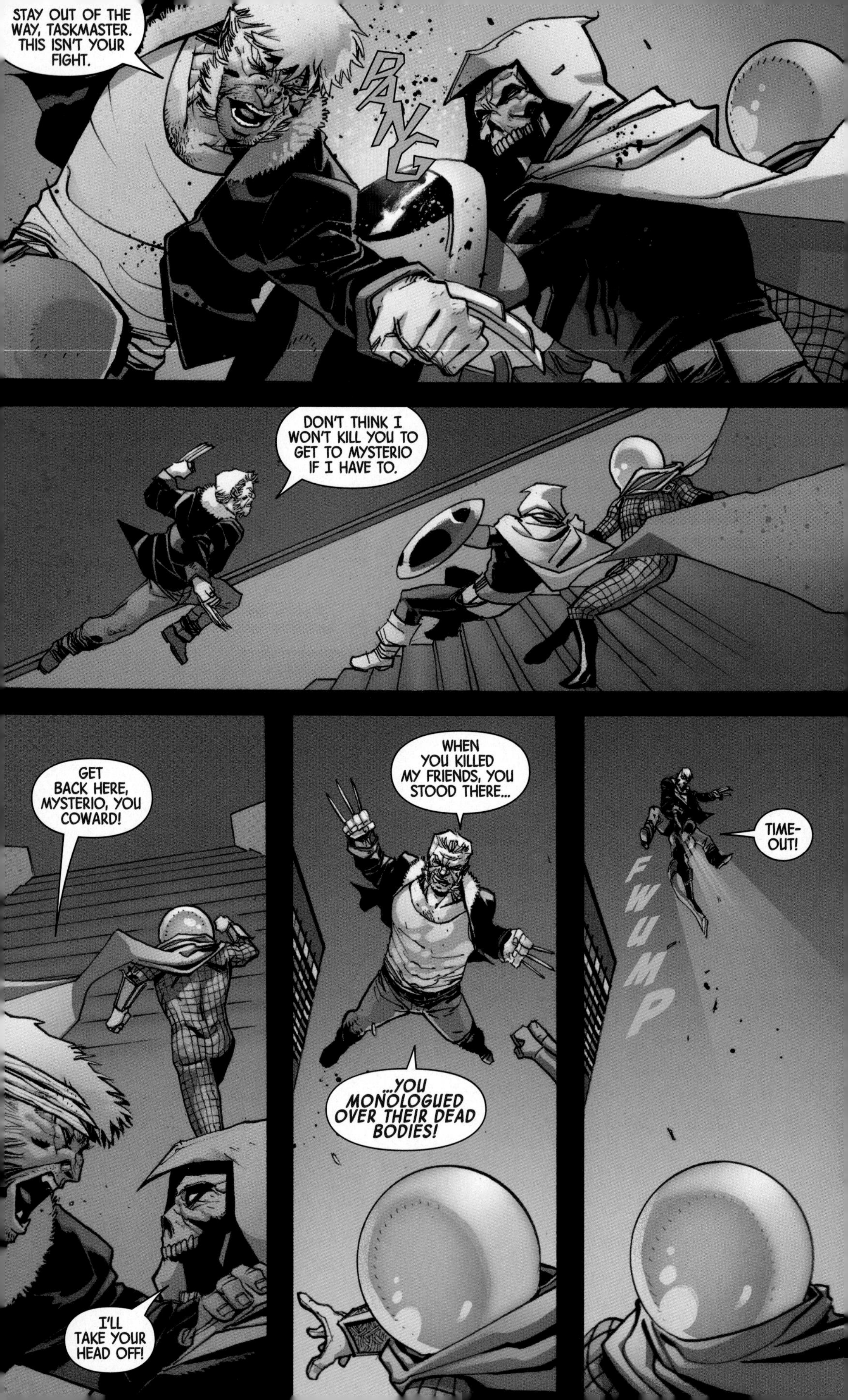
STAY OUT OF THE WAY, TASKMASTER. THIS ISN'T YOUR FIGHT.
BANG
DON'T THINK I WON'T KILL YOU TO GET TO MYSTERIO IF I HAVE TO.
GET BACK HERE, MYSTERIO, YOU COWARD!
I'LL TAKE YOUR HEAD OFF!
WHEN YOU KILLED MY FRIENDS, YOU STOOD THERE...
...YOU MONOLOGUED OVER THEIR DEAD BODIES!
TIME-OUT!
FWUMP

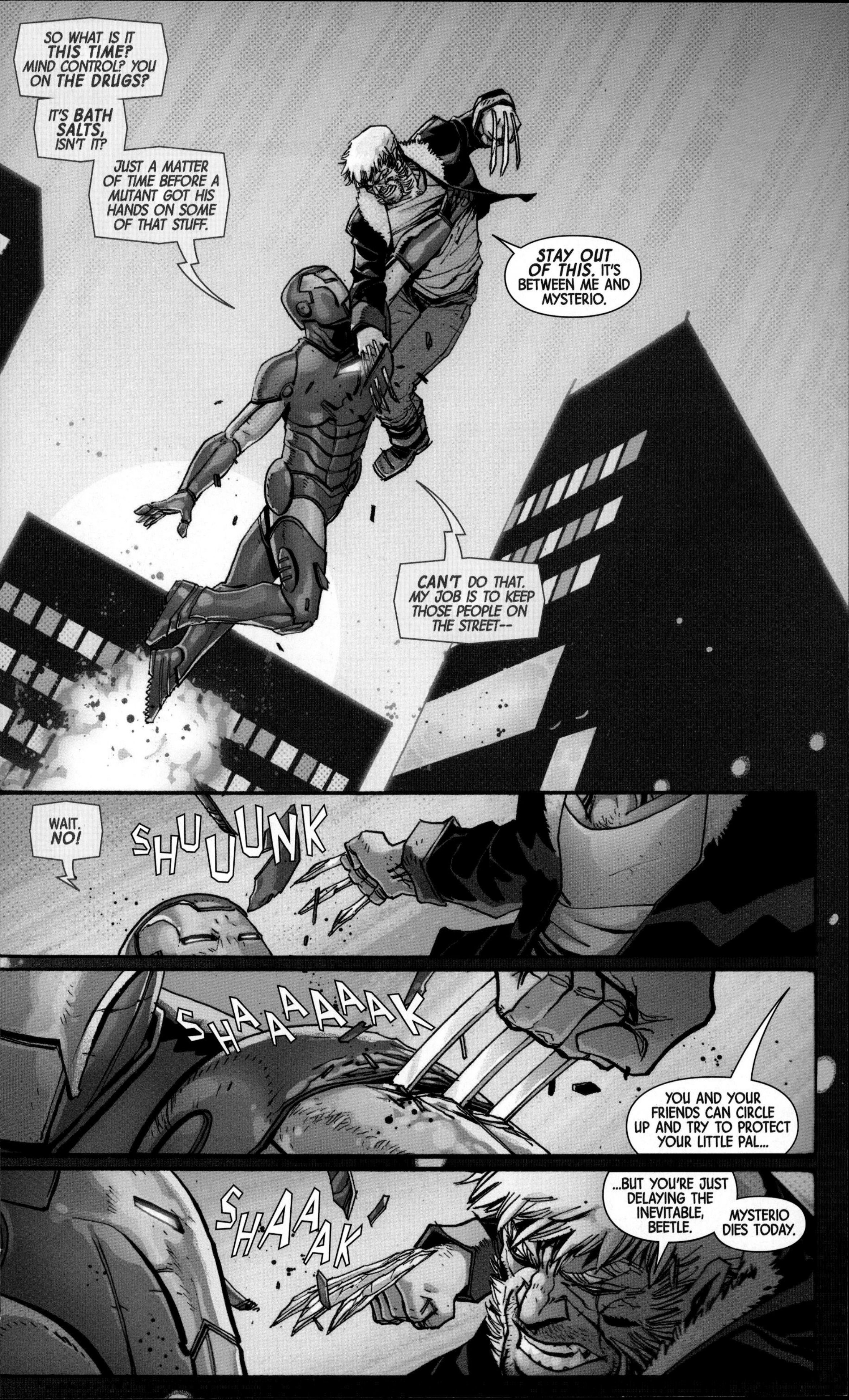

SO WHAT IS IT THIS TIME? MIND CONTROL? YOU ON THE DRUGS?
IT'S BATH SALTS, ISN'T IT?
JUST A MATTER OF TIME BEFORE A MUTANT GOT HIS HANDS ON SOME OF THAT STUFF.
STAY OUT OF THIS. IT'S BETWEEN ME AND MYSTERIO.
CAN'T DO THAT. MY JOB IS TO KEEP THOSE PEOPLE ON THE STREET--
WAIT. NO!
SHUUUNK
SHAAAAAAK
YOU AND YOUR FRIENDS CAN CIRCLE UP AND TRY TO PROTECT YOUR LITTLE PAL...
SHAAAK
...BUT YOU'RE JUST DELAYING THE INEVITABLE, BEETLE.
MYSTERIO DIES TODAY.

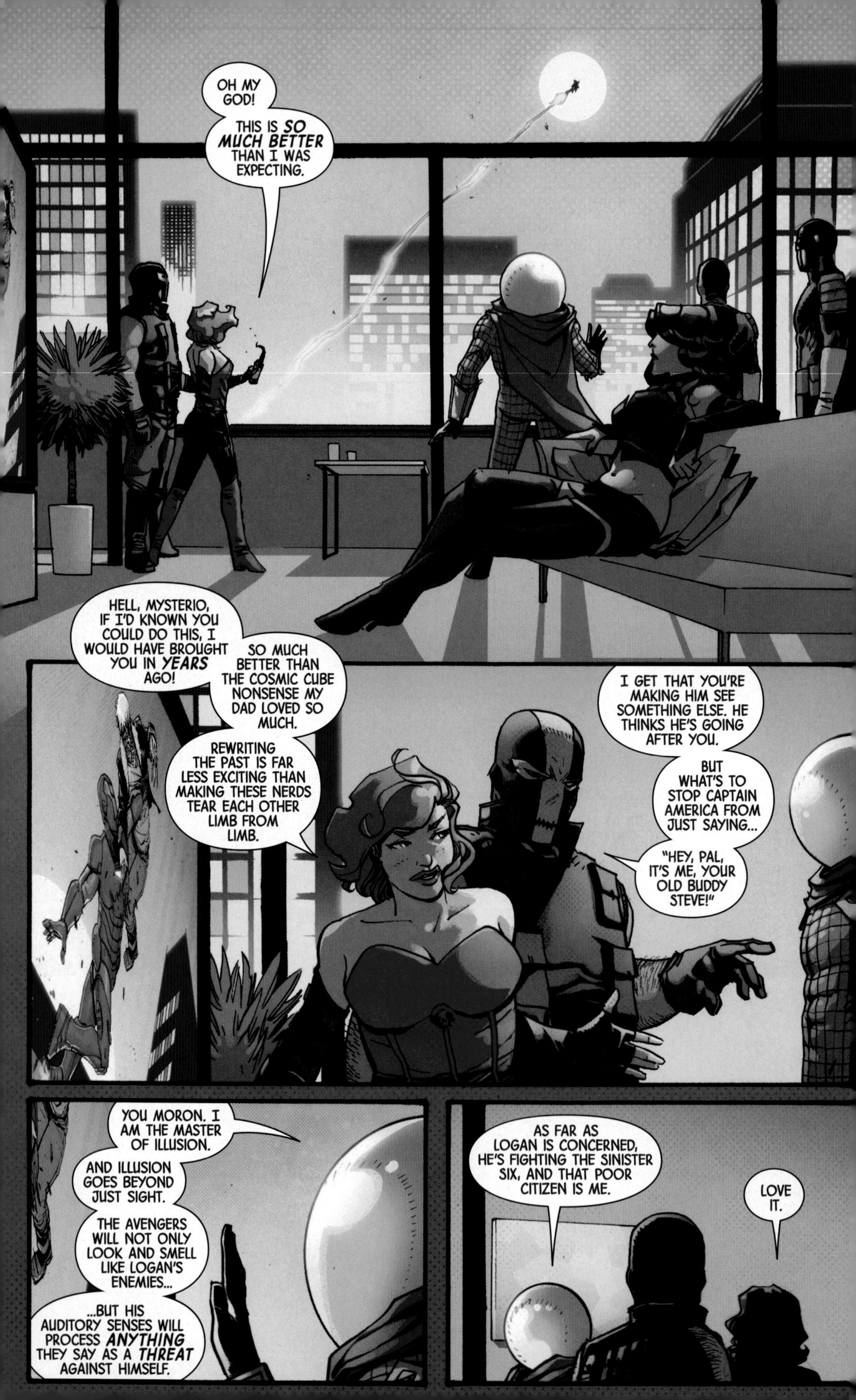
OH MY GOD!
THIS IS SO MUCH BETTER THAN I WAS EXPECTING.
HELL, MYSTERIO, IF I'D KNOWN YOU COULD DO THIS, I WOULD HAVE BROUGHT YOU IN YEARS AGO!
SO MUCH BETTER THAN THE COSMIC CUBE NONSENSE MY DAD LOVED SO MUCH.
REWRITING THE PAST IS FAR LESS EXCITING THAN MAKING THESE NERDS TEAR EACH OTHER LIMB FROM LIMB.
I GET THAT YOU'RE MAKING HIM SEE SOMETHING ELSE. HE THINKS HE'S GOING AFTER YOU.
BUT WHAT'S TO STOP CAPTAIN AMERICA FROM JUST SAYING...
"HEY, PAL, IT'S ME, YOUR OLD BUDDY STEVE!"
YOU MORON. I AM THE MASTER OF ILLUSION.
AND ILLUSION GOES BEYOND JUST SIGHT.
THE AVENGERS WILL NOT ONLY LOOK AND SMELL LIKE LOGAN'S ENEMIES...
...BUT HIS AUDITORY SENSES WILL PROCESS ANYTHING THEY SAY AS A THREAT AGAINST HIMSELF.
AS FAR AS LOGAN IS CONCERNED, HE'S FIGHTING THE SINISTER SIX, AND THAT POOR CITIZEN IS ME.
LOVE IT.

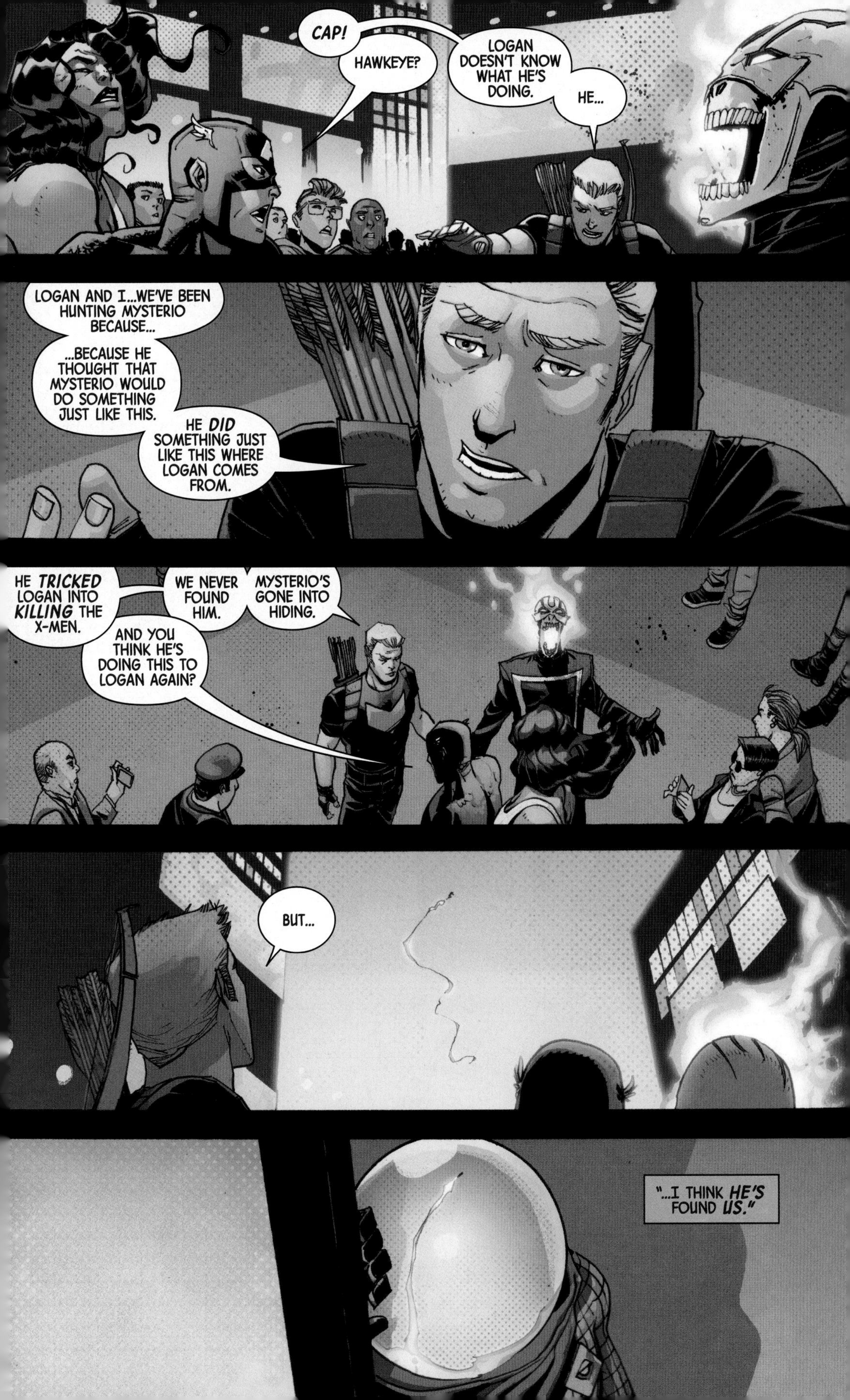
CAP!
HAWKEYE?
LOGAN DOESN'T KNOW WHAT HE'S DOING.
HE...
LOGAN AND I...WE'VE BEEN HUNTING MYSTERIO BECAUSE...
...BECAUSE HE THOUGHT THAT MYSTERIO WOULD DO SOMETHING JUST LIKE THIS.
HE DID SOMETHING JUST LIKE THIS WHERE LOGAN COMES FROM.
HE TRICKED LOGAN INTO KILLING THE X-MEN.
WE NEVER FOUND HIM.
MYSTERIO'S GONE INTO HIDING.
AND YOU THINK HE'S DOING THIS TO LOGAN AGAIN?
BUT...
"...I THINK HE'S FOUND US."

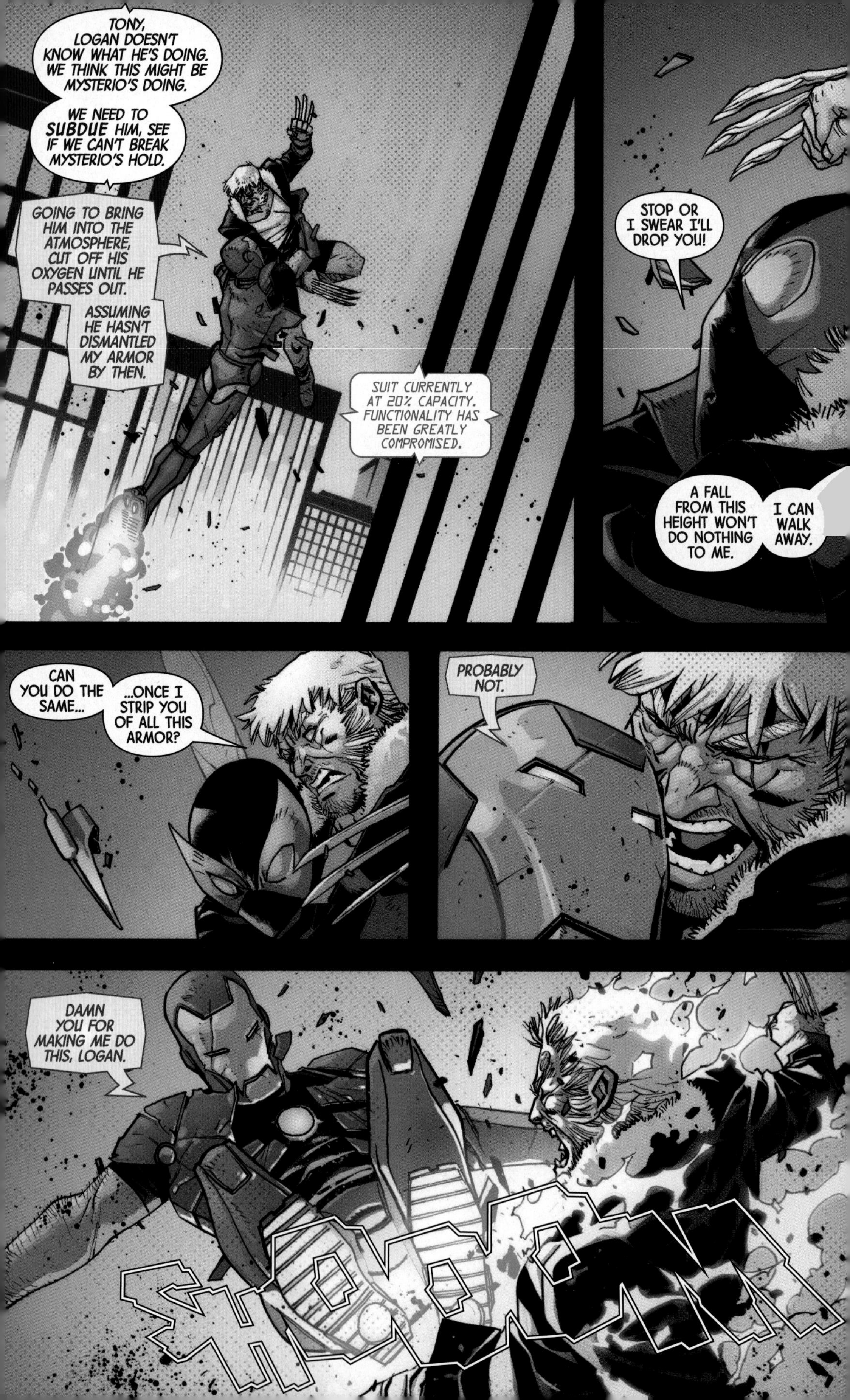
TONY, LOGAN DOESN'T KNOW WHAT HE'S DOING. WE THINK THIS MIGHT BE MYSTERIO'S DOING.
WE NEED TO SUBDUE HIM, SEE IF WE CAN'T BREAK MYSTERIO'S HOLD.
GOING TO BRING HIM INTO THE ATMOSPHERE, CUT OFF HIS OXYGEN UNTIL HE PASSES OUT.
ASSUMING HE HASN'T DISMANTLED MY ARMOR BY THEN.
SUIT CURRENTLY AT 20% CAPACITY. FUNCTIONALITY HAS BEEN GREATLY COMPROMISED.
STOP OR I SWEAR I'LL DROP YOU!
A FALL FROM THIS HEIGHT WON'T DO NOTHING TO ME.
I CAN WALK AWAY.
CAN YOU DO THE SAME...
...ONCE I STRIP YOU OF ALL THIS ARMOR?
PROBABLY NOT.
DAMN YOU FOR MAKING ME DO THIS, LOGAN.
SHOOOM

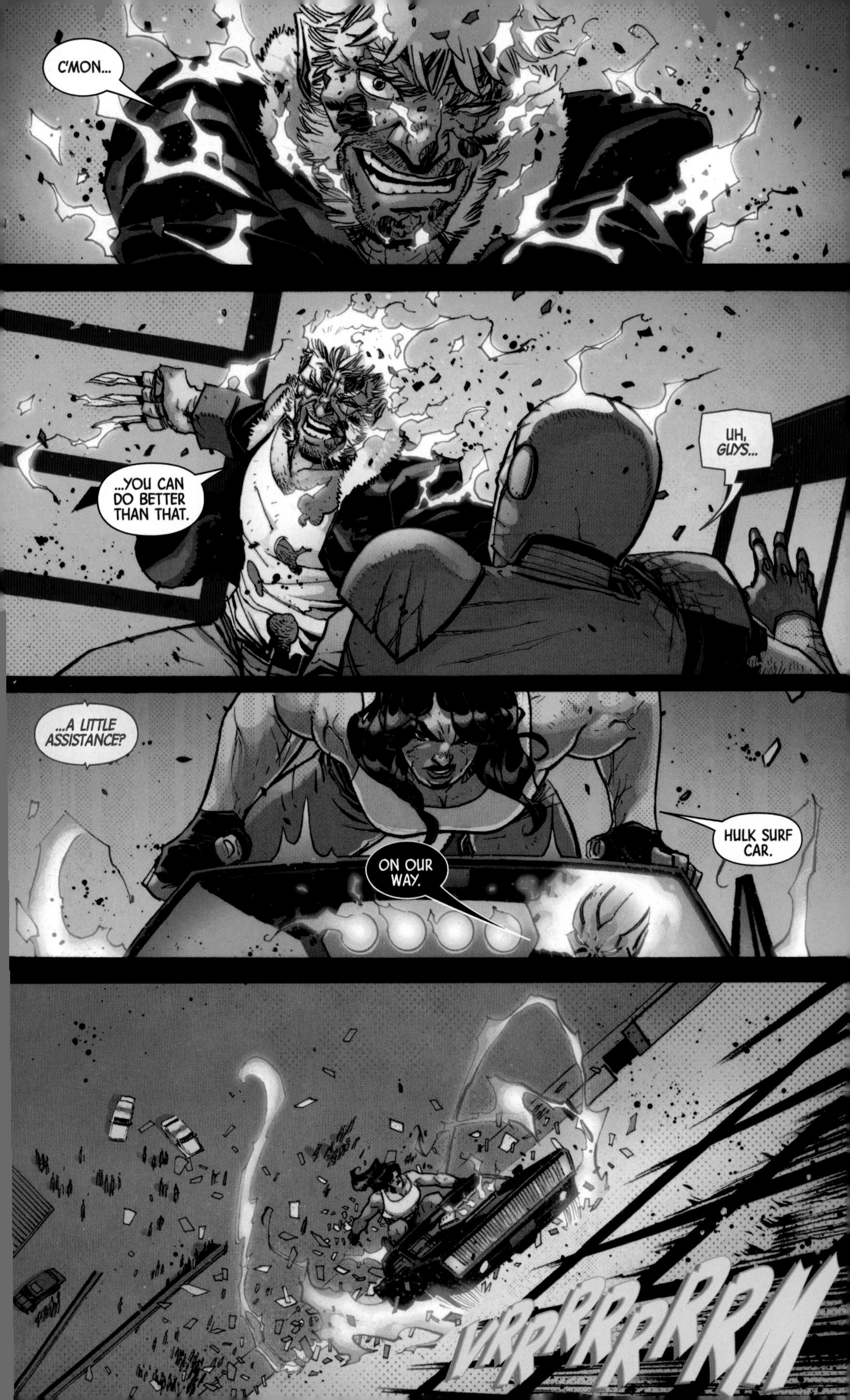
C'MON...
...YOU CAN DO BETTER THAN THAT.
UH, GUYS...
...A LITTLE ASSISTANCE?
HULK SURF CAR.
ON OUR WAY.
VRRRRRRRRM

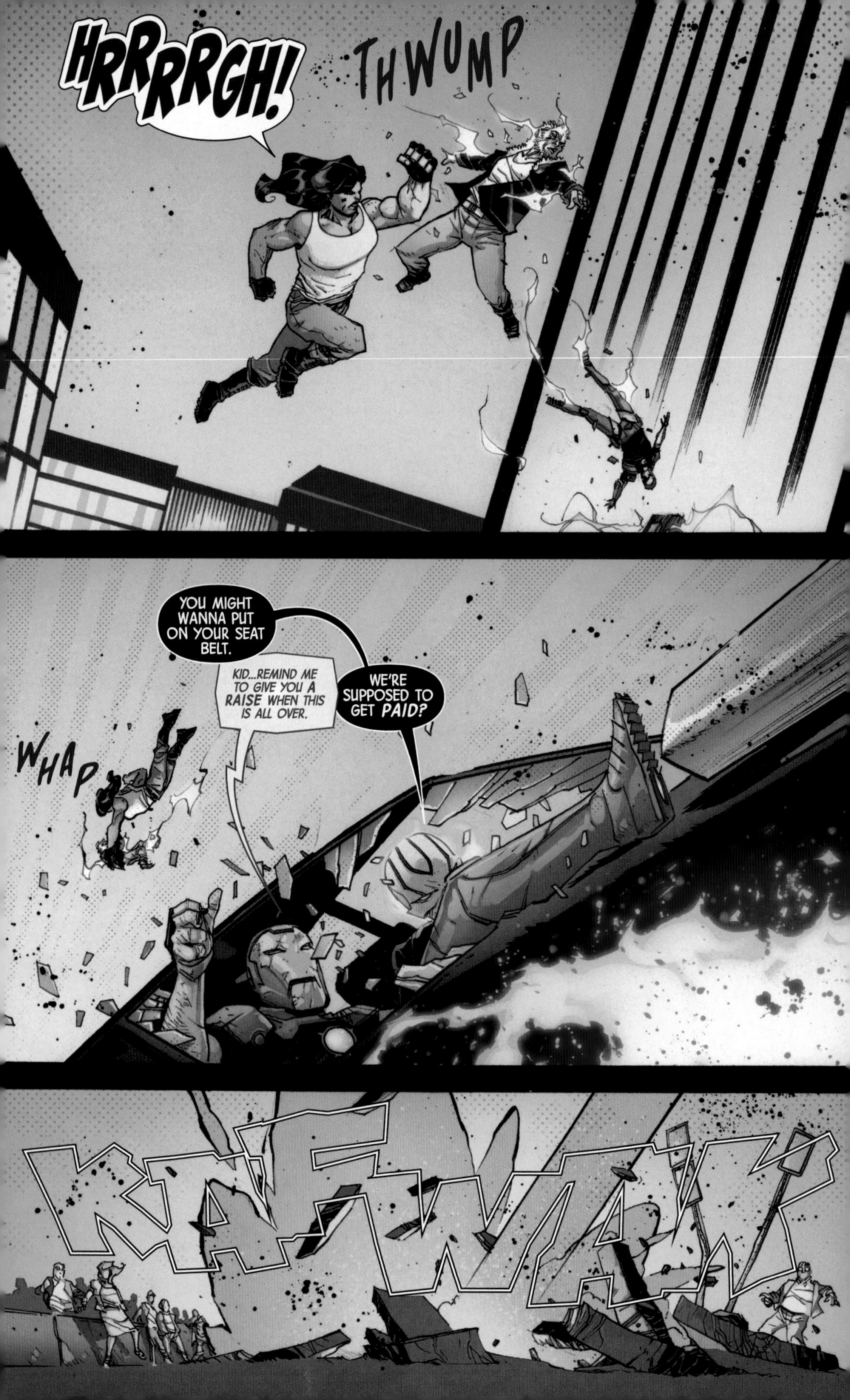
HRRRRGH!
THWUMP
YOU MIGHT WANNA PUT ON YOUR SEAT BELT.
KID...REMIND ME TO GIVE YOU A RAISE WHEN THIS IS ALL OVER.
WE'RE SUPPOSED TO GET PAID?
WHAP

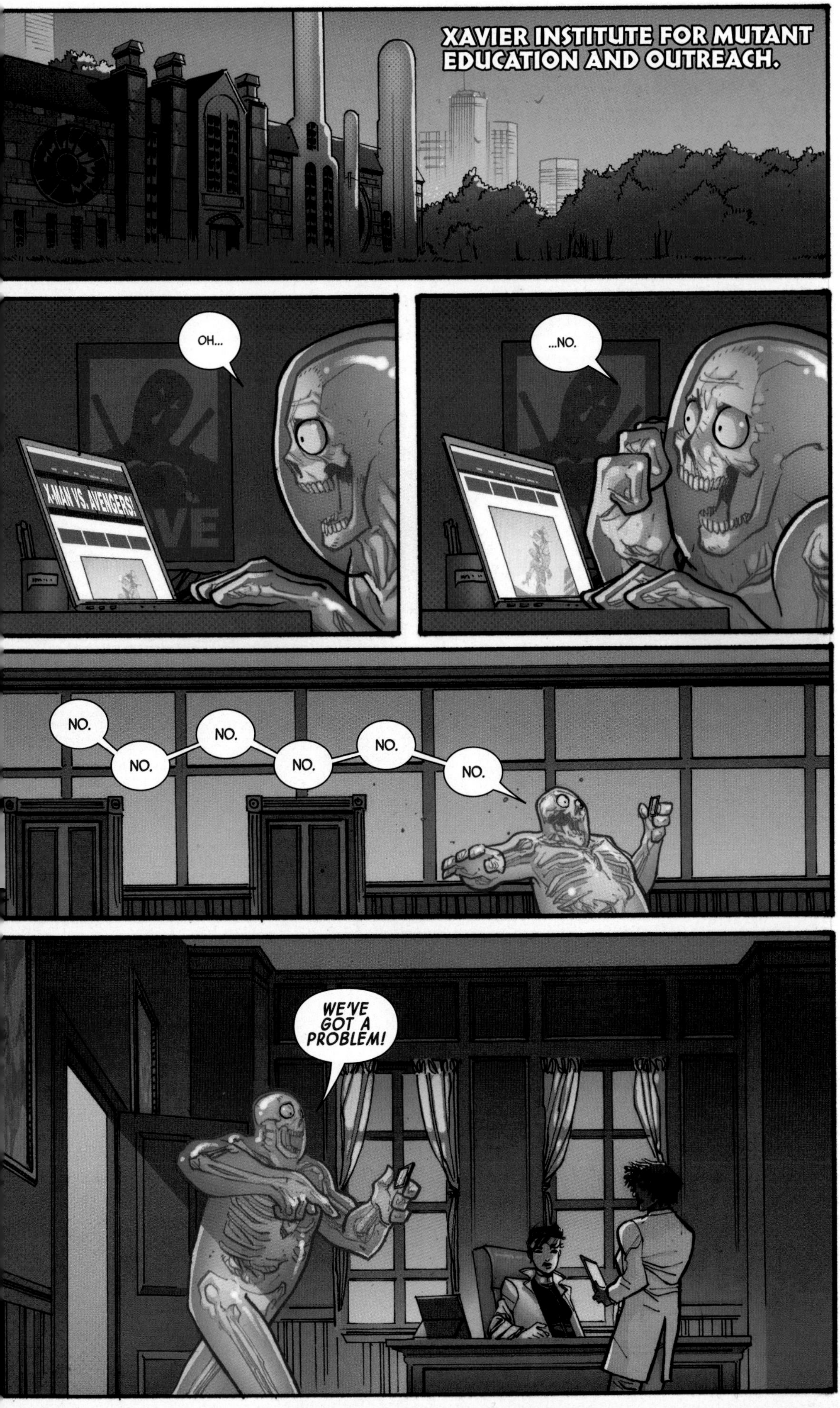
XAVIER INSTITUTE FOR MUTANT EDUCATION AND OUTREACH.
OH...
X-MAN VS. AVENGERS!
...NO.
NO.
NO.
NO.
NO.
NO.
NO.
WE'VE GOT A PROBLEM!

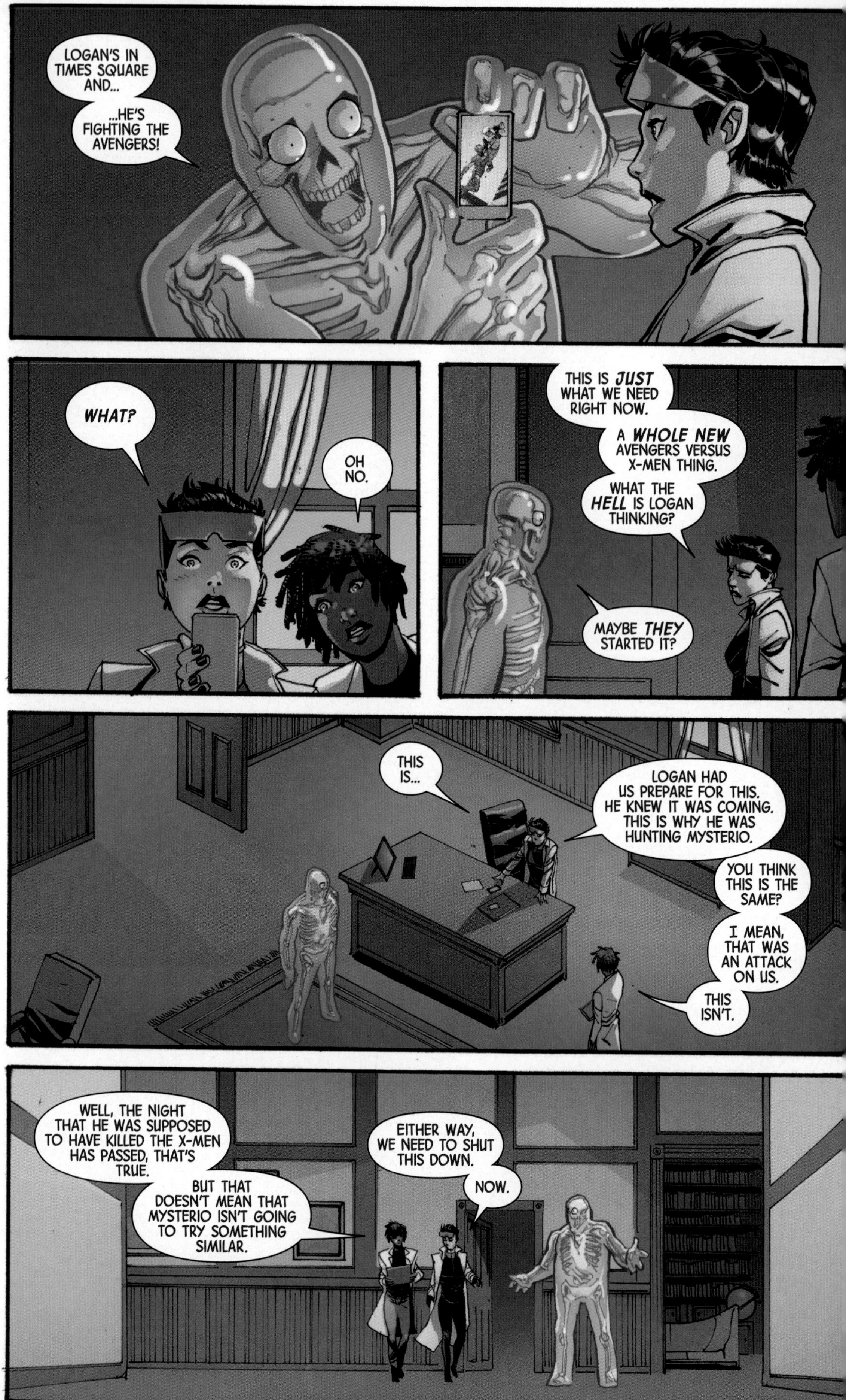

LOGAN'S IN TIMES SQUARE AND...
...HE'S FIGHTING THE AVENGERS!
WHAT?
OH NO.
THIS IS JUST WHAT WE NEED RIGHT NOW.
A WHOLE NEW AVENGERS VERSUS X-MEN THING.
WHAT THE HELL IS LOGAN THINKING?
MAYBE THEY STARTED IT?
THIS IS...
LOGAN HAD US PREPARE FOR THIS. HE KNEW IT WAS COMING. THIS IS WHY HE WAS HUNTING MYSTERIO.
YOU THINK THIS IS THE SAME?
I MEAN, THAT WAS AN ATTACK ON US.
THIS ISN'T.
WELL, THE NIGHT THAT HE WAS SUPPOSED TO HAVE KILLED THE X-MEN HAS PASSED, THAT'S TRUE.
BUT THAT DOESN'T MEAN THAT MYSTERIO ISN'T GOING TO TRY SOMETHING SIMILAR.
EITHER WAY, WE NEED TO SHUT THIS DOWN.
NOW.

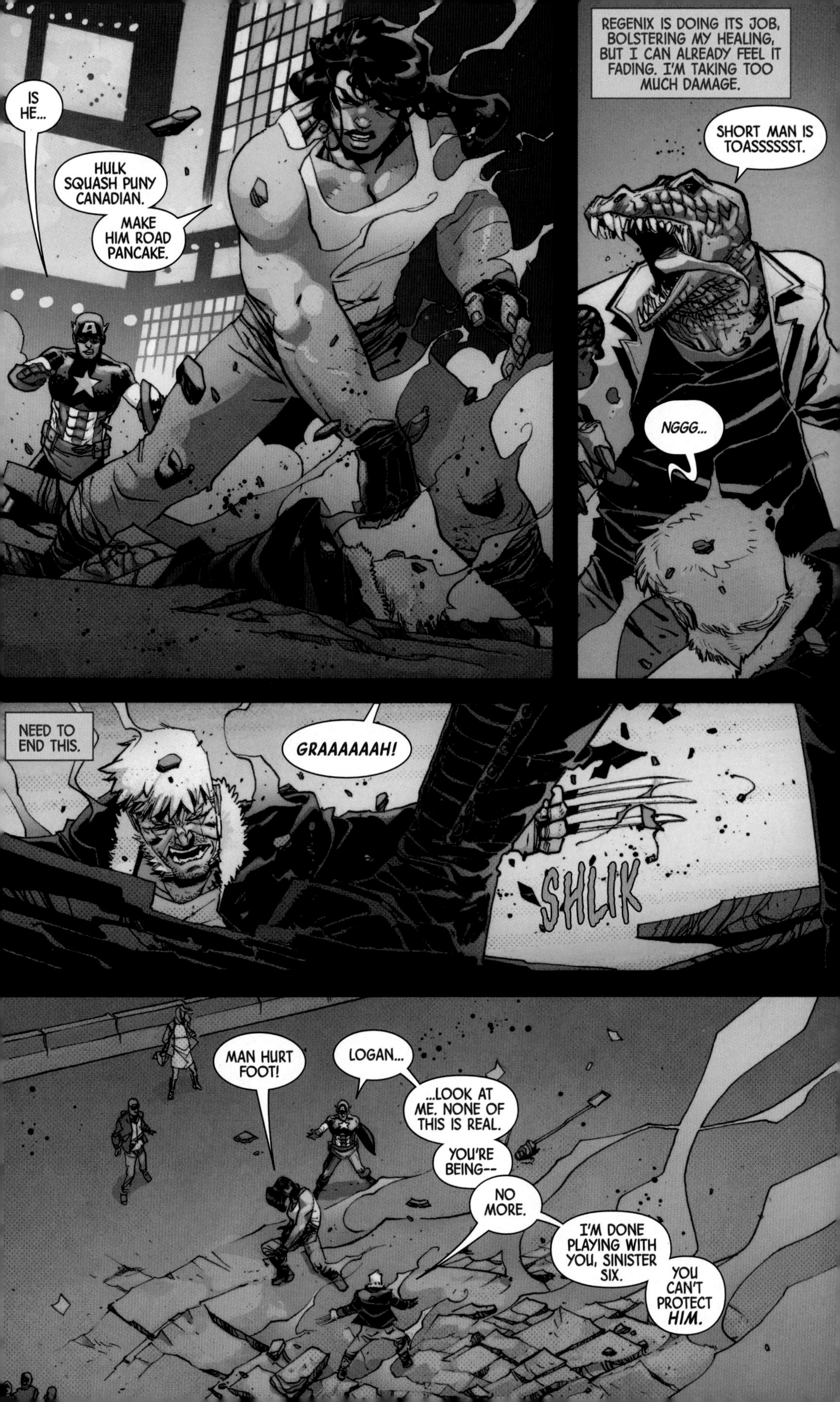
IS HE...
HULK SQUASH PUNY CANADIAN.
MAKE HIM ROAD PANCAKE.
REGENIX IS DOING ITS JOB, BOLSTERING MY HEALING, BUT I CAN ALREADY FEEL IT FADING. I'M TAKING TOO MUCH DAMAGE.
SHORT MAN IS TOASSSSSST.
NGGG...
NEED TO END THIS.
GRAAAAAAH!
SHLIK
MAN HURT FOOT!
LOGAN...
...LOOK AT ME. NONE OF THIS IS REAL.
YOU'RE BEING--
NO MORE.
I'M DONE PLAYING WITH YOU, SINISTER SIX.
YOU CAN'T PROTECT *HIM*.

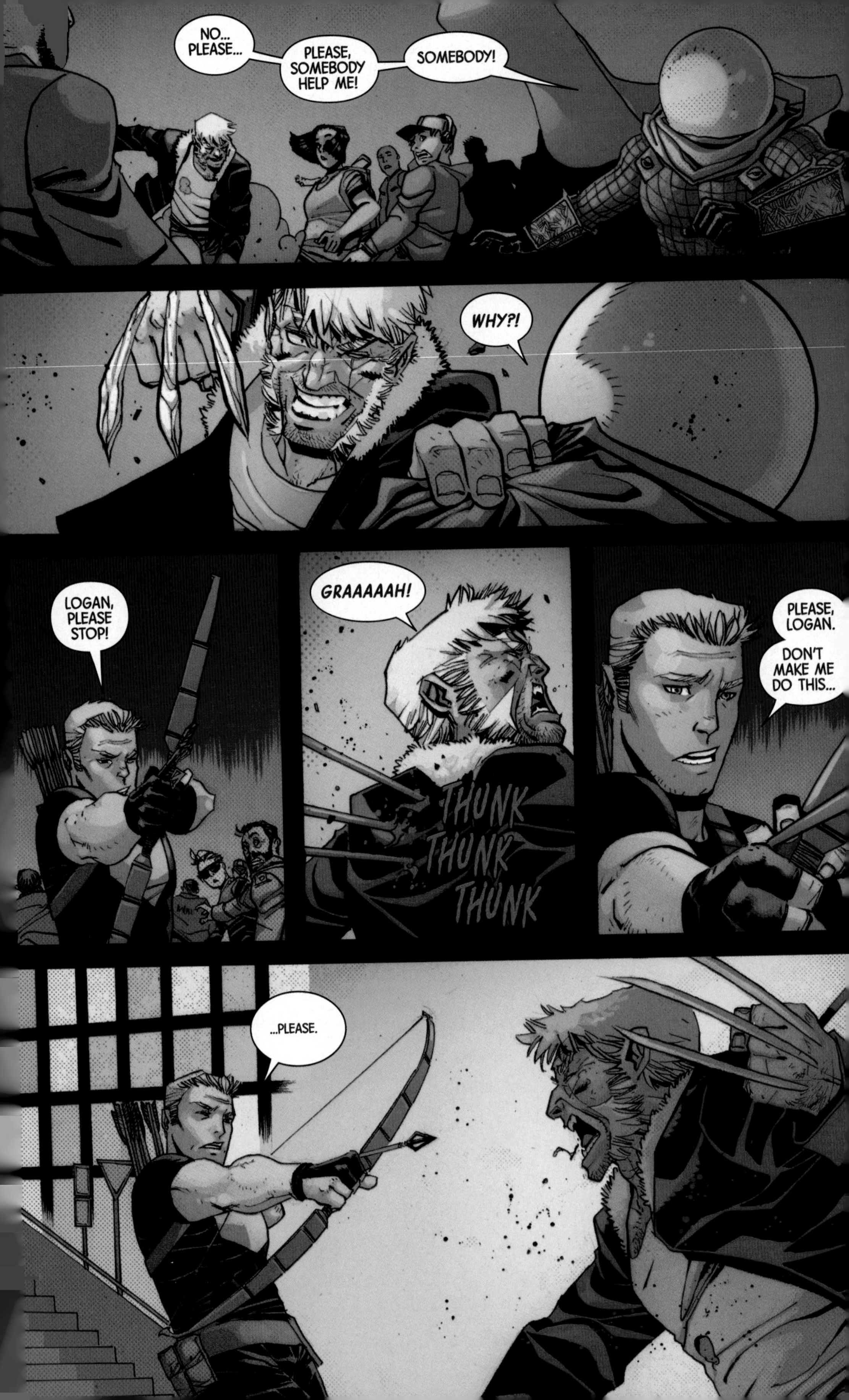
NO... PLEASE...
PLEASE, SOMEBODY HELP ME!
SOMEBODY!
WHY?!
LOGAN, PLEASE STOP!
GRAAAAAH!
THUNK THUNK THUNK
PLEASE, LOGAN.
DON'T MAKE ME DO THIS...
...PLEASE.

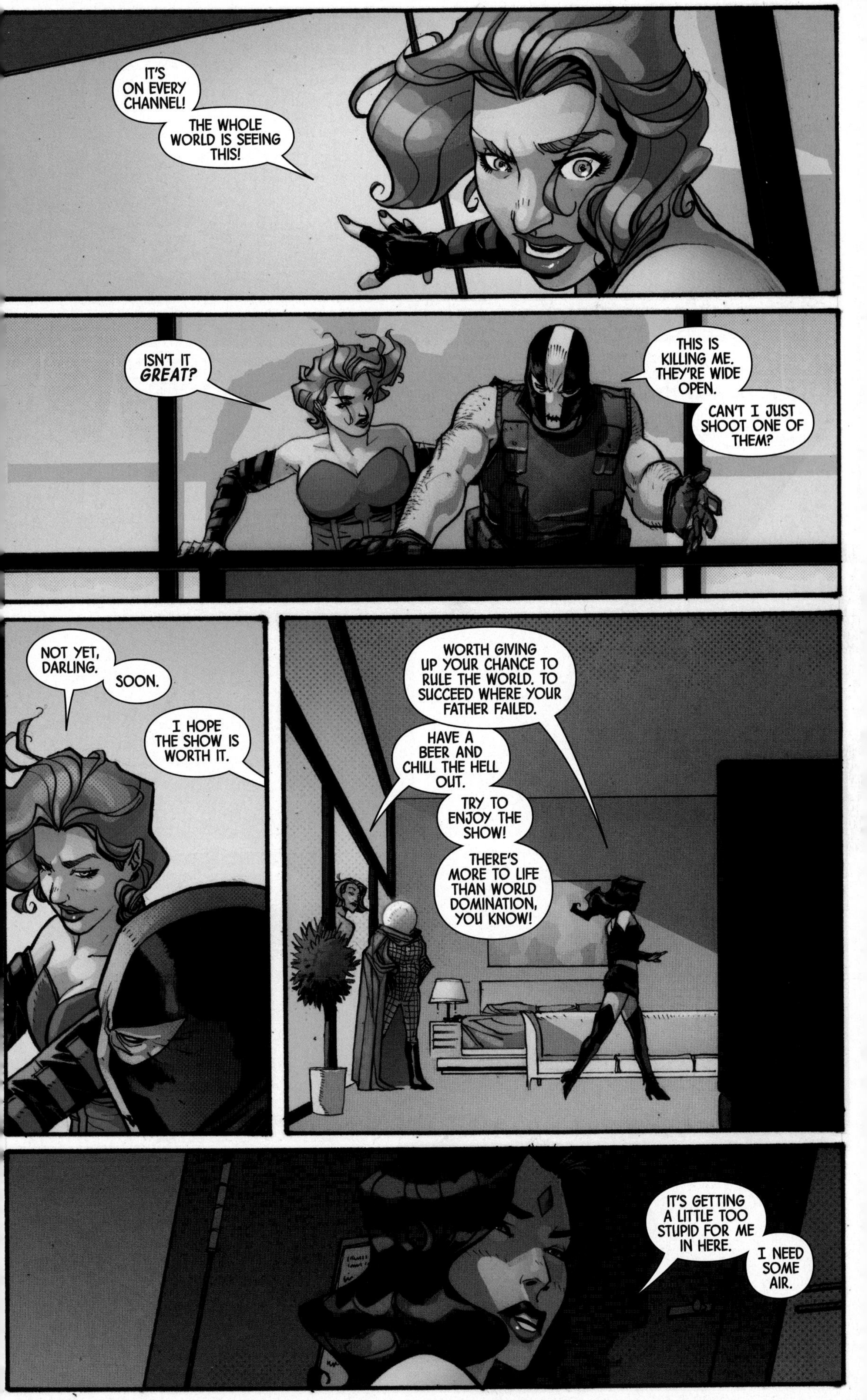
IT'S ON EVERY CHANNEL!
THE WHOLE WORLD IS SEEING THIS!
ISN'T IT *GREAT?*
THIS IS KILLING ME. THEY'RE WIDE OPEN.
CAN'T I JUST SHOOT ONE OF THEM?
NOT YET, DARLING.
SOON.
I HOPE THE SHOW IS WORTH IT.
WORTH GIVING UP YOUR CHANCE TO RULE THE WORLD. TO SUCCEED WHERE YOUR FATHER FAILED.
HAVE A BEER AND CHILL THE HELL OUT.
TRY TO ENJOY THE SHOW!
THERE'S MORE TO LIFE THAN WORLD DOMINATION, YOU KNOW!
IT'S GETTING A LITTLE TOO STUPID FOR ME IN HERE.
I NEED SOME AIR.

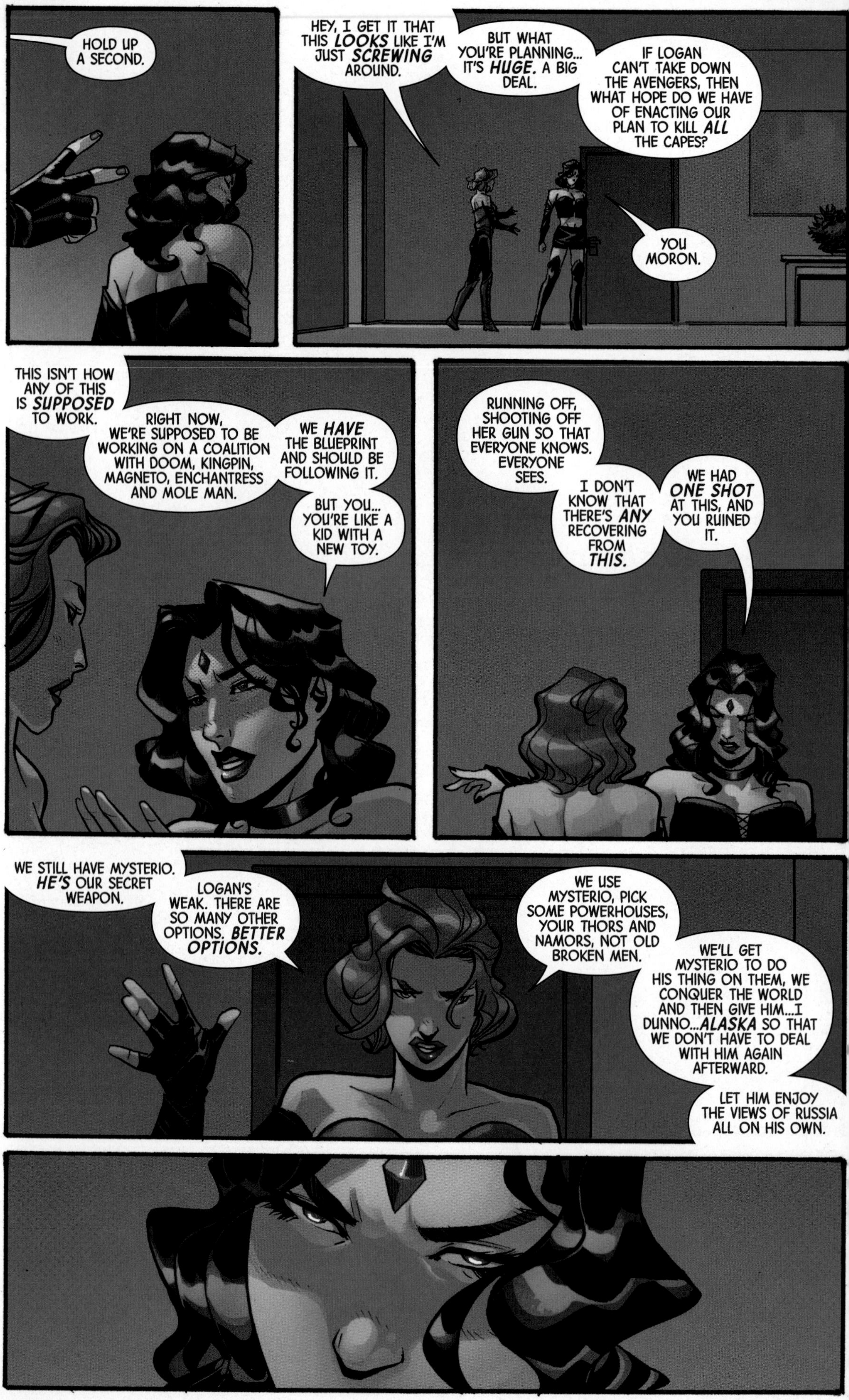
HOLD UP A SECOND.
HEY, I GET IT THAT THIS LOOKS LIKE I'M JUST SCREWING AROUND.
BUT WHAT YOU'RE PLANNING... IT'S HUGE. A BIG DEAL.
IF LOGAN CAN'T TAKE DOWN THE AVENGERS, THEN WHAT HOPE DO WE HAVE OF ENACTING OUR PLAN TO KILL ALL THE CAPES?
YOU MORON.
THIS ISN'T HOW ANY OF THIS IS SUPPOSED TO WORK.
RIGHT NOW, WE'RE SUPPOSED TO BE WORKING ON A COALITION WITH DOOM, KINGPIN, MAGNETO, ENCHANTRESS AND MOLE MAN.
WE HAVE THE BLUEPRINT AND SHOULD BE FOLLOWING IT.
BUT YOU... YOU'RE LIKE A KID WITH A NEW TOY.
RUNNING OFF, SHOOTING OFF HER GUN SO THAT EVERYONE KNOWS. EVERYONE SEES.
I DON'T KNOW THAT THERE'S ANY RECOVERING FROM THIS.
WE HAD ONE SHOT AT THIS, AND YOU RUINED IT.
WE STILL HAVE MYSTERIO. HE'S OUR SECRET WEAPON.
LOGAN'S WEAK. THERE ARE SO MANY OTHER OPTIONS. BETTER OPTIONS.
WE USE MYSTERIO, PICK SOME POWERHOUSES, YOUR THORS AND NAMORS, NOT OLD BROKEN MEN.
WE'LL GET MYSTERIO TO DO HIS THING ON THEM, WE CONQUER THE WORLD AND THEN GIVE HIM...I DUNNO...ALASKA SO THAT WE DON'T HAVE TO DEAL WITH HIM AGAIN AFTERWARD.
LET HIM ENJOY THE VIEWS OF RUSSIA ALL ON HIS OWN.

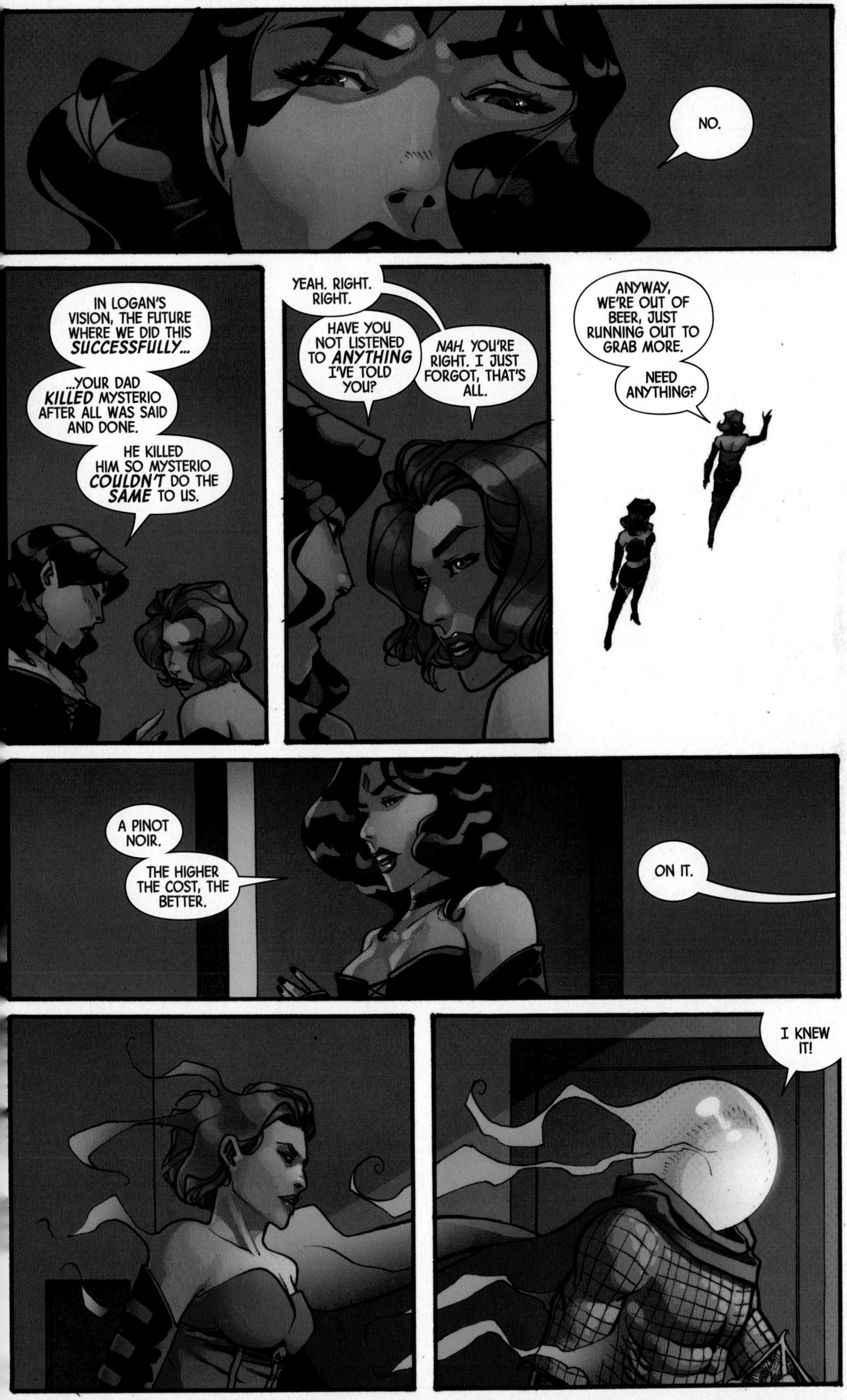
NO.
IN LOGAN'S VISION, THE FUTURE WHERE WE DID THIS *SUCCESSFULLY*...
...YOUR DAD *KILLED* MYSTERIO AFTER ALL WAS SAID AND DONE.
HE KILLED HIM SO MYSTERIO *COULDN'T* DO THE *SAME* TO US.
YEAH. RIGHT. RIGHT.
HAVE YOU NOT LISTENED TO *ANYTHING* I'VE TOLD YOU?
NAH. YOU'RE RIGHT. I JUST FORGOT, THAT'S ALL.
ANYWAY, WE'RE OUT OF BEER, JUST RUNNING OUT TO GRAB MORE.
NEED ANYTHING?
A PINOT NOIR.
THE HIGHER THE COST, THE BETTER.
ON IT.
I KNEW IT!

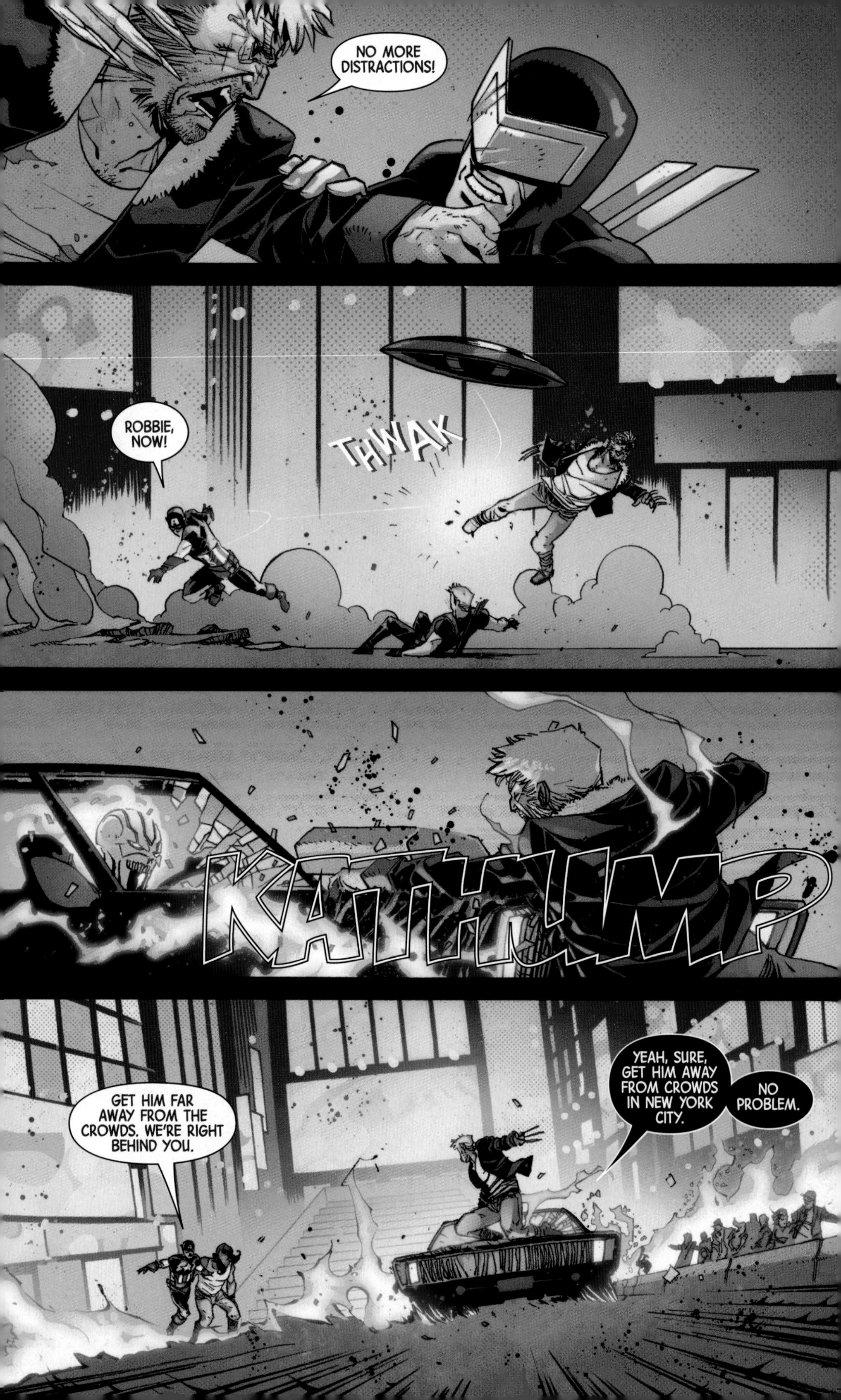
NO MORE DISTRACTIONS!
ROBBIE, NOW!
THWAK
KATHUMP
GET HIM FAR AWAY FROM THE CROWDS. WE'RE RIGHT BEHIND YOU.
YEAH, SURE, GET HIM AWAY FROM CROWDS IN NEW YORK CITY.
NO PROBLEM.

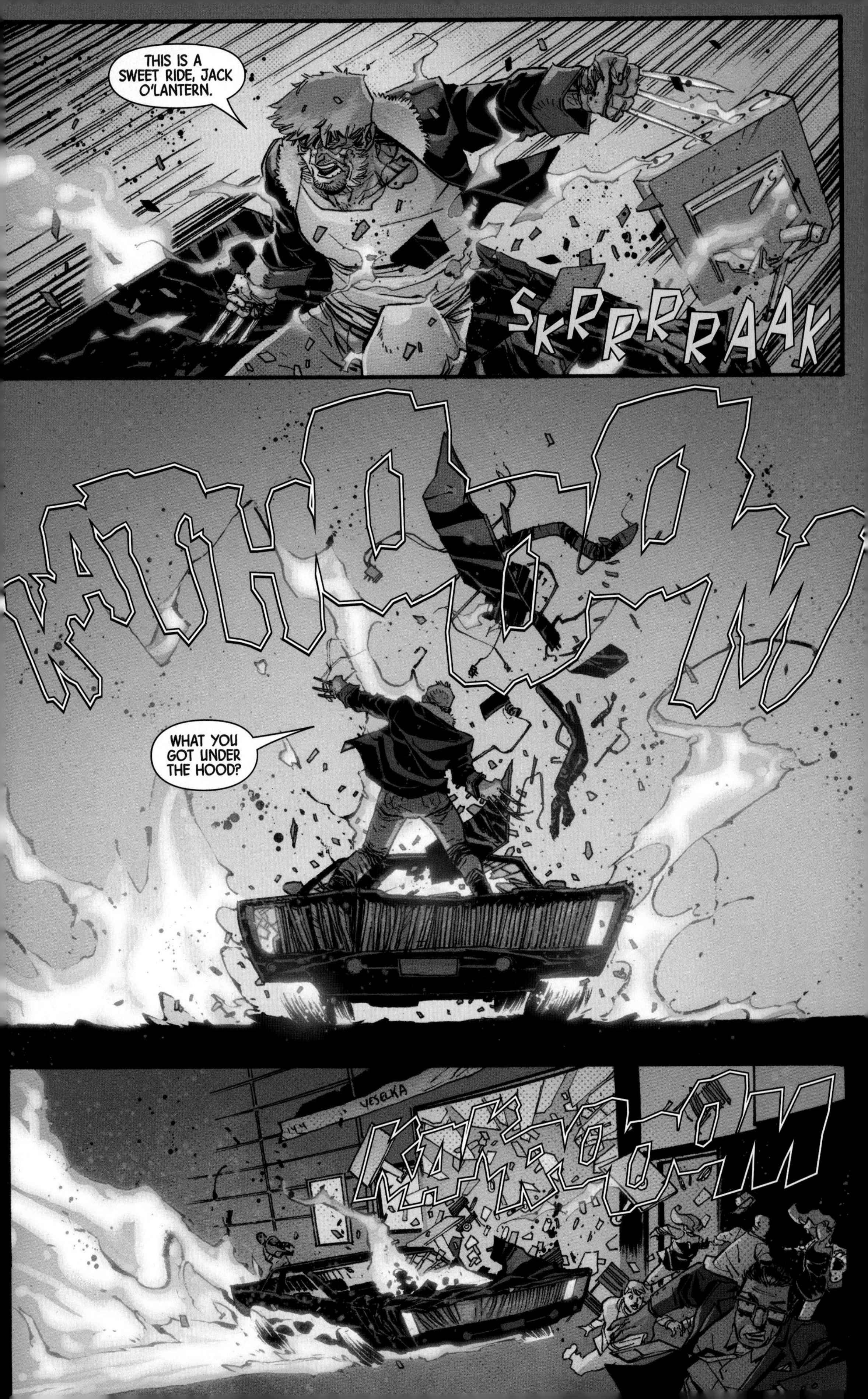
THIS IS A SWEET RIDE, JACK O'LANTERN.
SKRRRRAAK
WHAT YOU GOT UNDER THE HOOD?

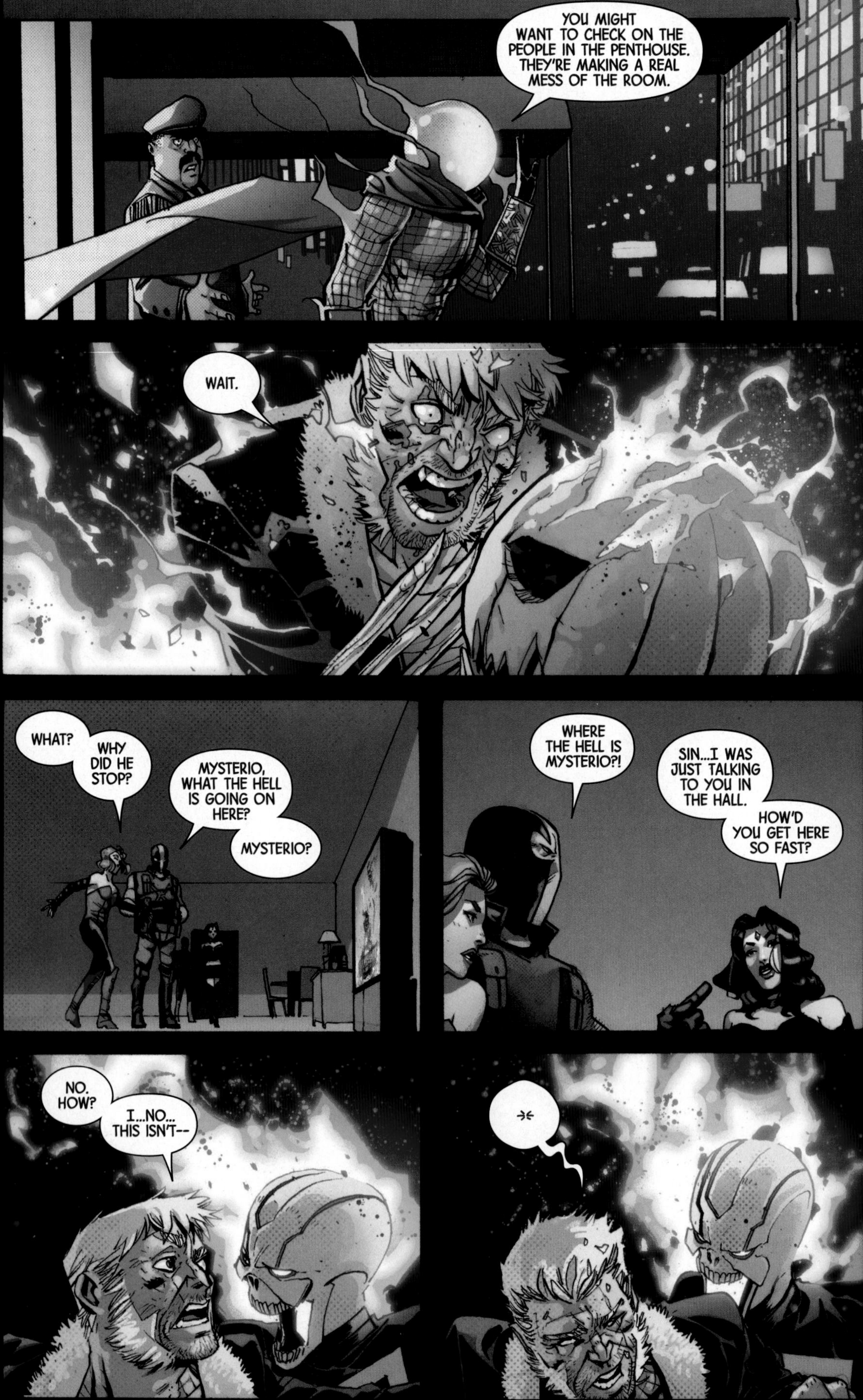
YOU MIGHT WANT TO CHECK ON THE PEOPLE IN THE PENTHOUSE. THEY'RE MAKING A REAL MESS OF THE ROOM.
WAIT.
WHAT?
WHY DID HE STOP?
MYSTERIO, WHAT THE HELL IS GOING ON HERE?
MYSTERIO?
WHERE THE HELL IS MYSTERIO?!
SIN...I WAS JUST TALKING TO YOU IN THE HALL.
HOW'D YOU GET HERE SO FAST?
NO. HOW?
I...NO... THIS ISN'T--

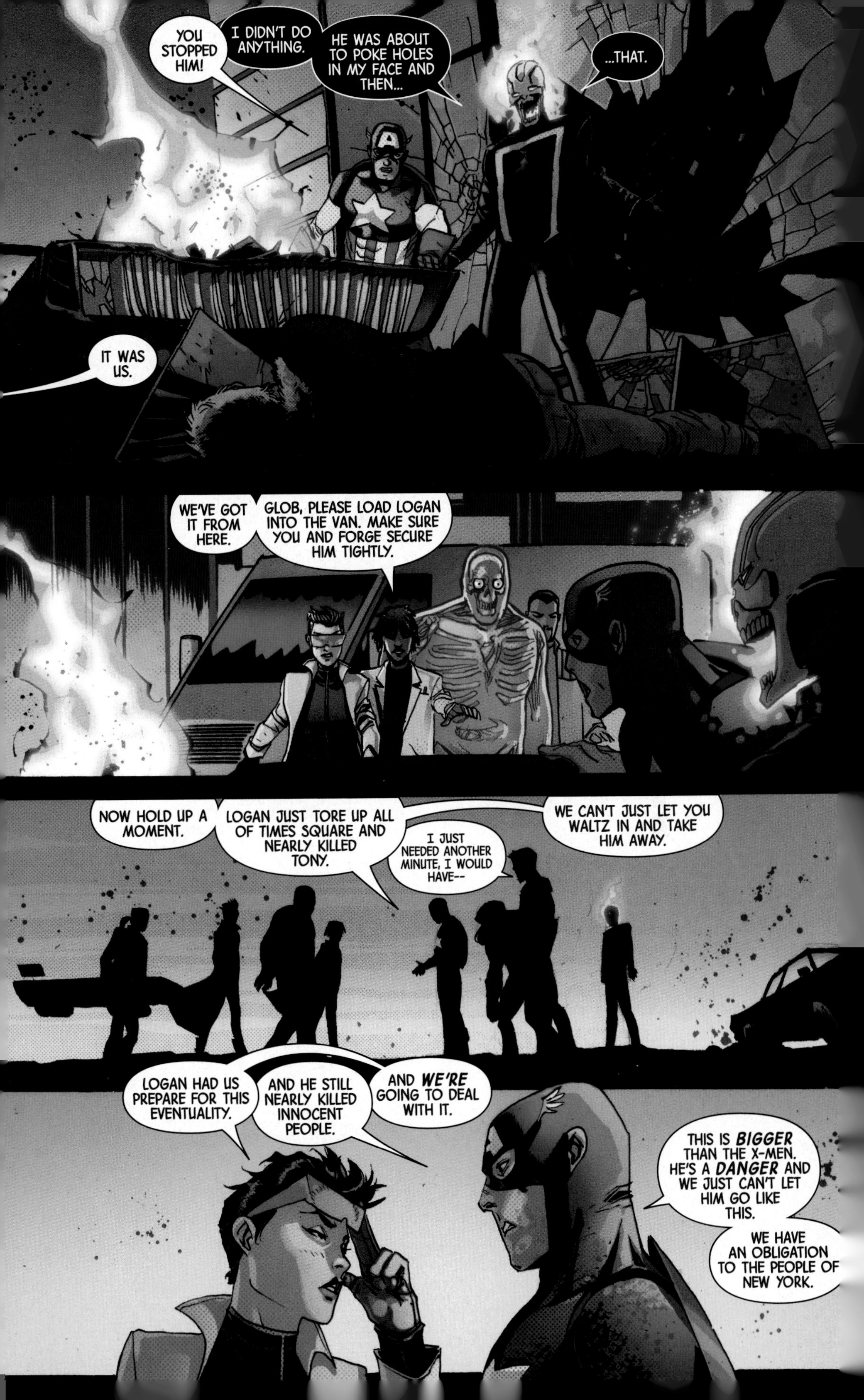
YOU STOPPED HIM!
I DIDN'T DO ANYTHING.
HE WAS ABOUT TO POKE HOLES IN MY FACE AND THEN...
...THAT.
IT WAS US.
WE'VE GOT IT FROM HERE.
GLOB, PLEASE LOAD LOGAN INTO THE VAN. MAKE SURE YOU AND FORGE SECURE HIM TIGHTLY.
NOW HOLD UP A MOMENT.
LOGAN JUST TORE UP ALL OF TIMES SQUARE AND NEARLY KILLED TONY.
I JUST NEEDED ANOTHER MINUTE, I WOULD HAVE--
WE CAN'T JUST LET YOU WALTZ IN AND TAKE HIM AWAY.
LOGAN HAD US PREPARE FOR THIS EVENTUALITY.
AND HE STILL NEARLY KILLED INNOCENT PEOPLE.
AND WE'RE GOING TO DEAL WITH IT.
THIS IS BIGGER THAN THE X-MEN. HE'S A DANGER AND WE JUST CAN'T LET HIM GO LIKE THIS.
WE HAVE AN OBLIGATION TO THE PEOPLE OF NEW YORK.

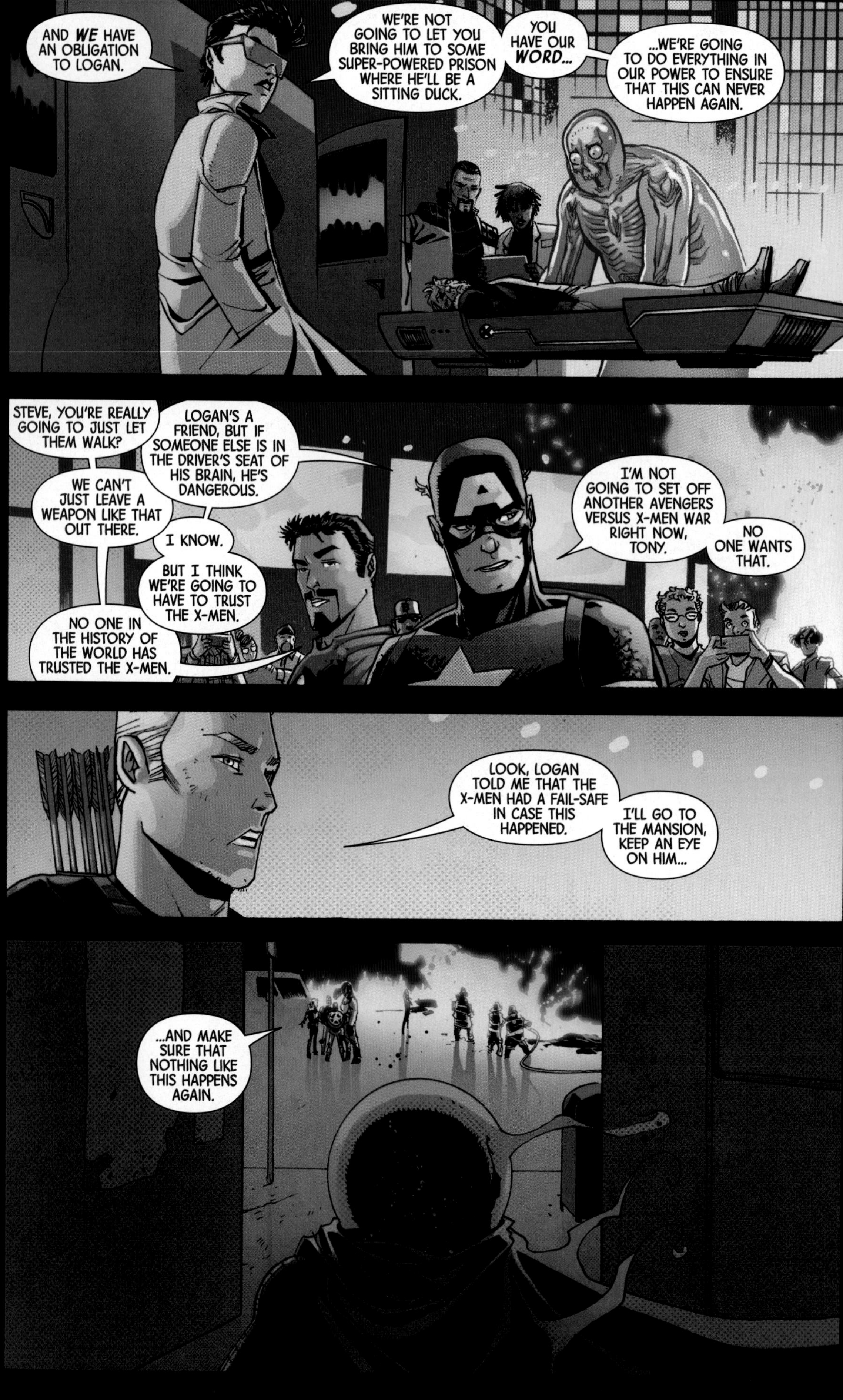
AND WE HAVE AN OBLIGATION TO LOGAN.
WE'RE NOT GOING TO LET YOU BRING HIM TO SOME SUPER-POWERED PRISON WHERE HE'LL BE A SITTING DUCK.
YOU HAVE OUR WORD...
...WE'RE GOING TO DO EVERYTHING IN OUR POWER TO ENSURE THAT THIS CAN NEVER HAPPEN AGAIN.
STEVE, YOU'RE REALLY GOING TO JUST LET THEM WALK?
LOGAN'S A FRIEND, BUT IF SOMEONE ELSE IS IN THE DRIVER'S SEAT OF HIS BRAIN, HE'S DANGEROUS.
WE CAN'T JUST LEAVE A WEAPON LIKE THAT OUT THERE.
I KNOW.
BUT I THINK WE'RE GOING TO HAVE TO TRUST THE X-MEN.
NO ONE IN THE HISTORY OF THE WORLD HAS TRUSTED THE X-MEN.
I'M NOT GOING TO SET OFF ANOTHER AVENGERS VERSUS X-MEN WAR RIGHT NOW, TONY.
NO ONE WANTS THAT.
LOOK, LOGAN TOLD ME THAT THE X-MEN HAD A FAIL-SAFE IN CASE THIS HAPPENED.
I'LL GO TO THE MANSION, KEEP AN EYE ON HIM...
...AND MAKE SURE THAT NOTHING LIKE THIS HAPPENS AGAIN.

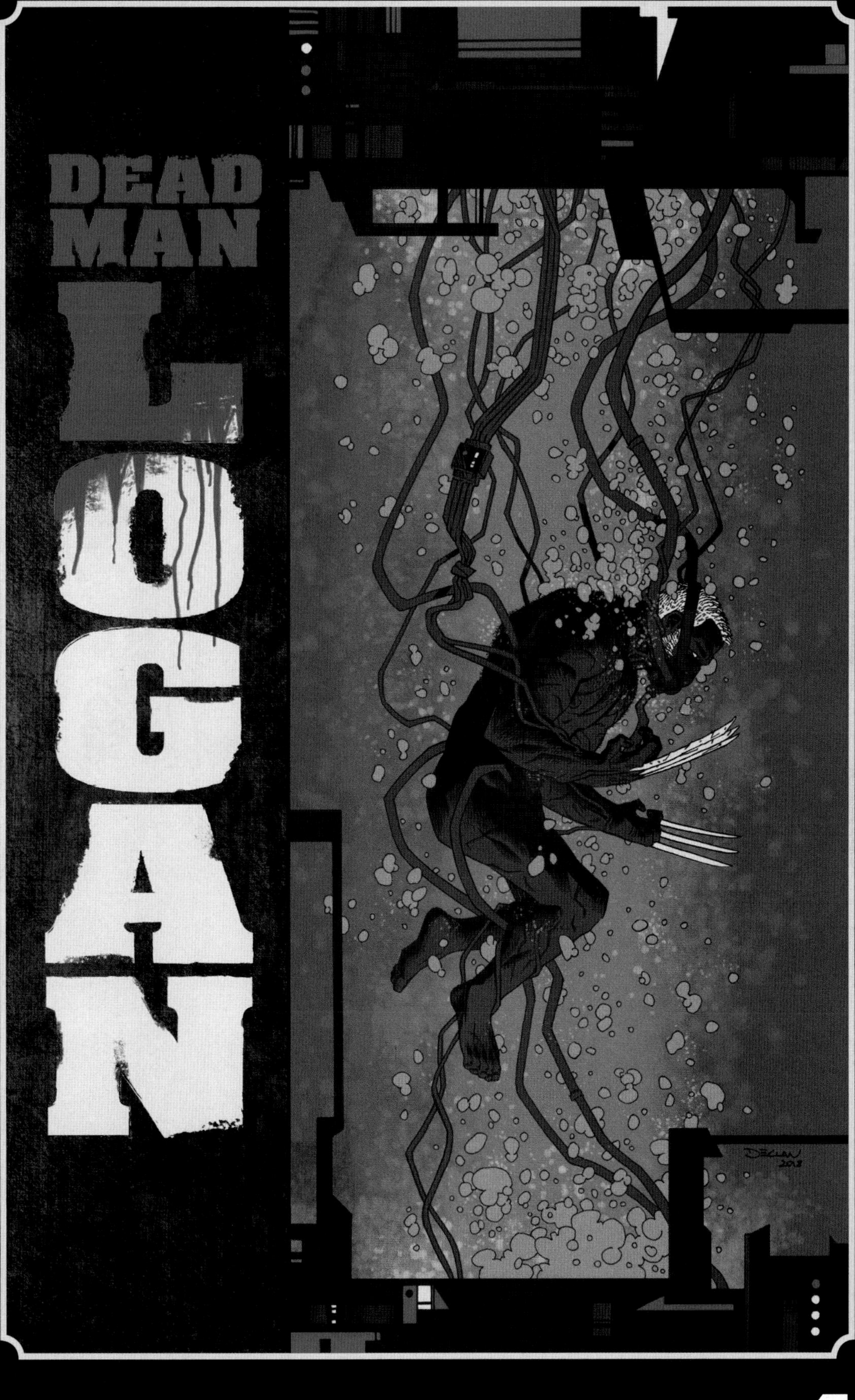
DEAD
MAN
LOGAN

4

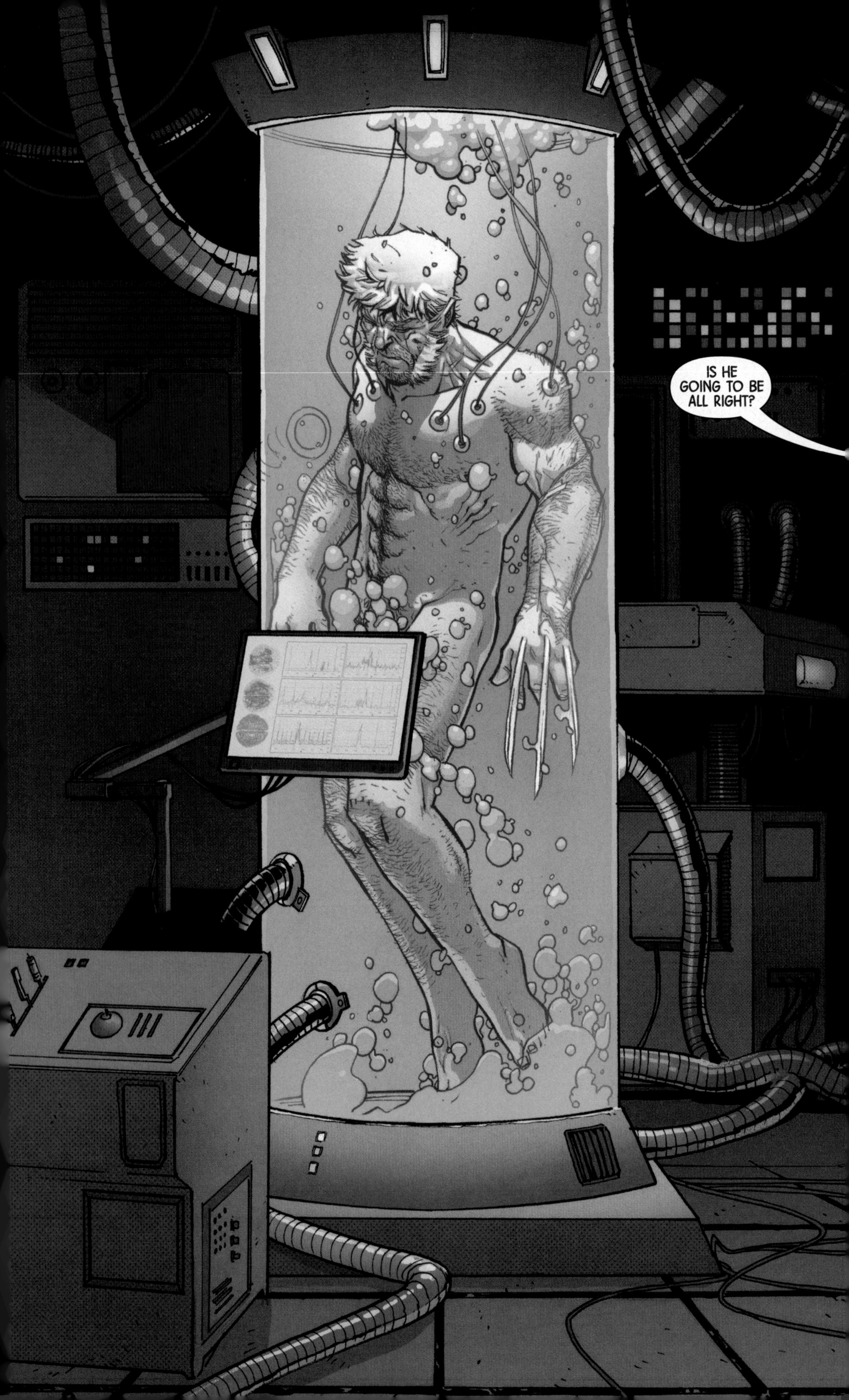
IS HE GOING TO BE ALL RIGHT?

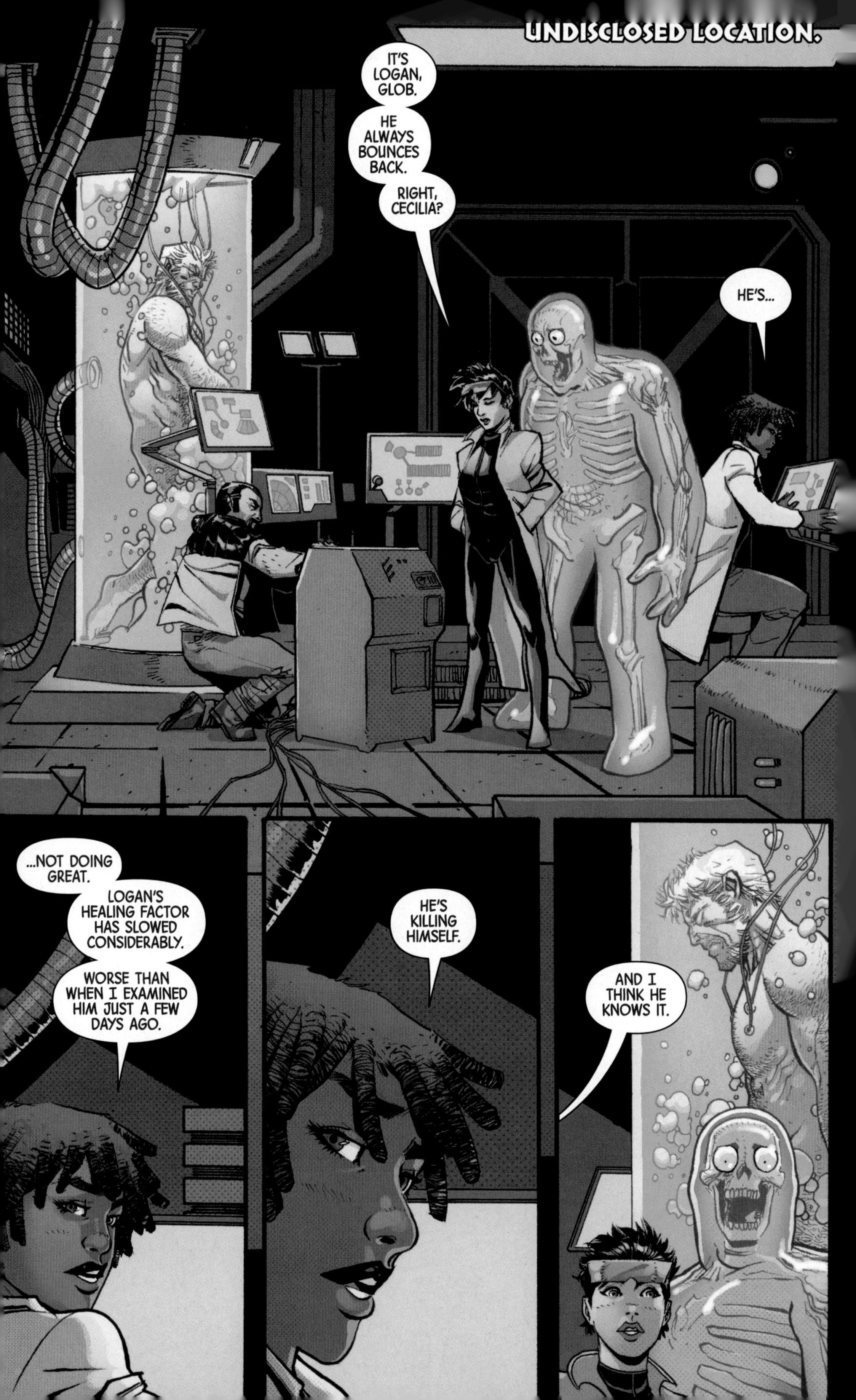
UNDISCLOSED LOCATION.
IT'S LOGAN, GLOB.
HE ALWAYS BOUNCES BACK.
RIGHT, CECILIA?
HE'S...
...NOT DOING GREAT.
LOGAN'S HEALING FACTOR HAS SLOWED CONSIDERABLY.
WORSE THAN WHEN I EXAMINED HIM JUST A FEW DAYS AGO.
HE'S KILLING HIMSELF.
AND I THINK HE KNOWS IT.

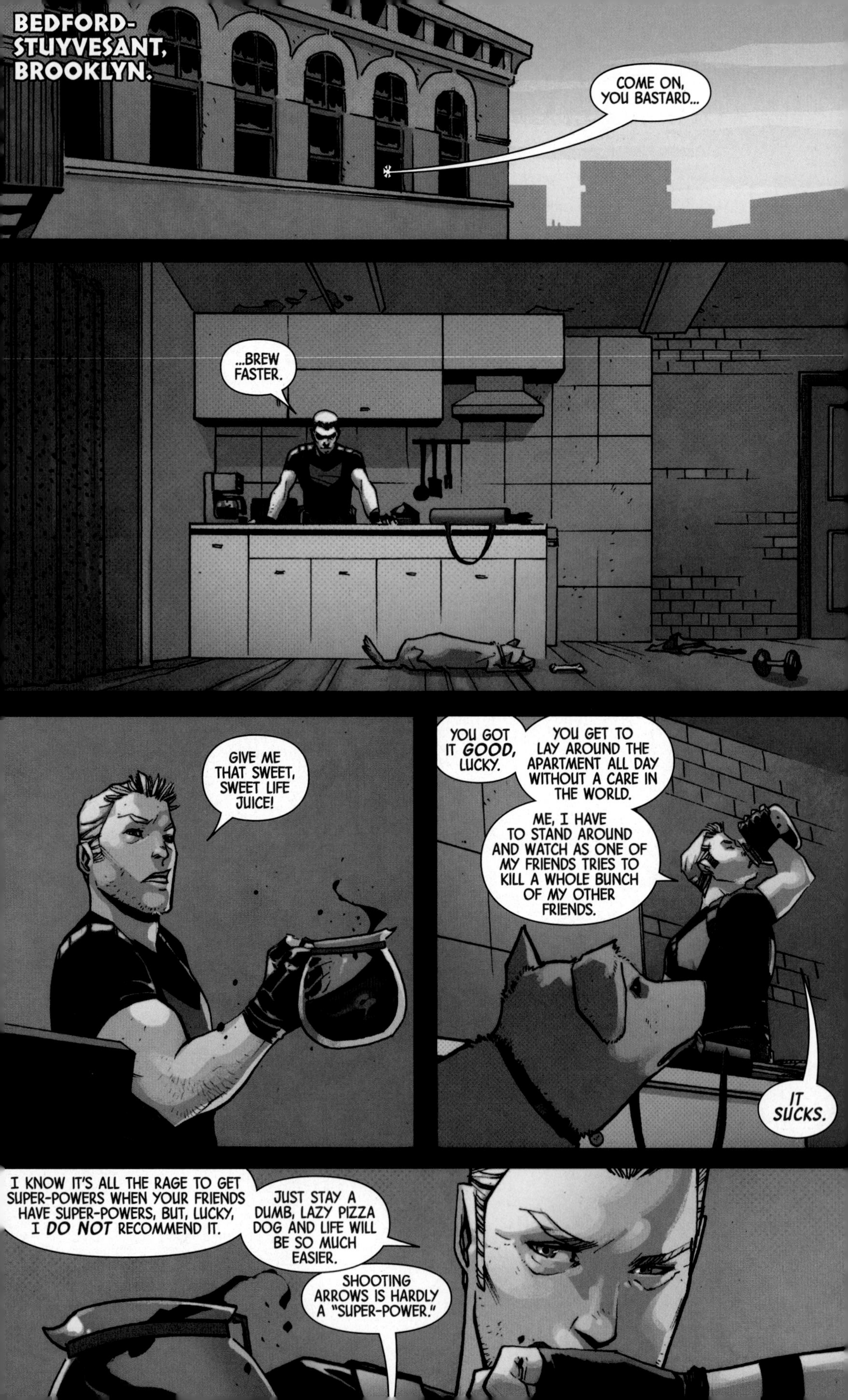
BEDFORD-STUYVESANT, BROOKLYN.
COME ON, YOU BASTARD...
...BREW FASTER.
GIVE ME THAT SWEET, SWEET LIFE JUICE!
YOU GOT IT GOOD, LUCKY.
YOU GET TO LAY AROUND THE APARTMENT ALL DAY WITHOUT A CARE IN THE WORLD.
ME, I HAVE TO STAND AROUND AND WATCH AS ONE OF MY FRIENDS TRIES TO KILL A WHOLE BUNCH OF MY OTHER FRIENDS.
IT SUCKS.
I KNOW IT'S ALL THE RAGE TO GET SUPER-POWERS WHEN YOUR FRIENDS HAVE SUPER-POWERS, BUT, LUCKY, I DO NOT RECOMMEND IT.
JUST STAY A DUMB, LAZY PIZZA DOG AND LIFE WILL BE SO MUCH EASIER.
SHOOTING ARROWS IS HARDLY A "SUPER-POWER."

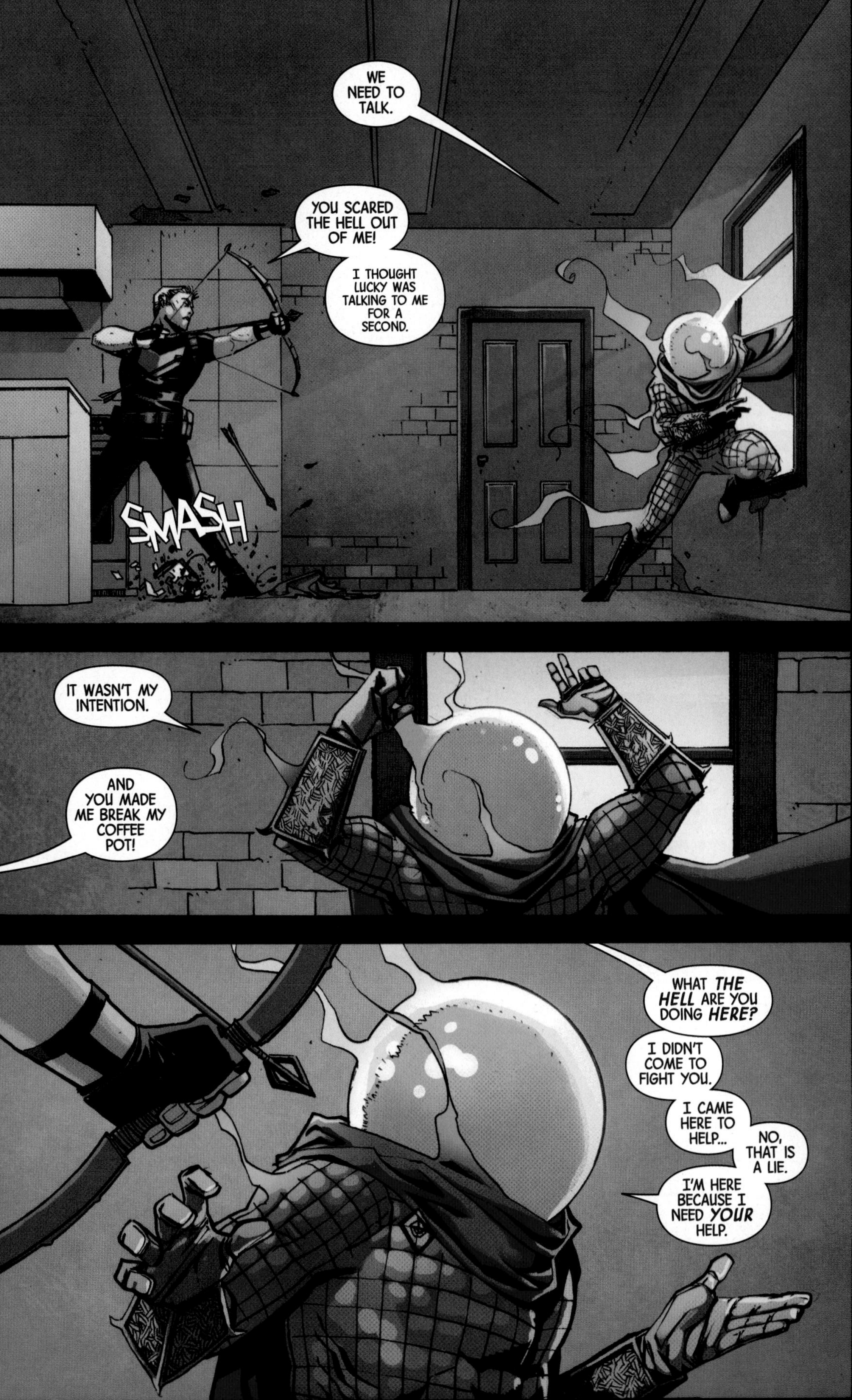

WE NEED TO TALK.
YOU SCARED THE HELL OUT OF ME!
I THOUGHT LUCKY WAS TALKING TO ME FOR A SECOND.
SMASH
IT WASN'T MY INTENTION.
AND YOU MADE ME BREAK MY COFFEE POT!
WHAT *THE HELL* ARE YOU DOING *HERE?*
I DIDN'T COME TO FIGHT YOU.
I CAME HERE TO HELP...
NO, THAT IS A LIE.
I'M HERE BECAUSE I NEED *YOUR* HELP.

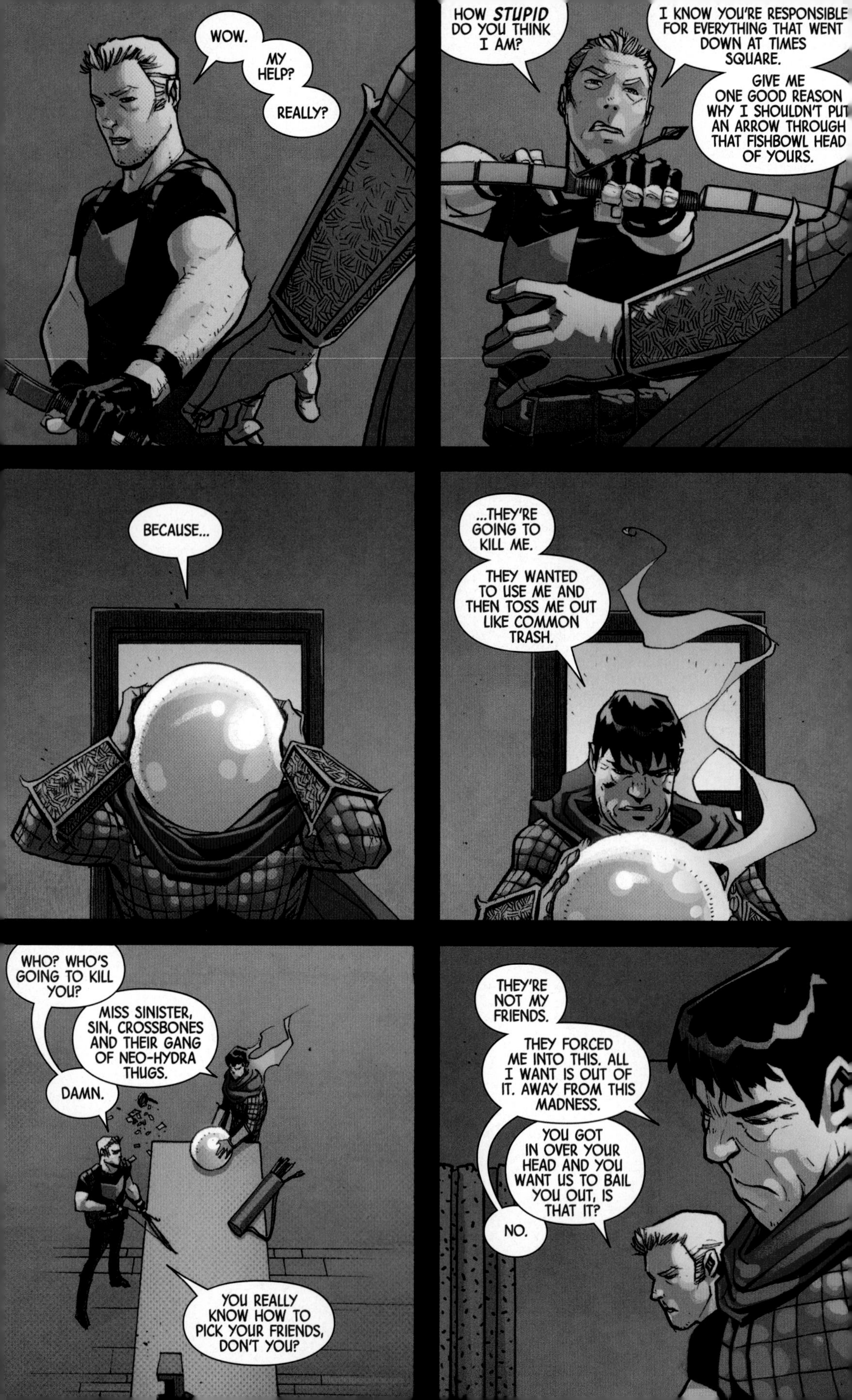
WOW.
MY HELP?
REALLY?
HOW STUPID DO YOU THINK I AM?
I KNOW YOU'RE RESPONSIBLE FOR EVERYTHING THAT WENT DOWN AT TIMES SQUARE.
GIVE ME ONE GOOD REASON WHY I SHOULDN'T PUT AN ARROW THROUGH THAT FISHBOWL HEAD OF YOURS.
BECAUSE...
...THEY'RE GOING TO KILL ME.
THEY WANTED TO USE ME AND THEN TOSS ME OUT LIKE COMMON TRASH.
WHO? WHO'S GOING TO KILL YOU?
MISS SINISTER, SIN, CROSSBONES AND THEIR GANG OF NEO-HYDRA THUGS.
DAMN.
YOU REALLY KNOW HOW TO PICK YOUR FRIENDS, DON'T YOU?
THEY'RE NOT MY FRIENDS.
THEY FORCED ME INTO THIS. ALL I WANT IS OUT OF IT. AWAY FROM THIS MADNESS.
YOU GOT IN OVER YOUR HEAD AND YOU WANT US TO BAIL YOU OUT, IS THAT IT?
NO.

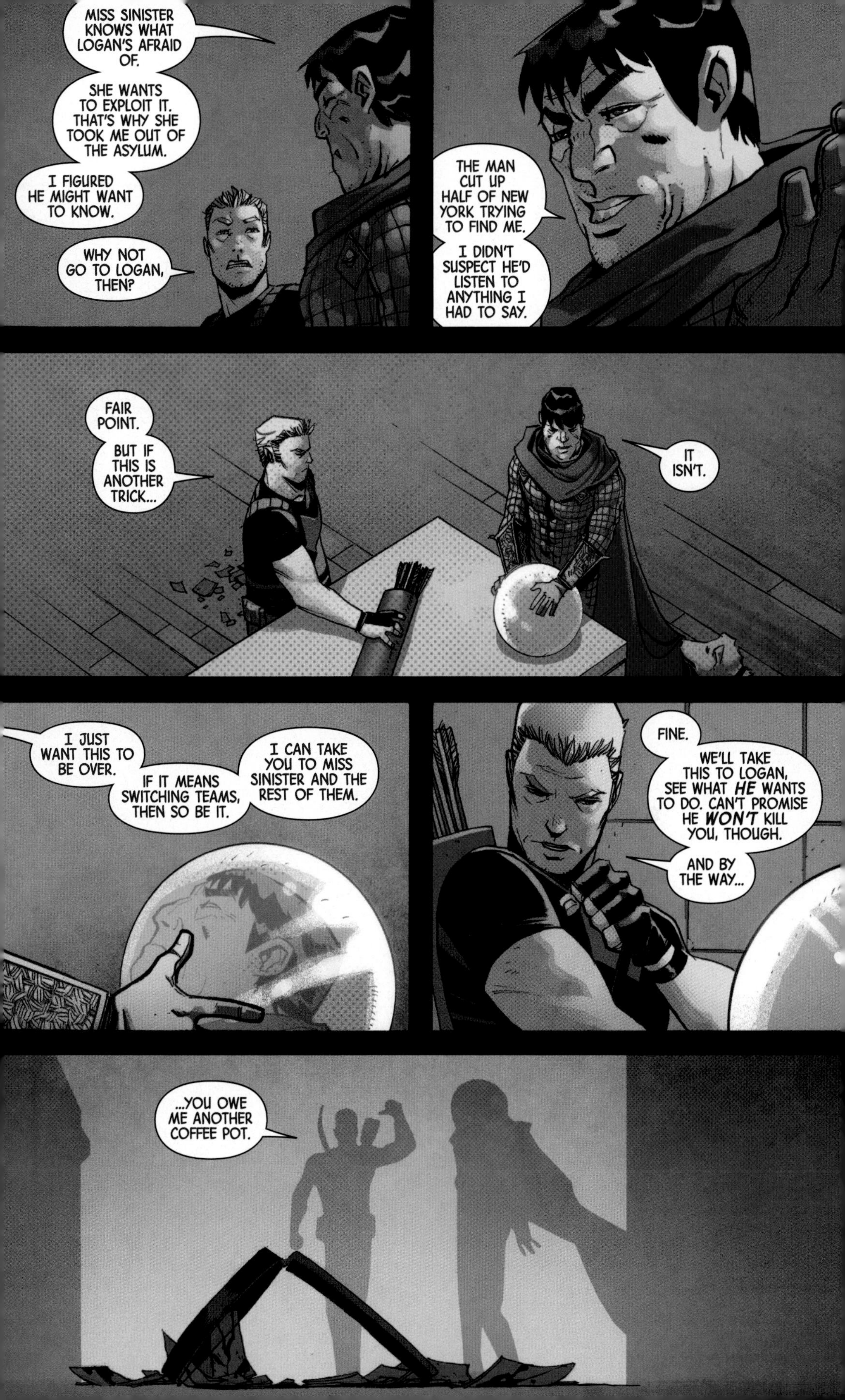
MISS SINISTER KNOWS WHAT LOGAN'S AFRAID OF.
SHE WANTS TO EXPLOIT IT. THAT'S WHY SHE TOOK ME OUT OF THE ASYLUM.
I FIGURED HE MIGHT WANT TO KNOW.
WHY NOT GO TO LOGAN, THEN?
THE MAN CUT UP HALF OF NEW YORK TRYING TO FIND ME.
I DIDN'T SUSPECT HE'D LISTEN TO ANYTHING I HAD TO SAY.
FAIR POINT.
BUT IF THIS IS ANOTHER TRICK...
IT ISN'T.
I JUST WANT THIS TO BE OVER.
IF IT MEANS SWITCHING TEAMS, THEN SO BE IT.
I CAN TAKE YOU TO MISS SINISTER AND THE REST OF THEM.
FINE.
WE'LL TAKE THIS TO LOGAN, SEE WHAT *HE* WANTS TO DO. CAN'T PROMISE HE *WON'T* KILL YOU, THOUGH.
AND BY THE WAY...
...YOU OWE ME ANOTHER COFFEE POT.

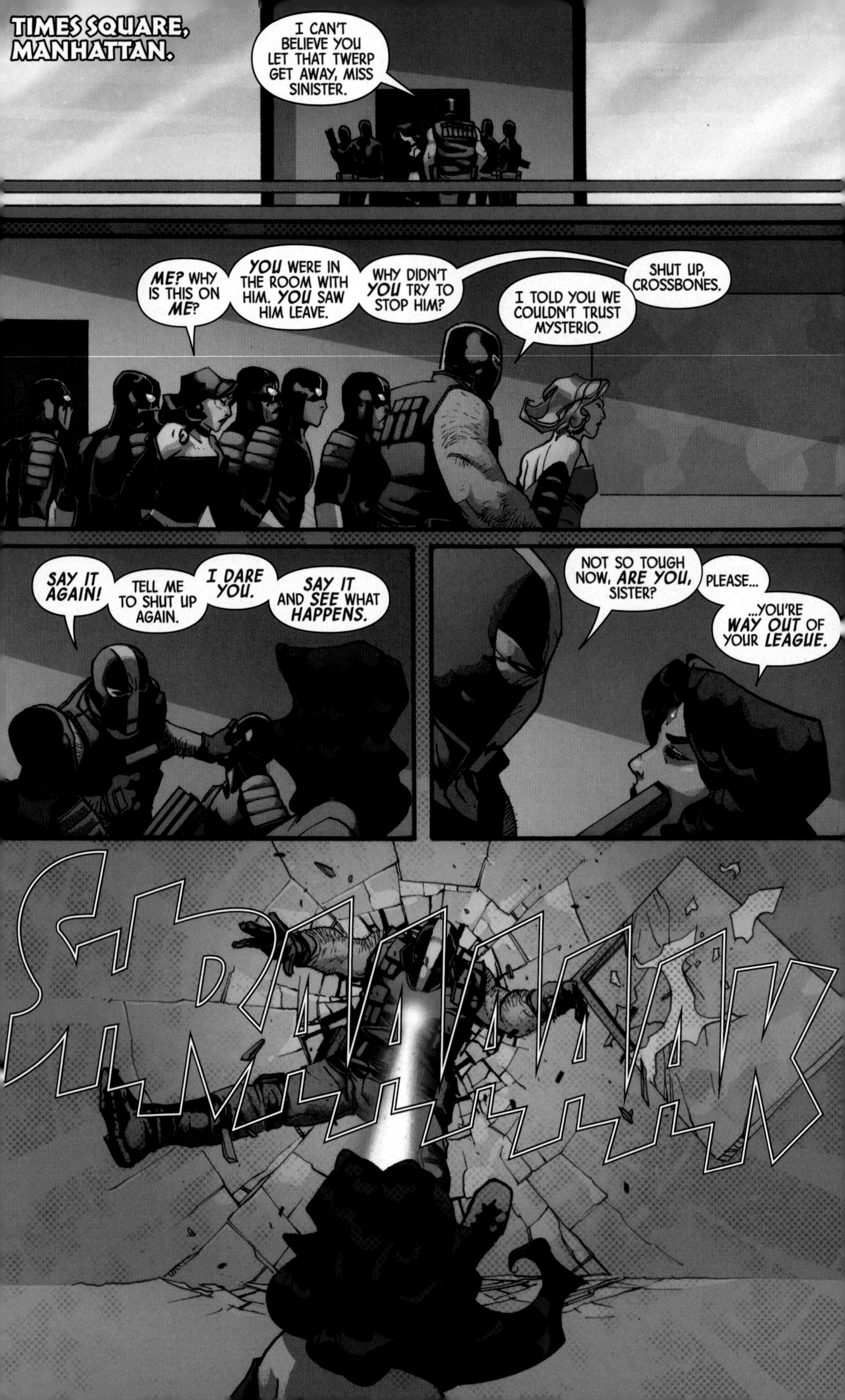
TIMES SQUARE, MANHATTAN.
I CAN'T BELIEVE YOU LET THAT TWERP GET AWAY, MISS SINISTER.
ME? WHY IS THIS ON ME?
YOU WERE IN THE ROOM WITH HIM. YOU SAW HIM LEAVE.
WHY DIDN'T YOU TRY TO STOP HIM?
SHUT UP, CROSSBONES.
I TOLD YOU WE COULDN'T TRUST MYSTERIO.
SAY IT AGAIN!
TELL ME TO SHUT UP AGAIN.
I DARE YOU.
SAY IT AND SEE WHAT HAPPENS.
NOT SO TOUGH NOW, ARE YOU, SISTER?
PLEASE...
...YOU'RE WAY OUT OF YOUR LEAGUE.
SHRAAAAAKK

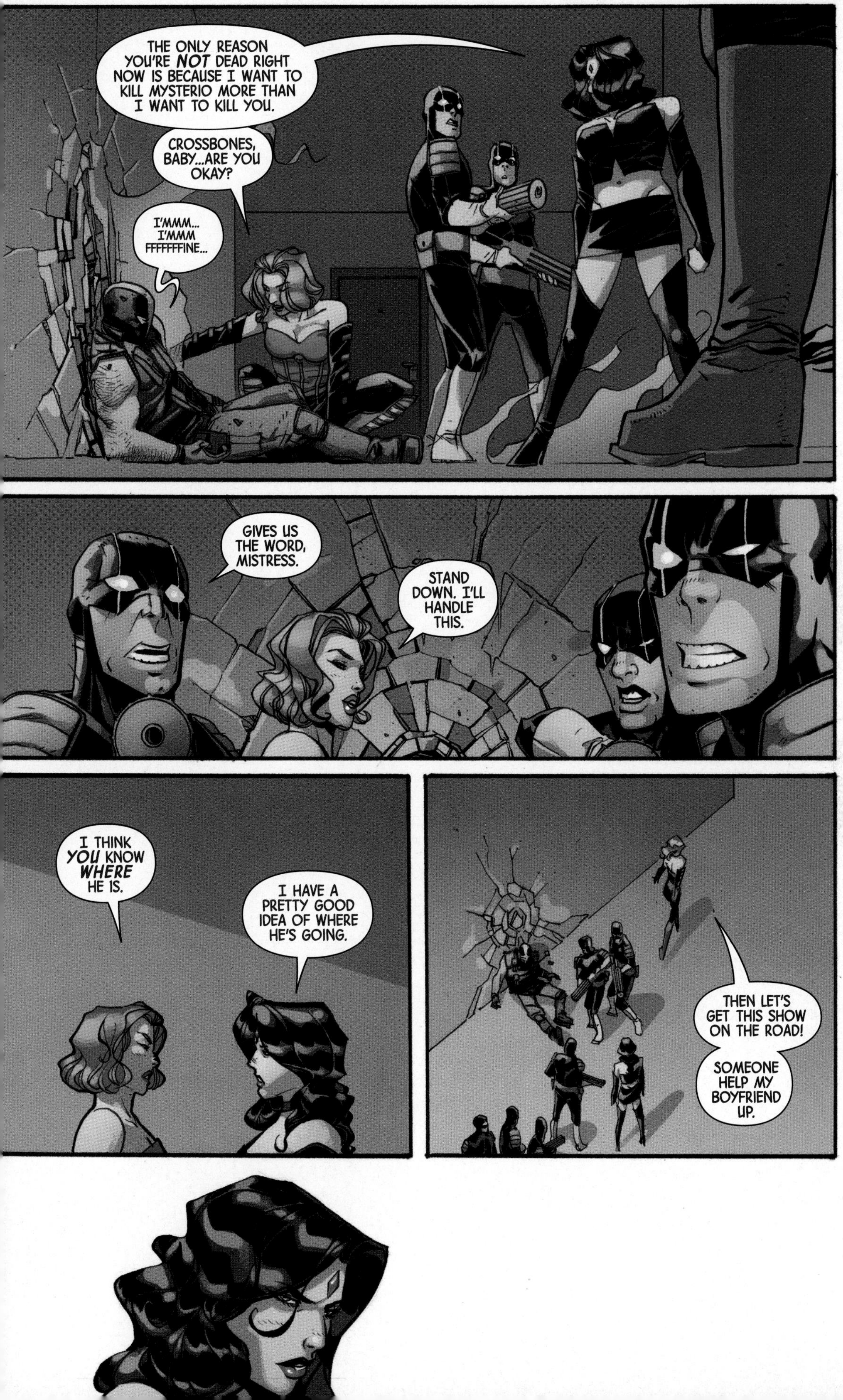

THE ONLY REASON YOU'RE NOT DEAD RIGHT NOW IS BECAUSE I WANT TO KILL MYSTERIO MORE THAN I WANT TO KILL YOU.
CROSSBONES, BABY...ARE YOU OKAY?
I'MMM... I'MMM FFFFFFFFINE...
GIVES US THE WORD, MISTRESS.
STAND DOWN. I'LL HANDLE THIS.
I THINK YOU KNOW WHERE HE IS.
I HAVE A PRETTY GOOD IDEA OF WHERE HE'S GOING.
THEN LET'S GET THIS SHOW ON THE ROAD!
SOMEONE HELP MY BOYFRIEND UP.

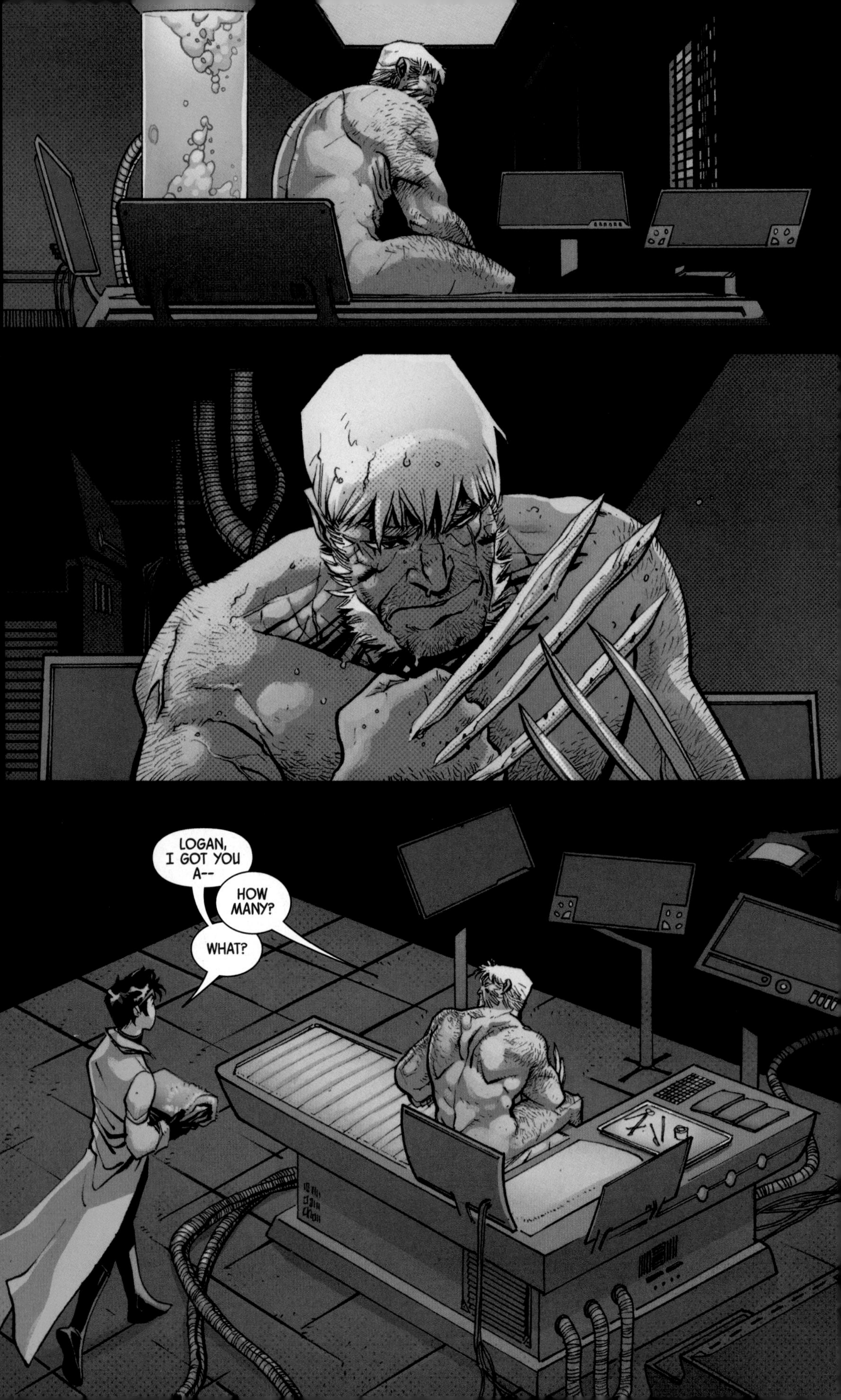
LOGAN, I GOT YOU A--
HOW MANY?
WHAT?

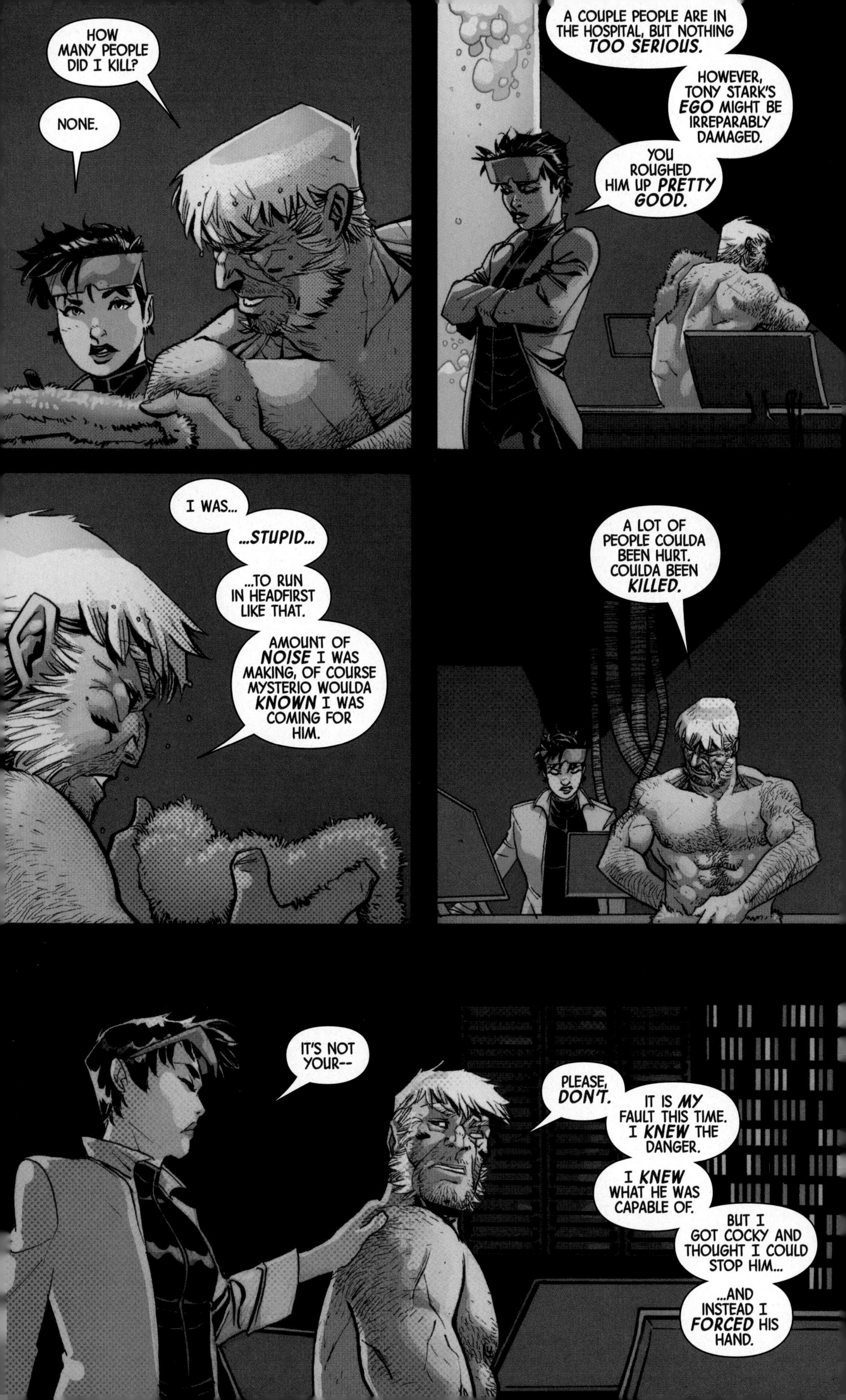
HOW MANY PEOPLE DID I KILL?
NONE.
A COUPLE PEOPLE ARE IN THE HOSPITAL, BUT NOTHING TOO SERIOUS.
HOWEVER, TONY STARK'S EGO MIGHT BE IRREPARABLY DAMAGED.
YOU ROUGHED HIM UP PRETTY GOOD.
I WAS...
...STUPID...
...TO RUN IN HEADFIRST LIKE THAT.
AMOUNT OF NOISE I WAS MAKING, OF COURSE MYSTERIO WOULDA KNOWN I WAS COMING FOR HIM.
A LOT OF PEOPLE COULDA BEEN HURT. COULDA BEEN KILLED.
IT'S NOT YOUR--
PLEASE, DON'T.
IT IS MY FAULT THIS TIME. I KNEW THE DANGER.
I KNEW WHAT HE WAS CAPABLE OF.
BUT I GOT COCKY AND THOUGHT I COULD STOP HIM...
...AND INSTEAD I FORCED HIS HAND.

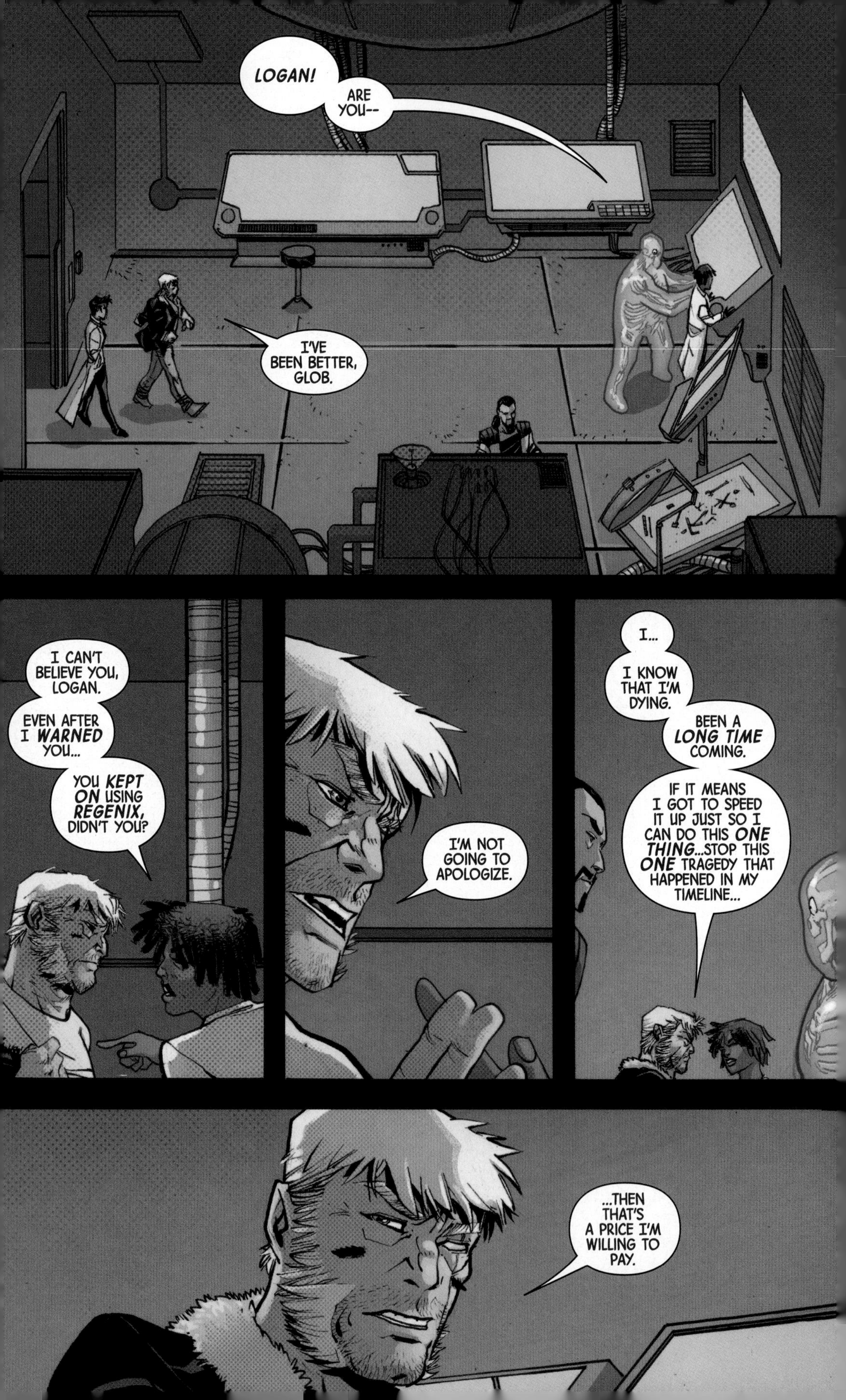
LOGAN!
ARE YOU--
I'VE BEEN BETTER, GLOB.
I CAN'T BELIEVE YOU, LOGAN.
EVEN AFTER I WARNED YOU...
YOU KEPT ON USING REGENIX, DIDN'T YOU?
I'M NOT GOING TO APOLOGIZE.
I...
I KNOW THAT I'M DYING.
BEEN A LONG TIME COMING.
IF IT MEANS I GOT TO SPEED IT UP JUST SO I CAN DO THIS ONE THING...STOP THIS ONE TRAGEDY THAT HAPPENED IN MY TIMELINE...
...THEN THAT'S A PRICE I'M WILLING TO PAY.

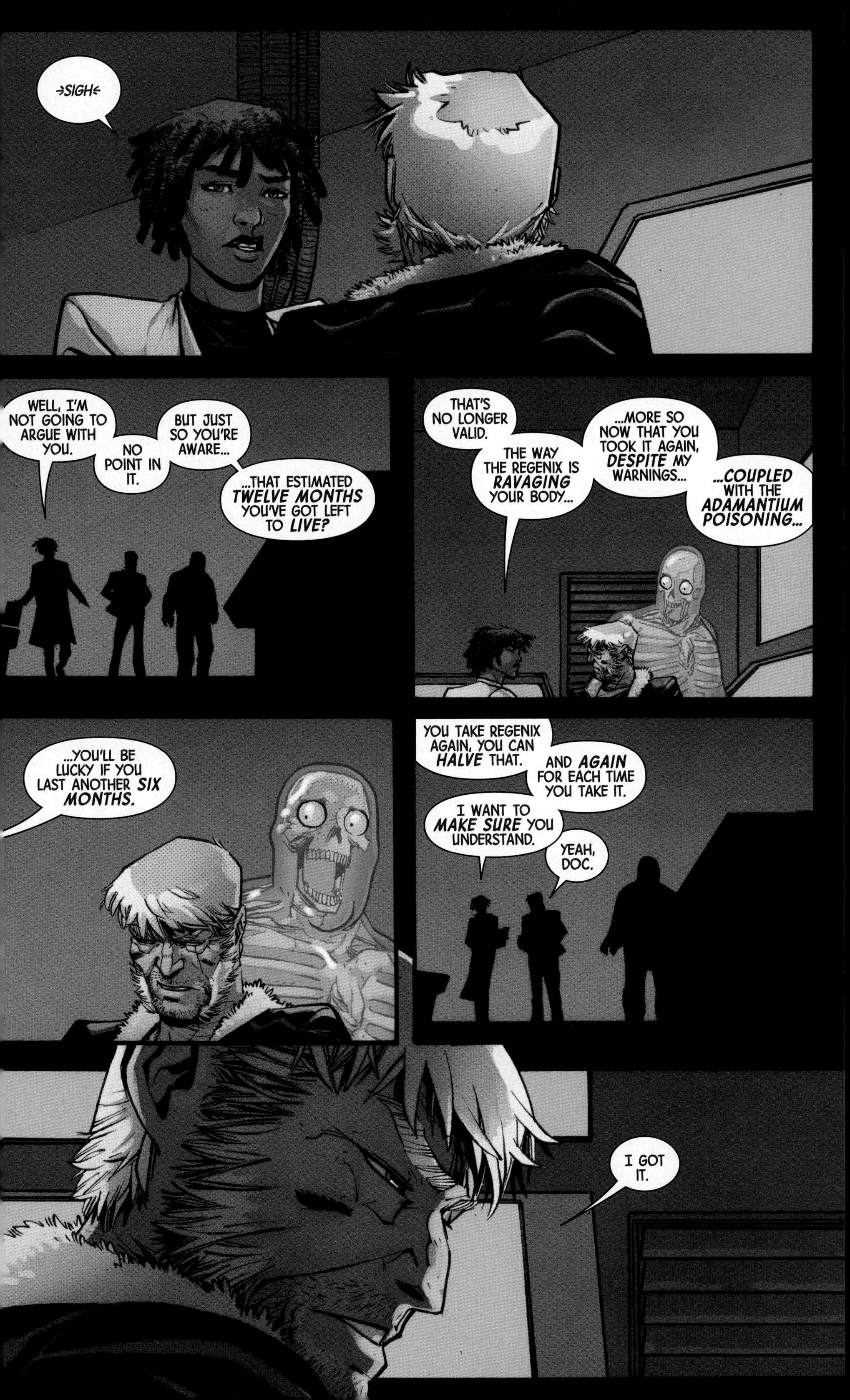
→SIGH←
WELL, I'M NOT GOING TO ARGUE WITH YOU.
NO POINT IN IT.
BUT JUST SO YOU'RE AWARE...
...THAT ESTIMATED TWELVE MONTHS YOU'VE GOT LEFT TO LIVE?
THAT'S NO LONGER VALID.
THE WAY THE REGENIX IS RAVAGING YOUR BODY...
...MORE SO NOW THAT YOU TOOK IT AGAIN, DESPITE MY WARNINGS...
...COUPLED WITH THE ADAMANTIUM POISONING...
...YOU'LL BE LUCKY IF YOU LAST ANOTHER SIX MONTHS.
YOU TAKE REGENIX AGAIN, YOU CAN HALVE THAT.
AND AGAIN FOR EACH TIME YOU TAKE IT.
I WANT TO MAKE SURE YOU UNDERSTAND.
YEAH, DOC.
I GOT IT.

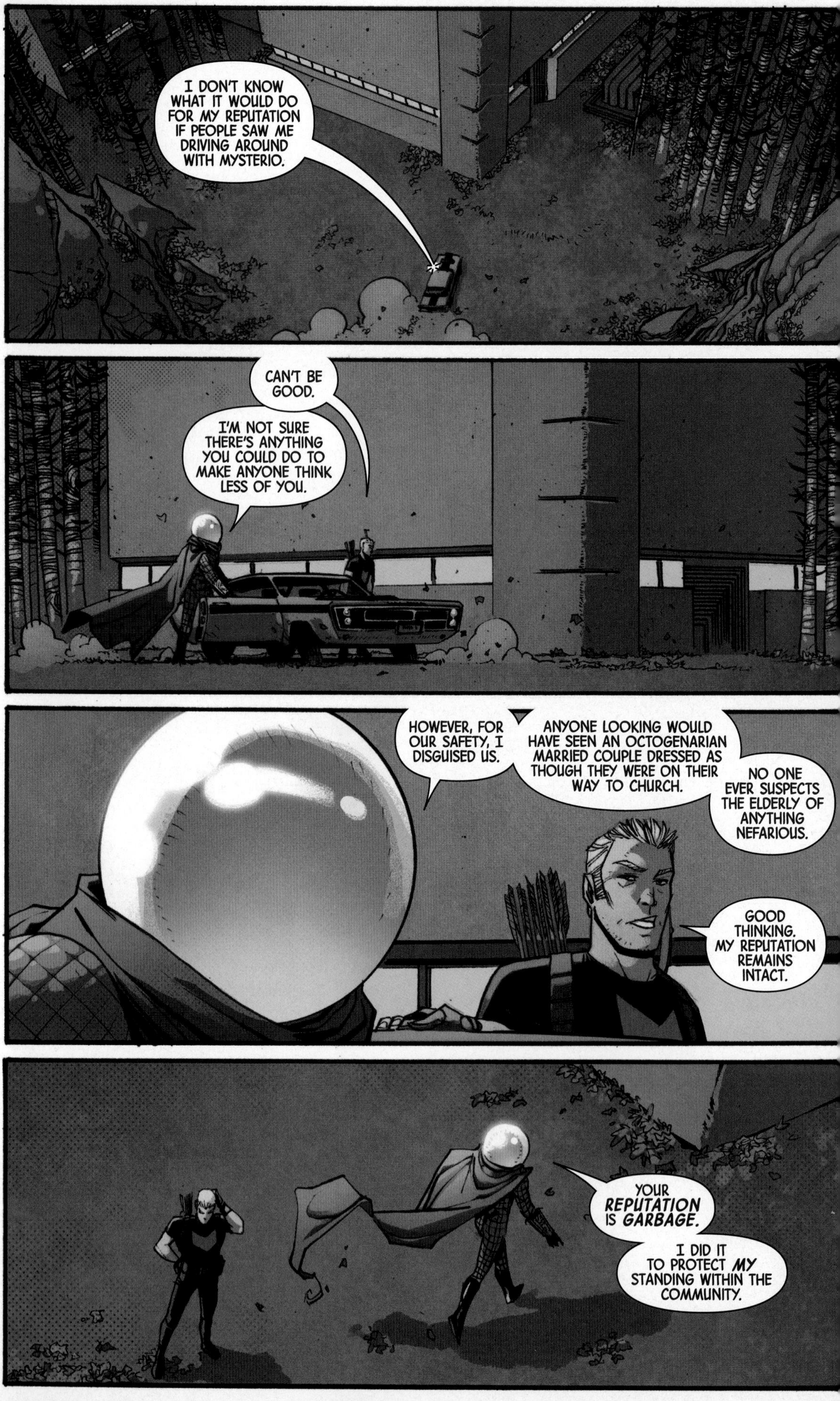
I DON'T KNOW WHAT IT WOULD DO FOR MY REPUTATION IF PEOPLE SAW ME DRIVING AROUND WITH MYSTERIO.
CAN'T BE GOOD.
I'M NOT SURE THERE'S ANYTHING YOU COULD DO TO MAKE ANYONE THINK LESS OF YOU.
HOWEVER, FOR OUR SAFETY, I DISGUISED US.
ANYONE LOOKING WOULD HAVE SEEN AN OCTOGENARIAN MARRIED COUPLE DRESSED AS THOUGH THEY WERE ON THEIR WAY TO CHURCH.
NO ONE EVER SUSPECTS THE ELDERLY OF ANYTHING NEFARIOUS.
GOOD THINKING. MY REPUTATION REMAINS INTACT.
YOUR *REPUTATION* IS *GARBAGE*.
I DID IT TO PROTECT *MY* STANDING WITHIN THE COMMUNITY.

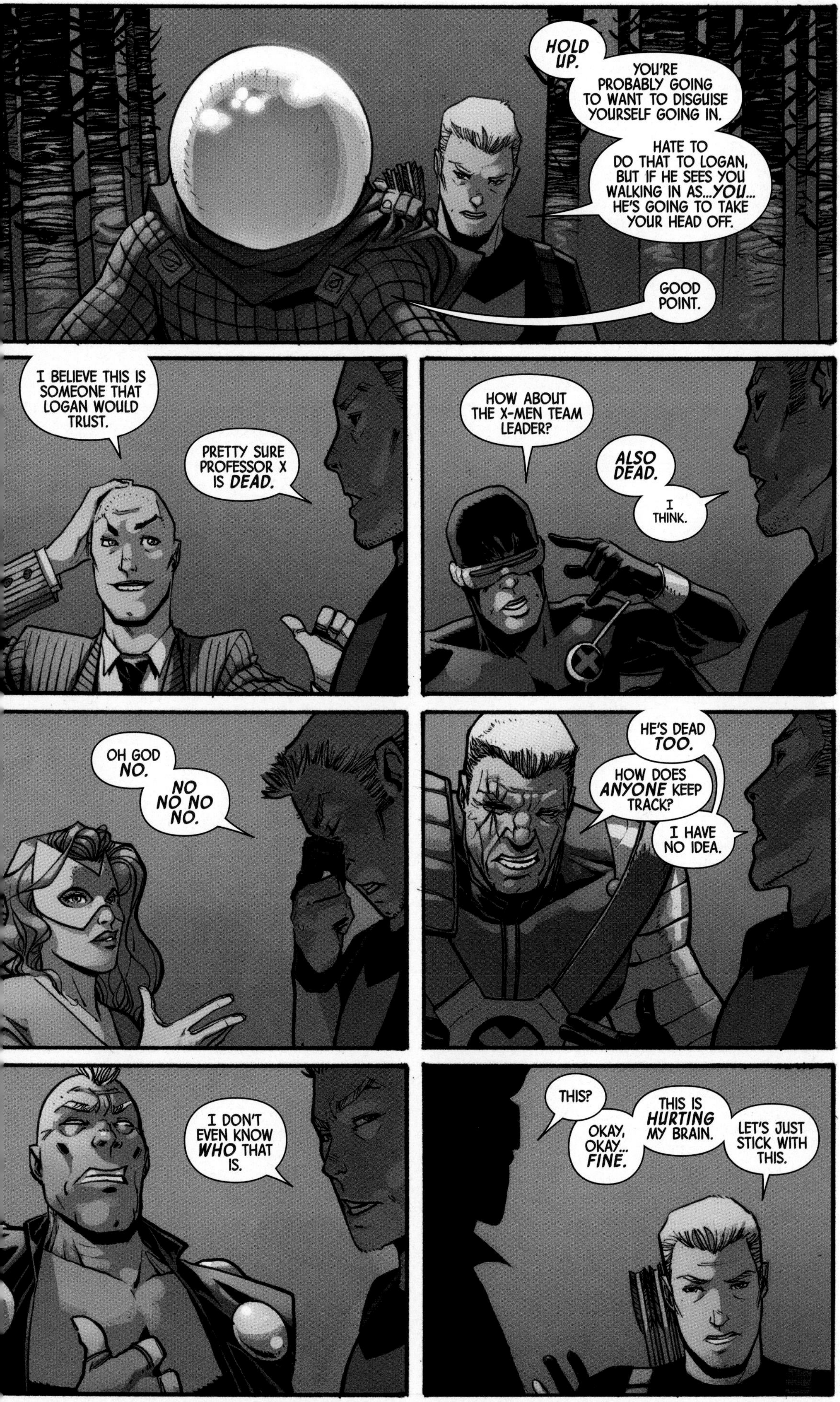
HOLD UP.
YOU'RE PROBABLY GOING TO WANT TO DISGUISE YOURSELF GOING IN.
HATE TO DO THAT TO LOGAN, BUT IF HE SEES YOU WALKING IN AS...YOU... HE'S GOING TO TAKE YOUR HEAD OFF.
GOOD POINT.
I BELIEVE THIS IS SOMEONE THAT LOGAN WOULD TRUST.
PRETTY SURE PROFESSOR X IS DEAD.
HOW ABOUT THE X-MEN TEAM LEADER?
ALSO DEAD.
I THINK.
OH GOD NO.
NO NO NO NO.
HE'S DEAD TOO.
HOW DOES ANYONE KEEP TRACK?
I HAVE NO IDEA.
I DON'T EVEN KNOW WHO THAT IS.
THIS?
OKAY, OKAY... FINE.
THIS IS HURTING MY BRAIN.
LET'S JUST STICK WITH THIS.

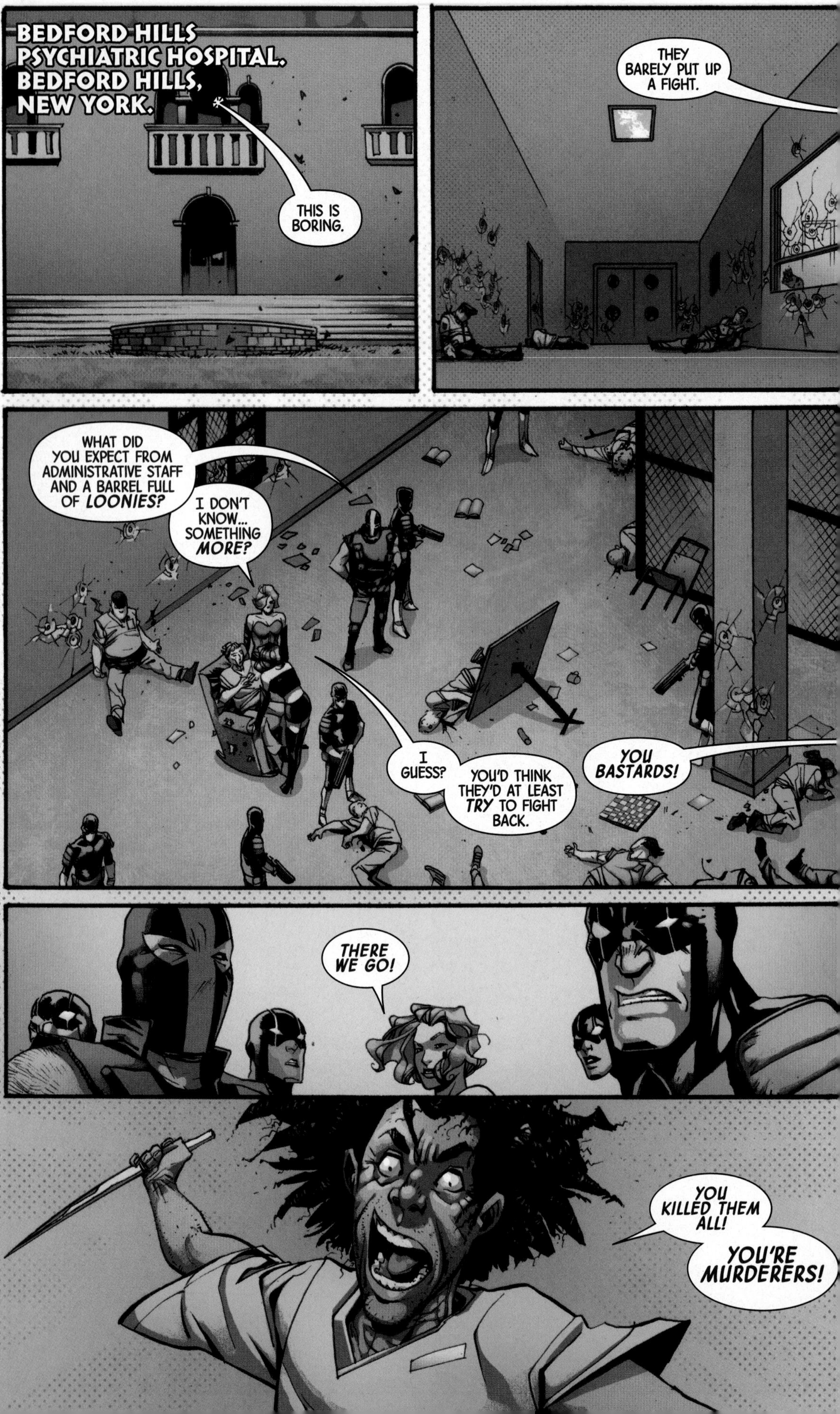
BEDFORD HILLS PSYCHIATRIC HOSPITAL. BEDFORD HILLS, NEW YORK.
THIS IS BORING.
THEY BARELY PUT UP A FIGHT.
WHAT DID YOU EXPECT FROM ADMINISTRATIVE STAFF AND A BARREL FULL OF *LOONIES?*
I DON'T KNOW... SOMETHING *MORE?*
I GUESS?
YOU'D THINK THEY'D AT LEAST *TRY* TO FIGHT BACK.
YOU BASTARDS!
THERE WE GO!
YOU KILLED THEM ALL!
YOU'RE MURDERERS!

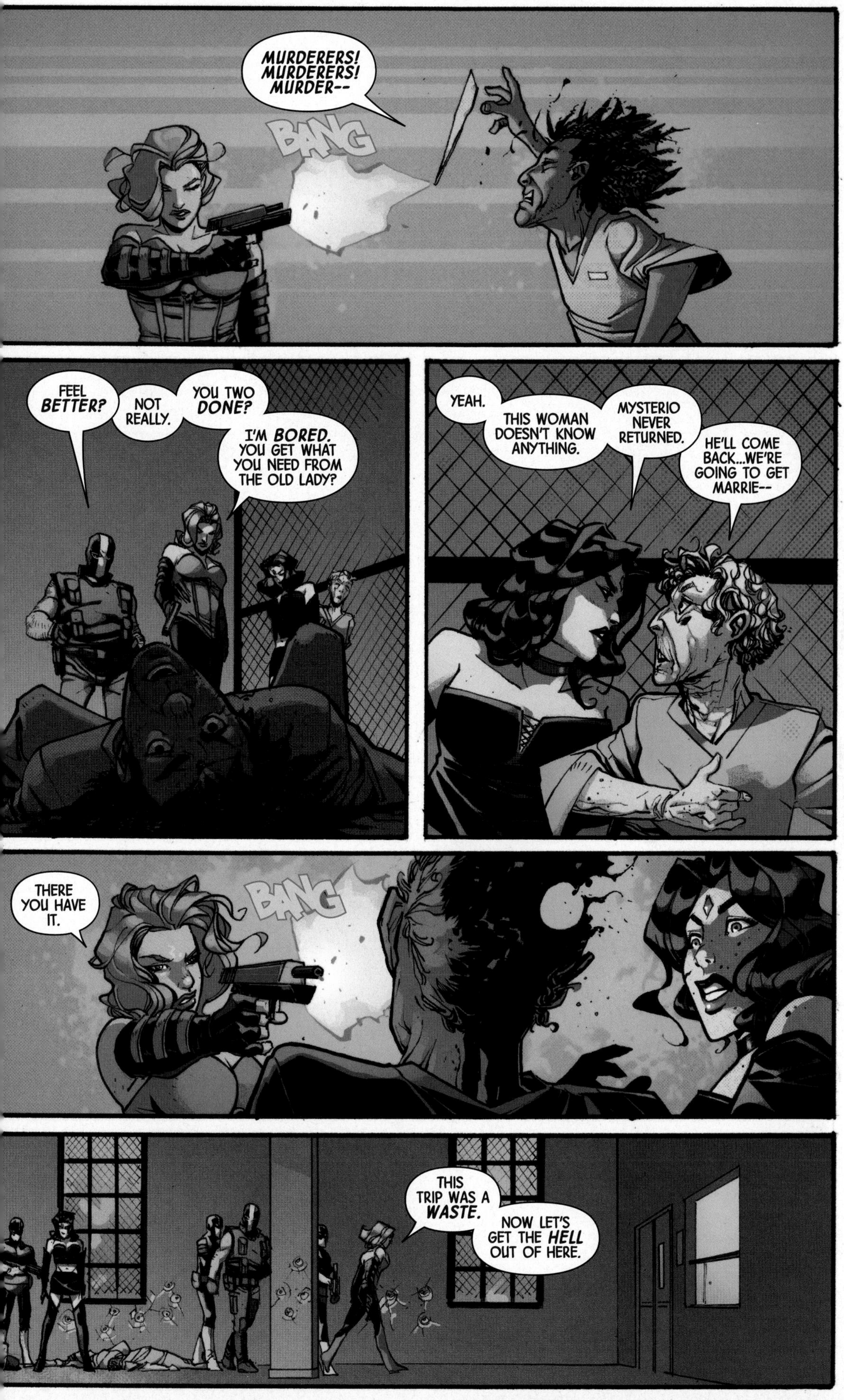
MURDERERS! MURDERERS! MURDER--
BANG
FEEL BETTER?
NOT REALLY.
YOU TWO DONE?
I'M BORED. YOU GET WHAT YOU NEED FROM THE OLD LADY?
YEAH.
THIS WOMAN DOESN'T KNOW ANYTHING.
MYSTERIO NEVER RETURNED.
HE'LL COME BACK...WE'RE GOING TO GET MARRIE--
THERE YOU HAVE IT.
BANG
THIS TRIP WAS A WASTE.
NOW LET'S GET THE HELL OUT OF HERE.

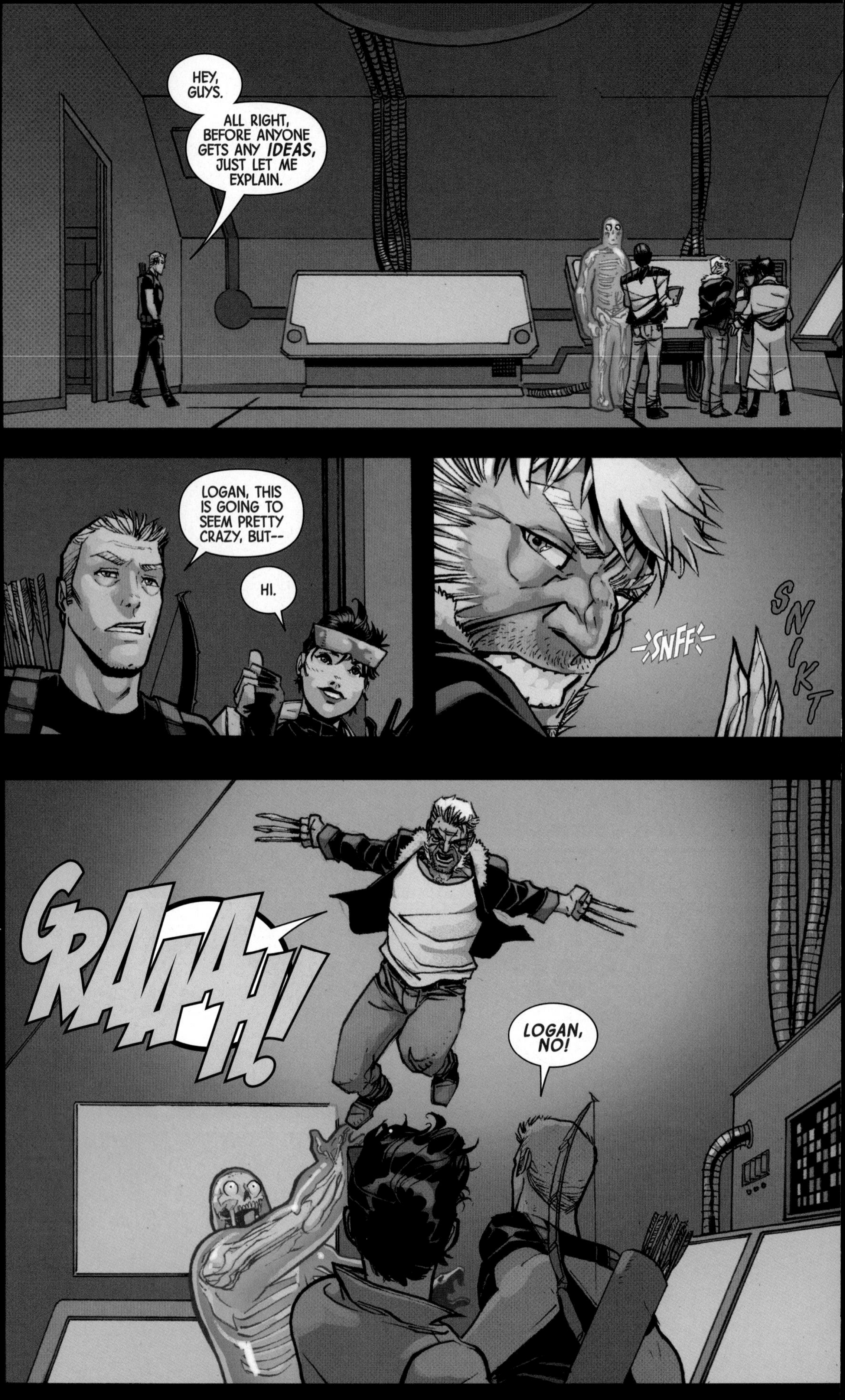
HEY, GUYS.
ALL RIGHT, BEFORE ANYONE GETS ANY *IDEAS,* JUST LET ME EXPLAIN.
LOGAN, THIS IS GOING TO SEEM PRETTY CRAZY, BUT--
HI.
SNFF
SNIKT
GRAAAH!
LOGAN, NO!

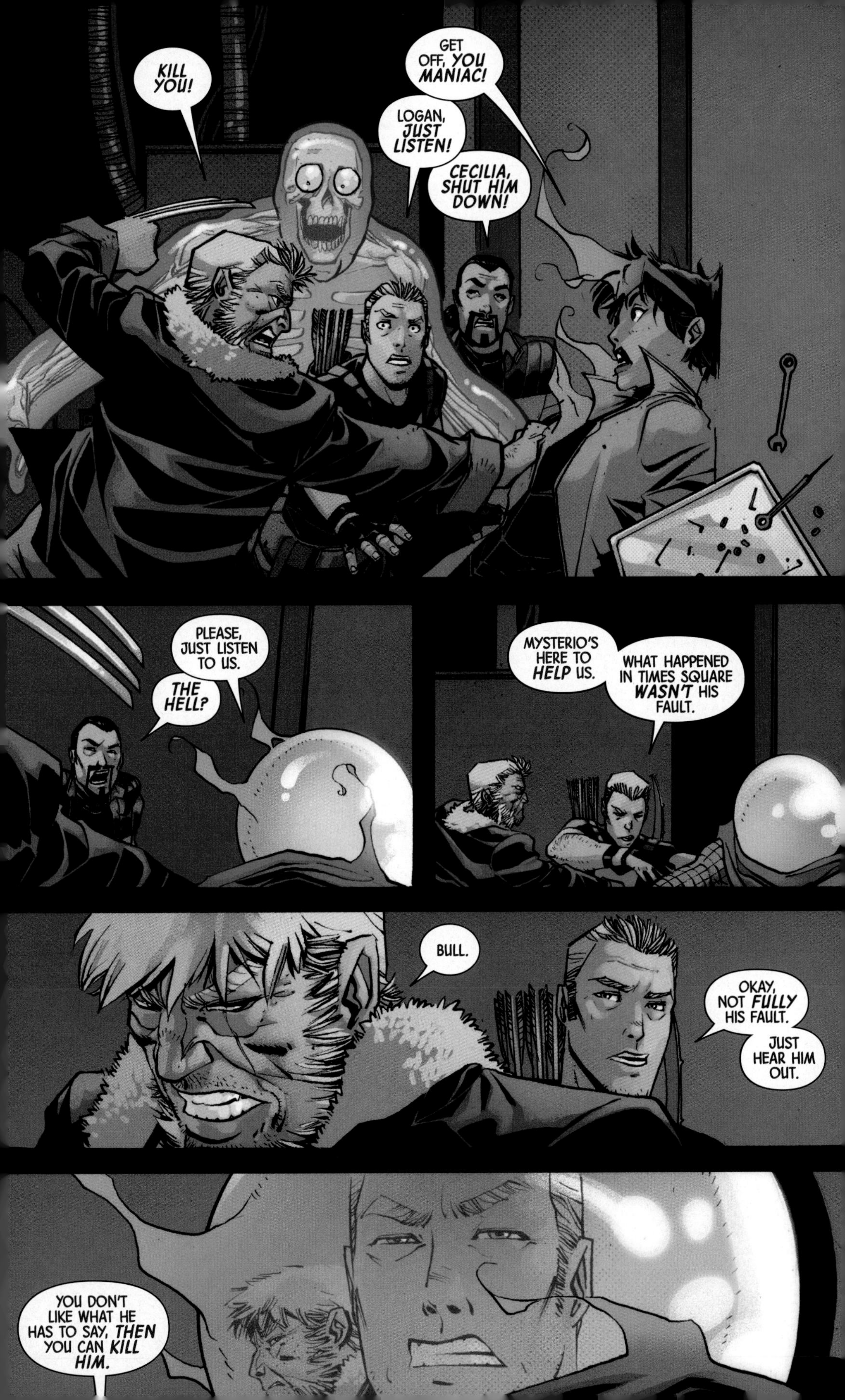
KILL YOU!
GET OFF, YOU MANIAC!
LOGAN, JUST LISTEN!
CECILIA, SHUT HIM DOWN!
PLEASE, JUST LISTEN TO US.
THE HELL?
MYSTERIO'S HERE TO HELP US.
WHAT HAPPENED IN TIMES SQUARE WASN'T HIS FAULT.
BULL.
OKAY, NOT FULLY HIS FAULT.
JUST HEAR HIM OUT.
YOU DON'T LIKE WHAT HE HAS TO SAY, THEN YOU CAN KILL HIM.

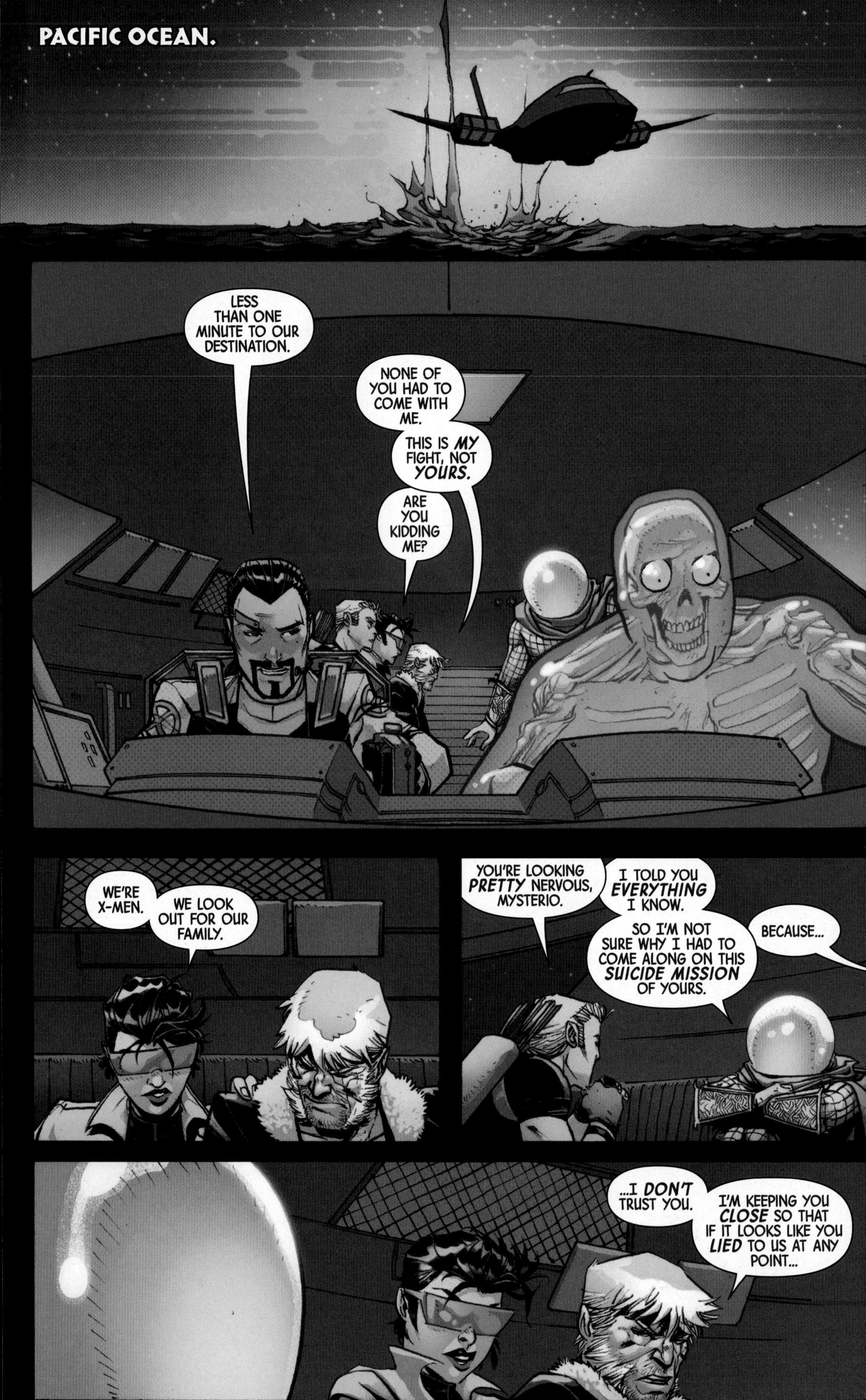
PACIFIC OCEAN.
LESS THAN ONE MINUTE TO OUR DESTINATION.
NONE OF YOU HAD TO COME WITH ME.
THIS IS MY FIGHT, NOT YOURS.
ARE YOU KIDDING ME?
WE'RE X-MEN.
WE LOOK OUT FOR OUR FAMILY.
YOU'RE LOOKING PRETTY NERVOUS, MYSTERIO.
I TOLD YOU EVERYTHING I KNOW.
SO I'M NOT SURE WHY I HAD TO COME ALONG ON THIS SUICIDE MISSION OF YOURS.
BECAUSE...
...I DON'T TRUST YOU.
I'M KEEPING YOU CLOSE SO THAT IF IT LOOKS LIKE YOU LIED TO US AT ANY POINT...

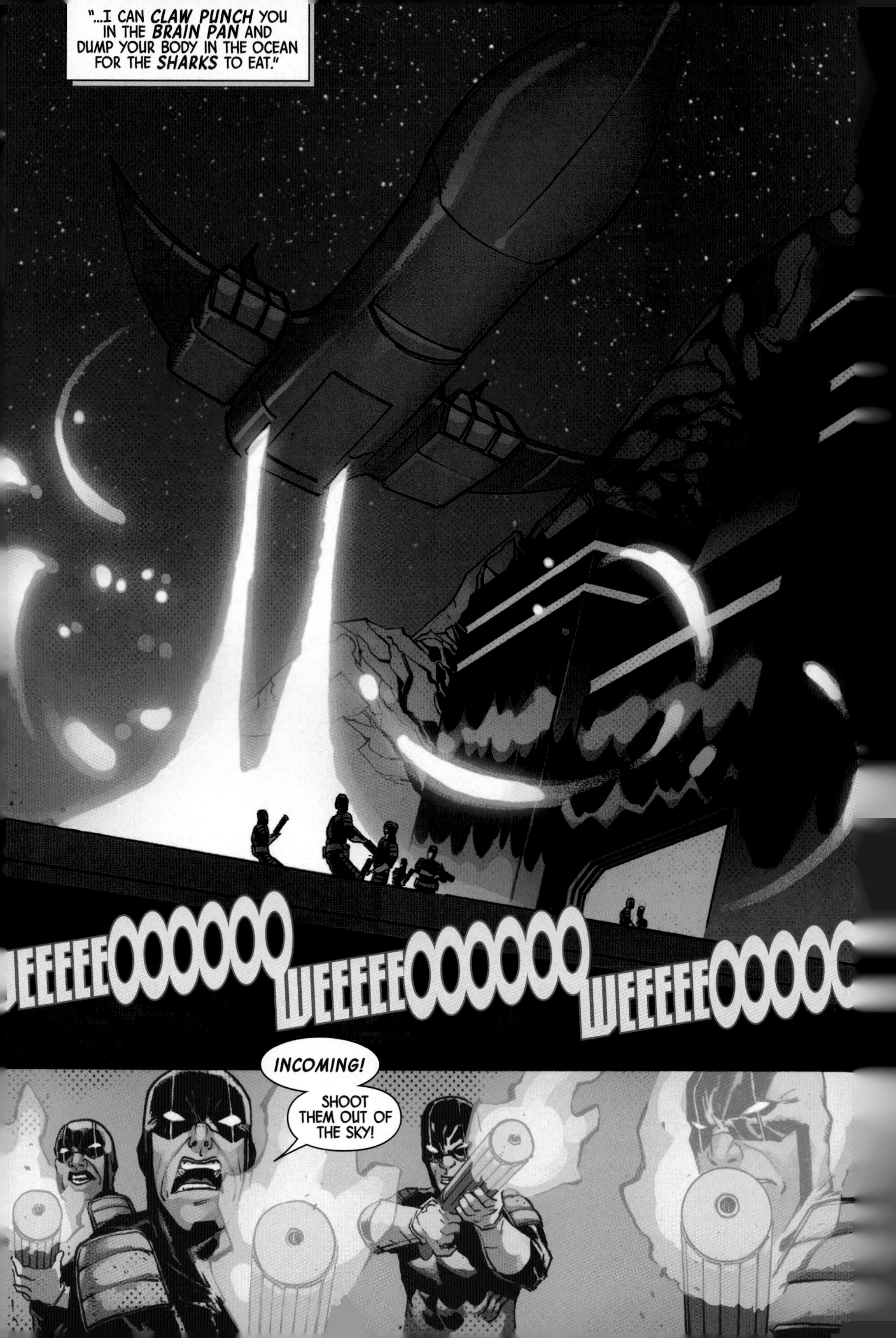
"...I CAN CLAW PUNCH YOU IN THE BRAIN PAN AND DUMP YOUR BODY IN THE OCEAN FOR THE SHARKS TO EAT."
WEEEEEOOOOOO WEEEEEOOOOOO WEEEEEOOOO
INCOMING!
SHOOT THEM OUT OF THE SKY!

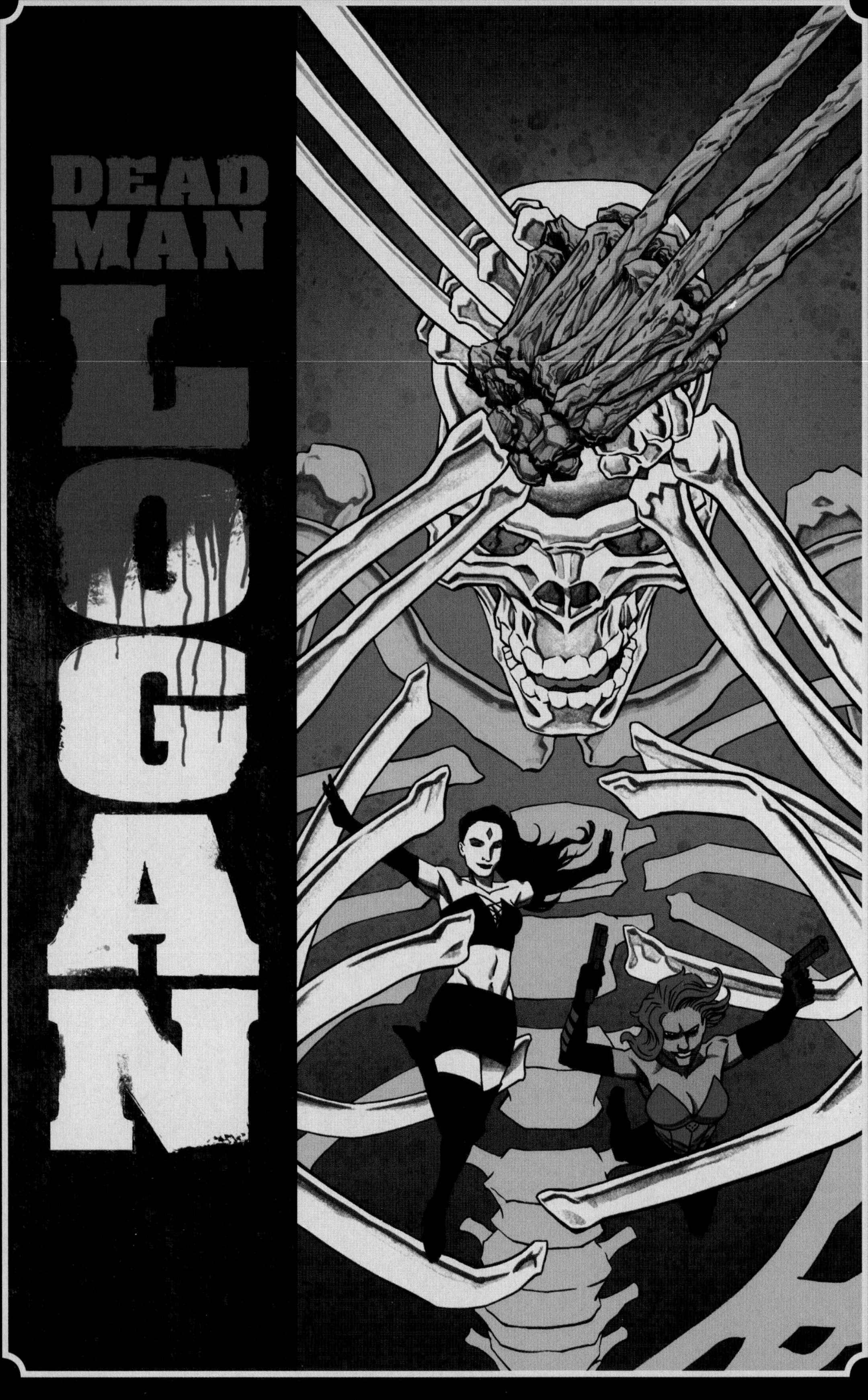
DEAD MAN
LOGAN

5

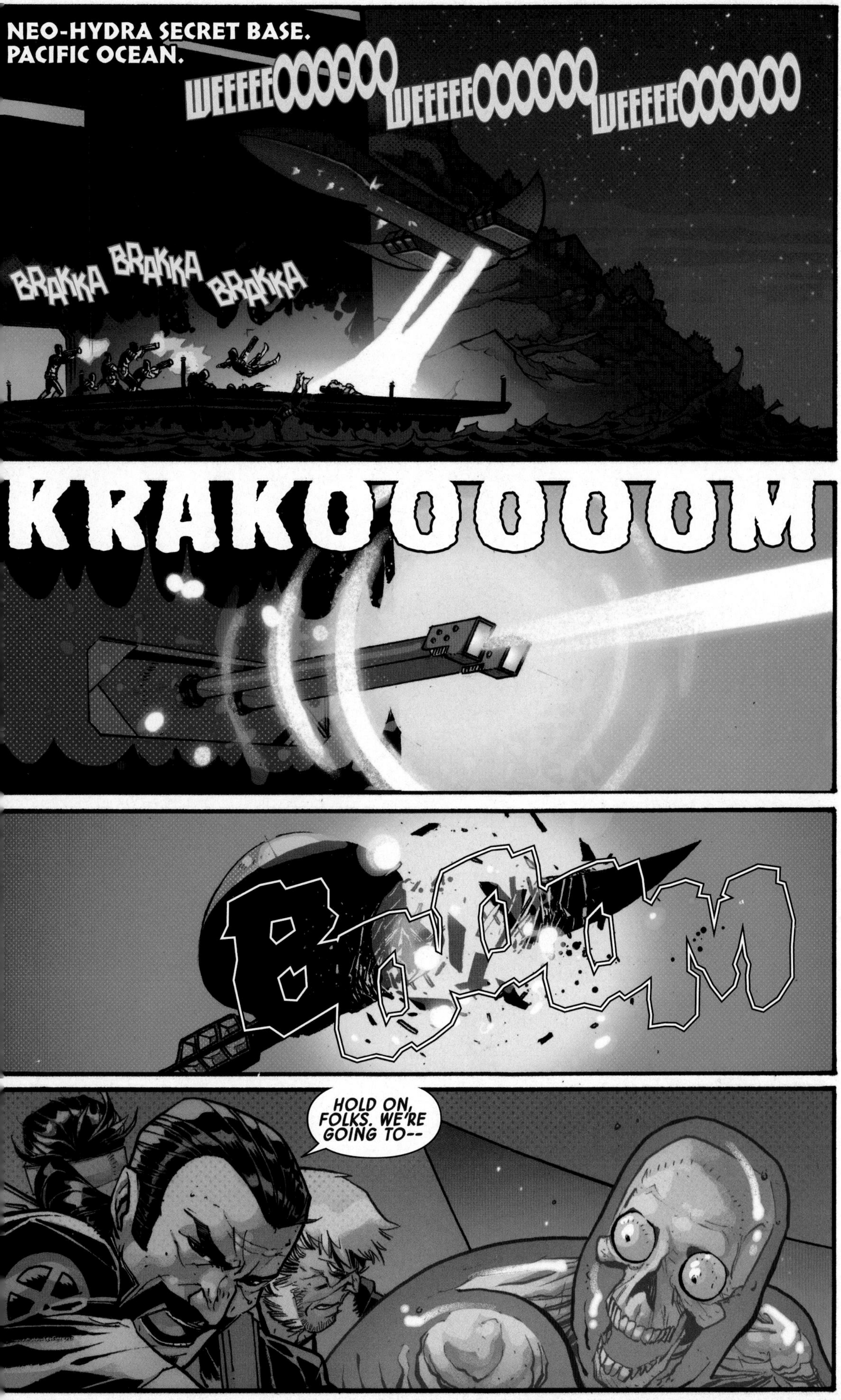
NEO-HYDRA SECRET BASE.
PACIFIC OCEAN.
WEEEEEOOOOOO WEEEEEOOOOOO WEEEEEOOOOOO
BRAKKA BRAKKA BRAKKA
KRAKOOOOOM
BOOOM
HOLD ON, FOLKS. WE'RE GOING TO--

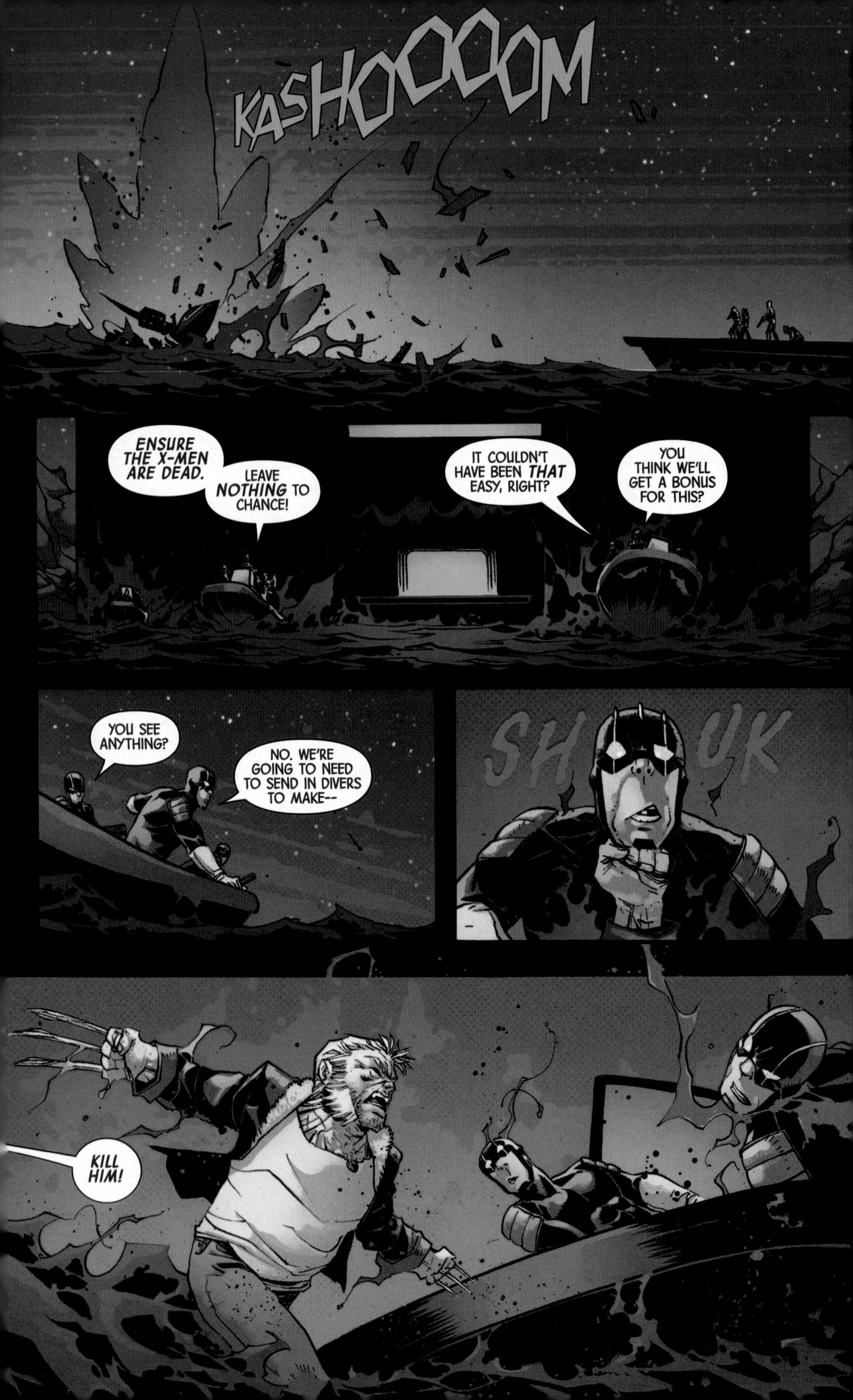
KASHOOOOM
ENSURE THE X-MEN ARE DEAD.
LEAVE NOTHING TO CHANCE!
IT COULDN'T HAVE BEEN THAT EASY, RIGHT?
YOU THINK WE'LL GET A BONUS FOR THIS?
YOU SEE ANYTHING?
NO. WE'RE GOING TO NEED TO SEND IN DIVERS TO MAKE--
KILL HIM!

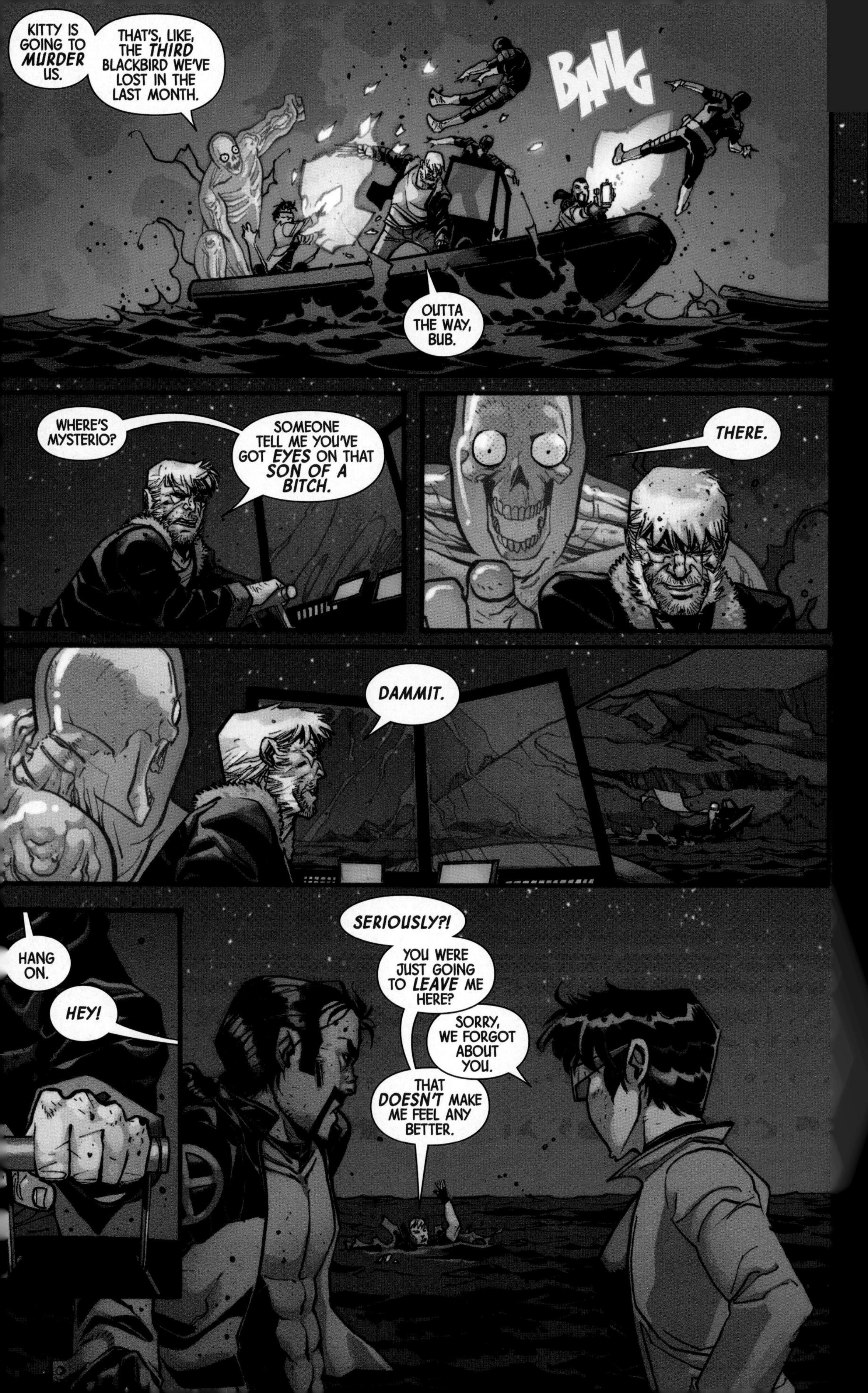
KITTY IS GOING TO MURDER US.
THAT'S, LIKE, THE THIRD BLACKBIRD WE'VE LOST IN THE LAST MONTH.
BANG
OUTTA THE WAY, BUB.
WHERE'S MYSTERIO?
SOMEONE TELL ME YOU'VE GOT EYES ON THAT SON OF A BITCH.
THERE.
DAMMIT.
HANG ON.
HEY!
SERIOUSLY?!
YOU WERE JUST GOING TO LEAVE ME HERE?
SORRY, WE FORGOT ABOUT YOU.
THAT DOESN'T MAKE ME FEEL ANY BETTER.

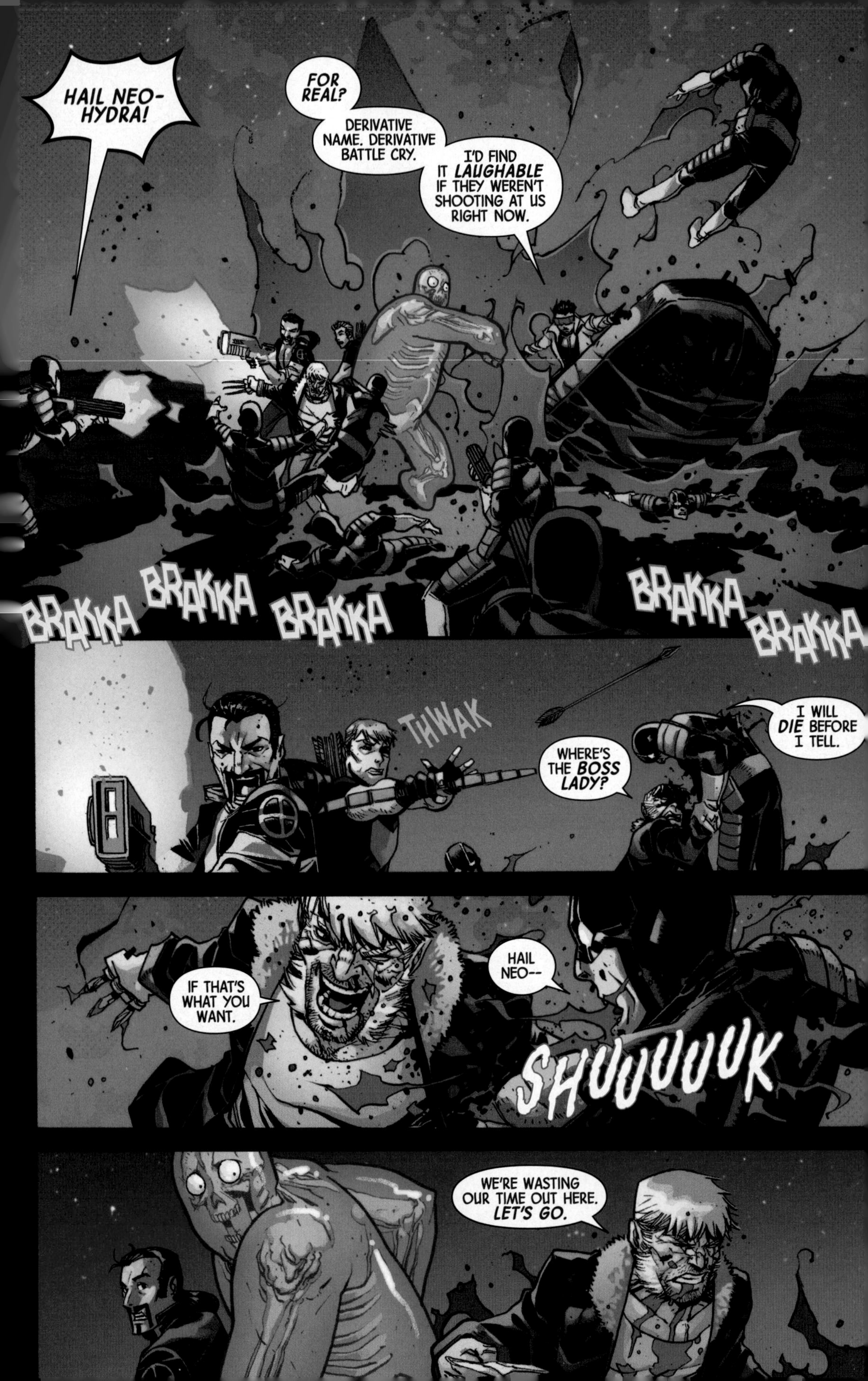
HAIL NEO-HYDRA!
FOR REAL?
DERIVATIVE NAME. DERIVATIVE BATTLE CRY.
I'D FIND IT LAUGHABLE IF THEY WEREN'T SHOOTING AT US RIGHT NOW.
BRAKKA BRAKKA BRAKKA
BRAKKA BRAKKA
THWAK
WHERE'S THE BOSS LADY?
I WILL DIE BEFORE I TELL.
IF THAT'S WHAT YOU WANT.
HAIL NEO--
SHUUUUUK
WE'RE WASTING OUR TIME OUT HERE. LET'S GO.

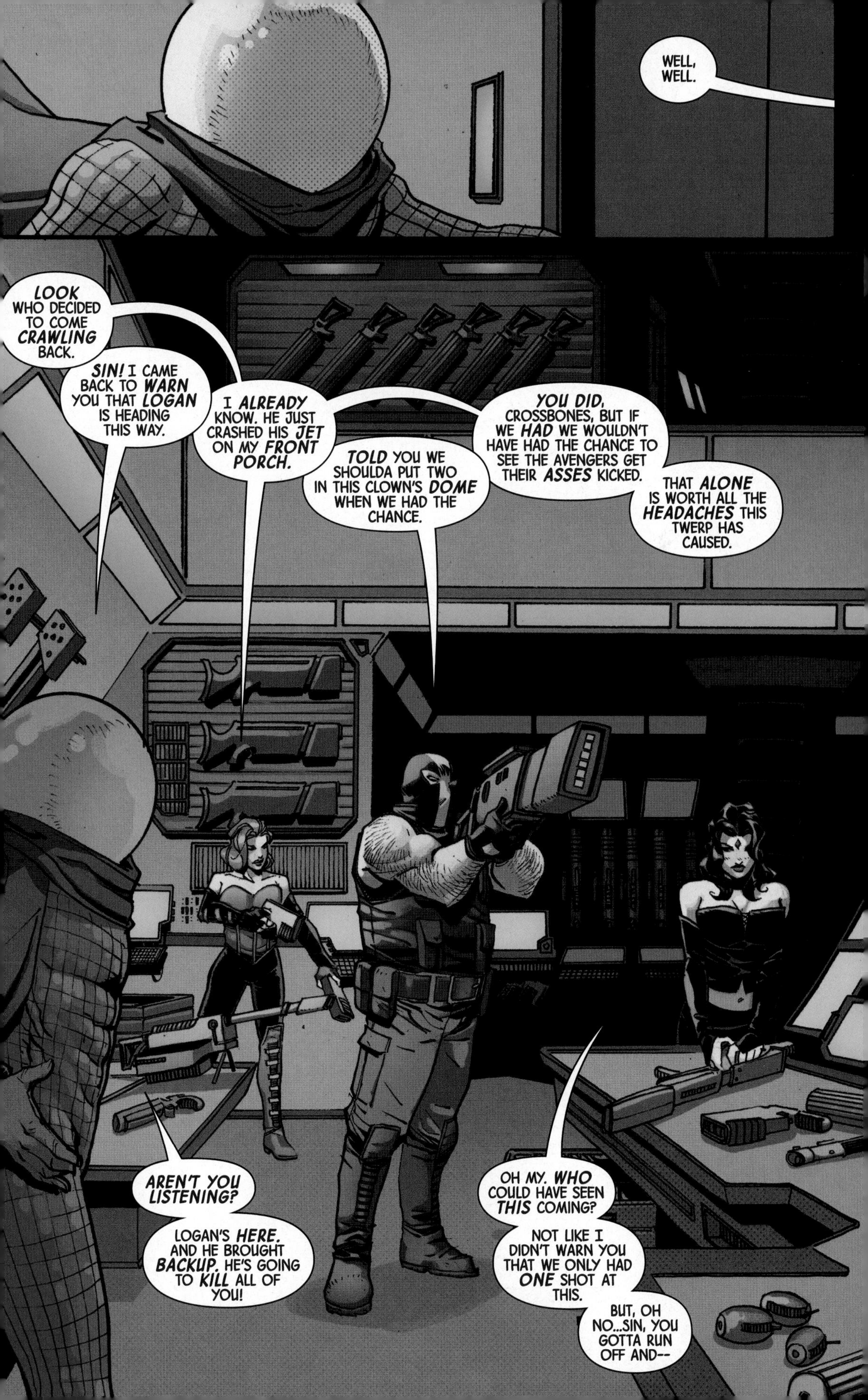
WELL, WELL.
LOOK WHO DECIDED TO COME CRAWLING BACK.
SIN! I CAME BACK TO WARN YOU THAT LOGAN IS HEADING THIS WAY.
I ALREADY KNOW. HE JUST CRASHED HIS JET ON MY FRONT PORCH.
TOLD YOU WE SHOULDA PUT TWO IN THIS CLOWN'S DOME WHEN WE HAD THE CHANCE.
YOU DID, CROSSBONES, BUT IF WE HAD WE WOULDN'T HAVE HAD THE CHANCE TO SEE THE AVENGERS GET THEIR ASSES KICKED.
THAT ALONE IS WORTH ALL THE HEADACHES THIS TWERP HAS CAUSED.
AREN'T YOU LISTENING?
LOGAN'S HERE. AND HE BROUGHT BACKUP. HE'S GOING TO KILL ALL OF YOU!
OH MY. WHO COULD HAVE SEEN THIS COMING?
NOT LIKE I DIDN'T WARN YOU THAT WE ONLY HAD ONE SHOT AT THIS.
BUT, OH NO...SIN, YOU GOTTA RUN OFF AND--

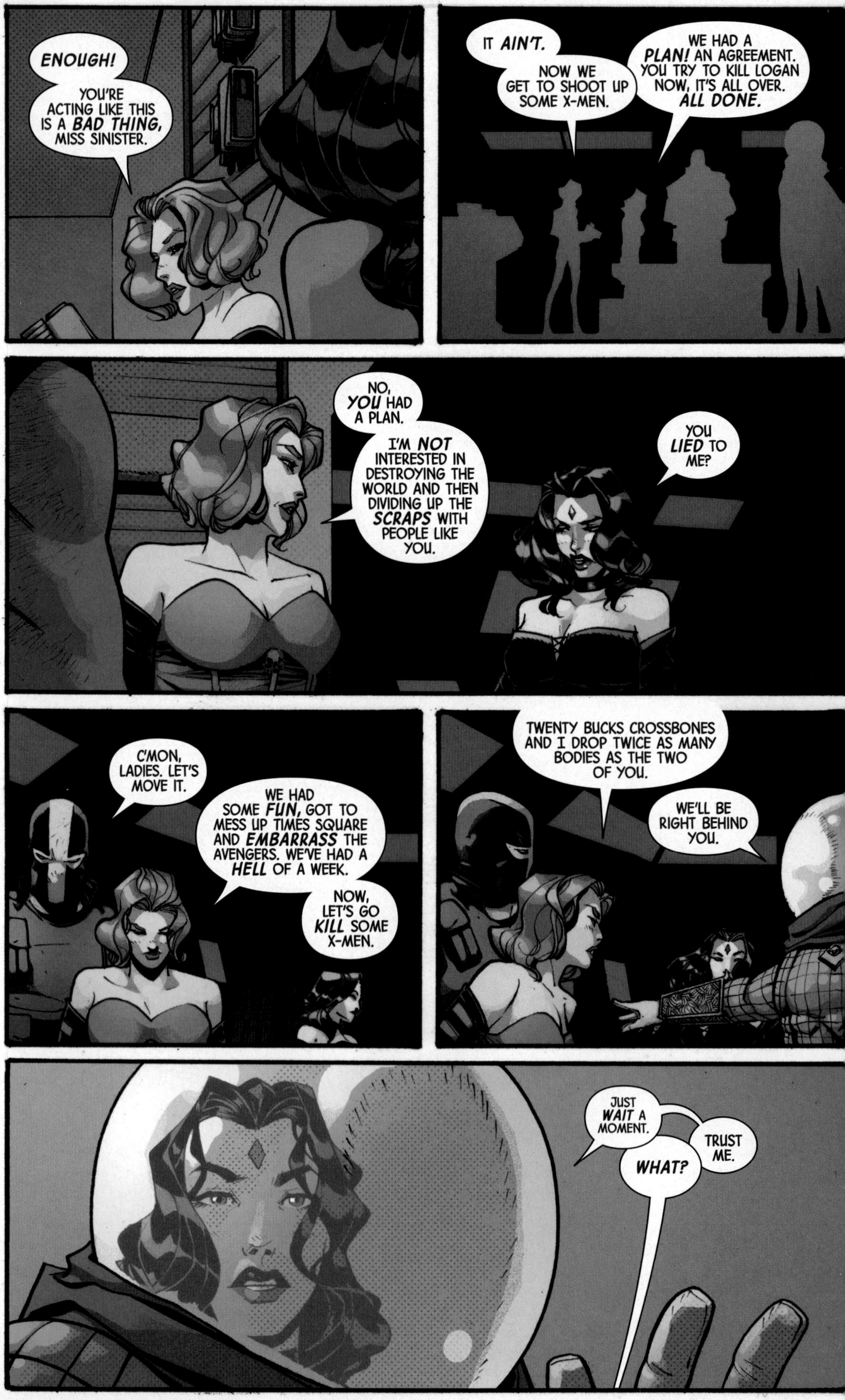

ENOUGH!
YOU'RE ACTING LIKE THIS IS A BAD THING, MISS SINISTER.
IT AIN'T.
NOW WE GET TO SHOOT UP SOME X-MEN.
WE HAD A PLAN! AN AGREEMENT. YOU TRY TO KILL LOGAN NOW, IT'S ALL OVER. ALL DONE.
NO, YOU HAD A PLAN.
I'M NOT INTERESTED IN DESTROYING THE WORLD AND THEN DIVIDING UP THE SCRAPS WITH PEOPLE LIKE YOU.
YOU LIED TO ME?
C'MON, LADIES. LET'S MOVE IT.
WE HAD SOME FUN, GOT TO MESS UP TIMES SQUARE AND EMBARRASS THE AVENGERS. WE'VE HAD A HELL OF A WEEK.
NOW, LET'S GO KILL SOME X-MEN.
TWENTY BUCKS CROSSBONES AND I DROP TWICE AS MANY BODIES AS THE TWO OF YOU.
WE'LL BE RIGHT BEHIND YOU.
JUST WAIT A MOMENT.
TRUST ME.
WHAT?

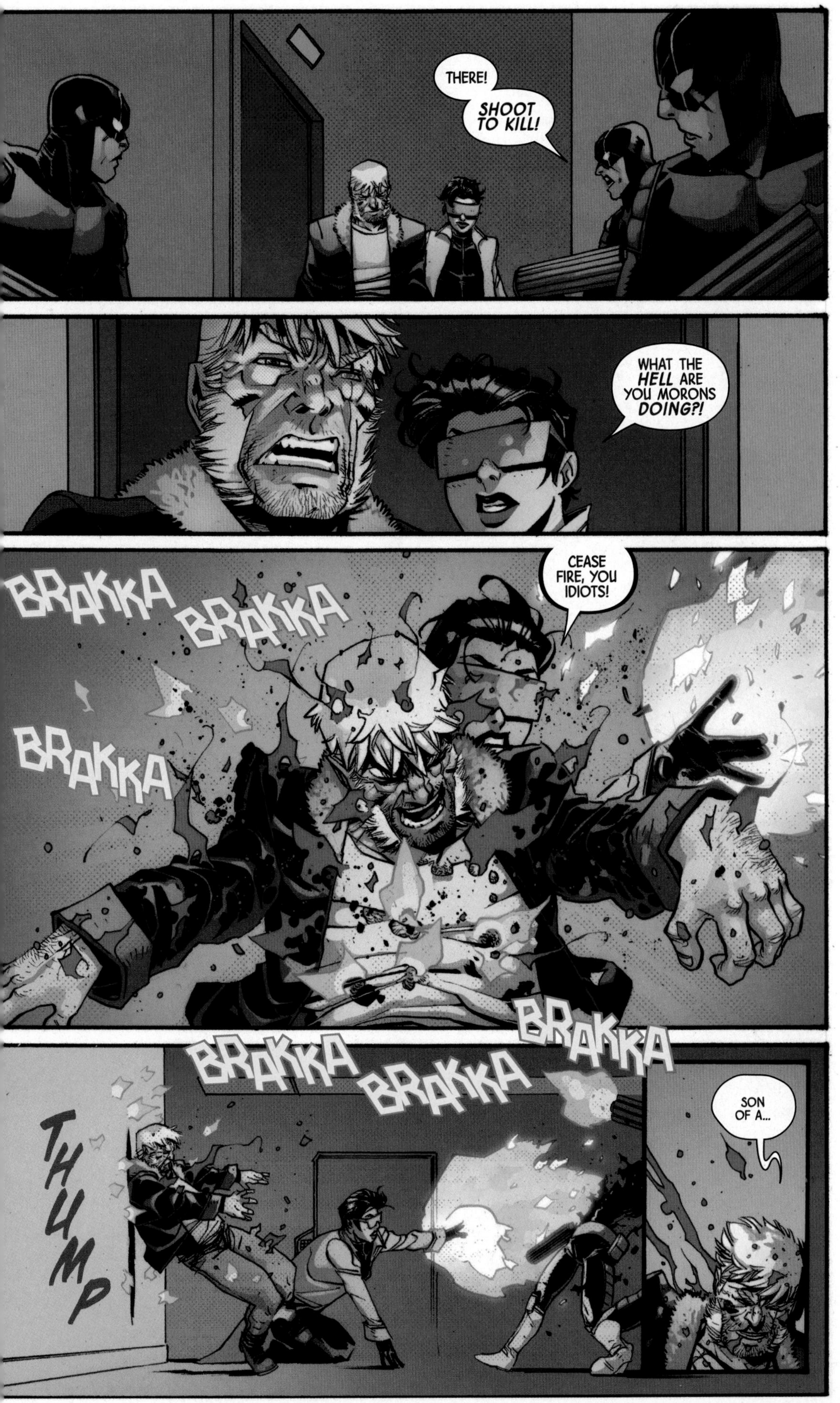
THERE!
SHOOT TO KILL!
WHAT THE HELL ARE YOU MORONS DOING?!
BRAKKA
BRAKKA
CEASE FIRE, YOU IDIOTS!
BRAKKA
BRAKKA
BRAKKA
BRAKKA
THUMP
SON OF A...

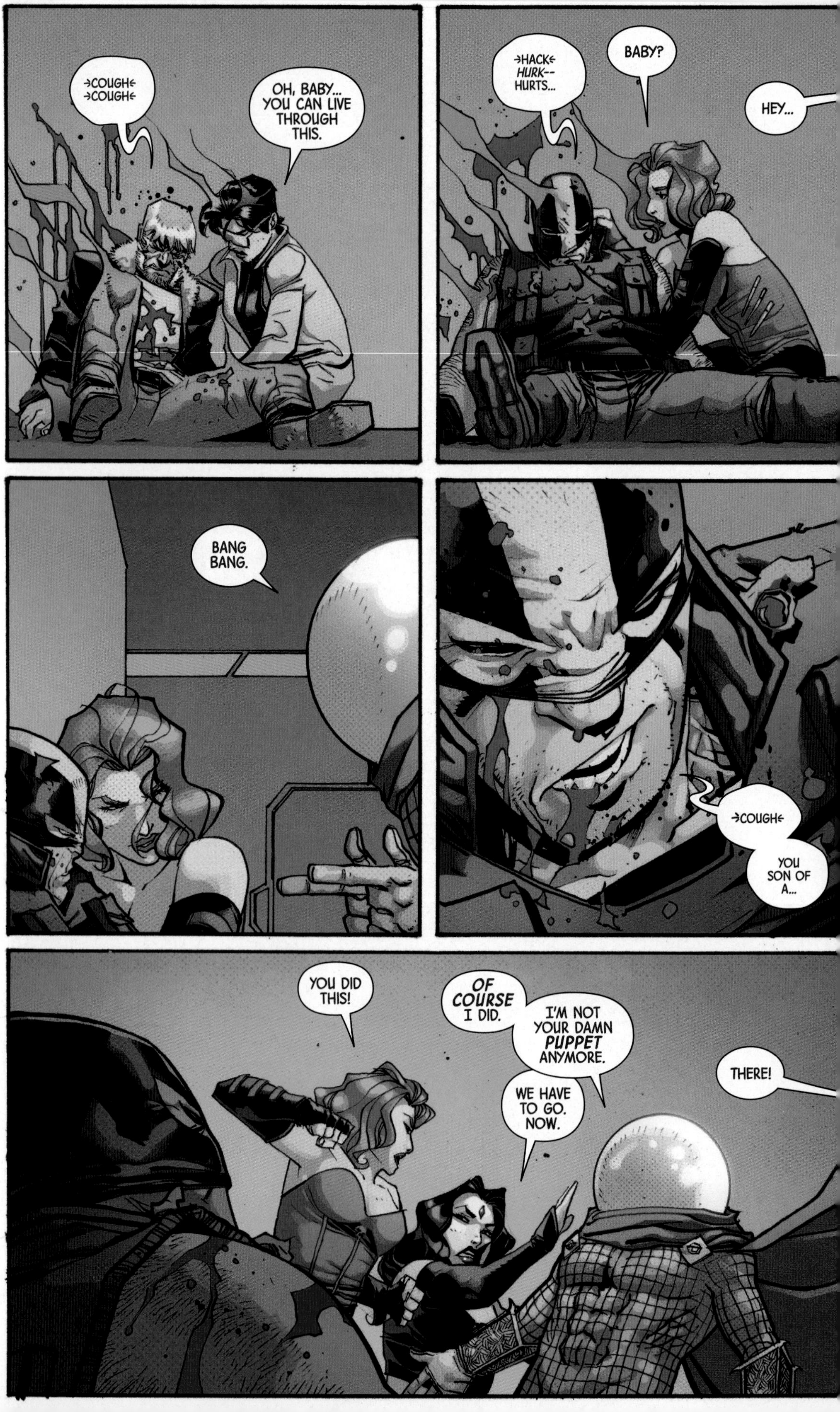

→COUGH←
→COUGH←
OH, BABY... YOU CAN LIVE THROUGH THIS.
→HACK←
HURK--
HURTS...
BABY?
HEY...
BANG BANG.
→COUGH←
YOU SON OF A...
YOU DID THIS!
OF COURSE I DID.
I'M NOT YOUR DAMN PUPPET ANYMORE.
WE HAVE TO GO. NOW.
THERE!

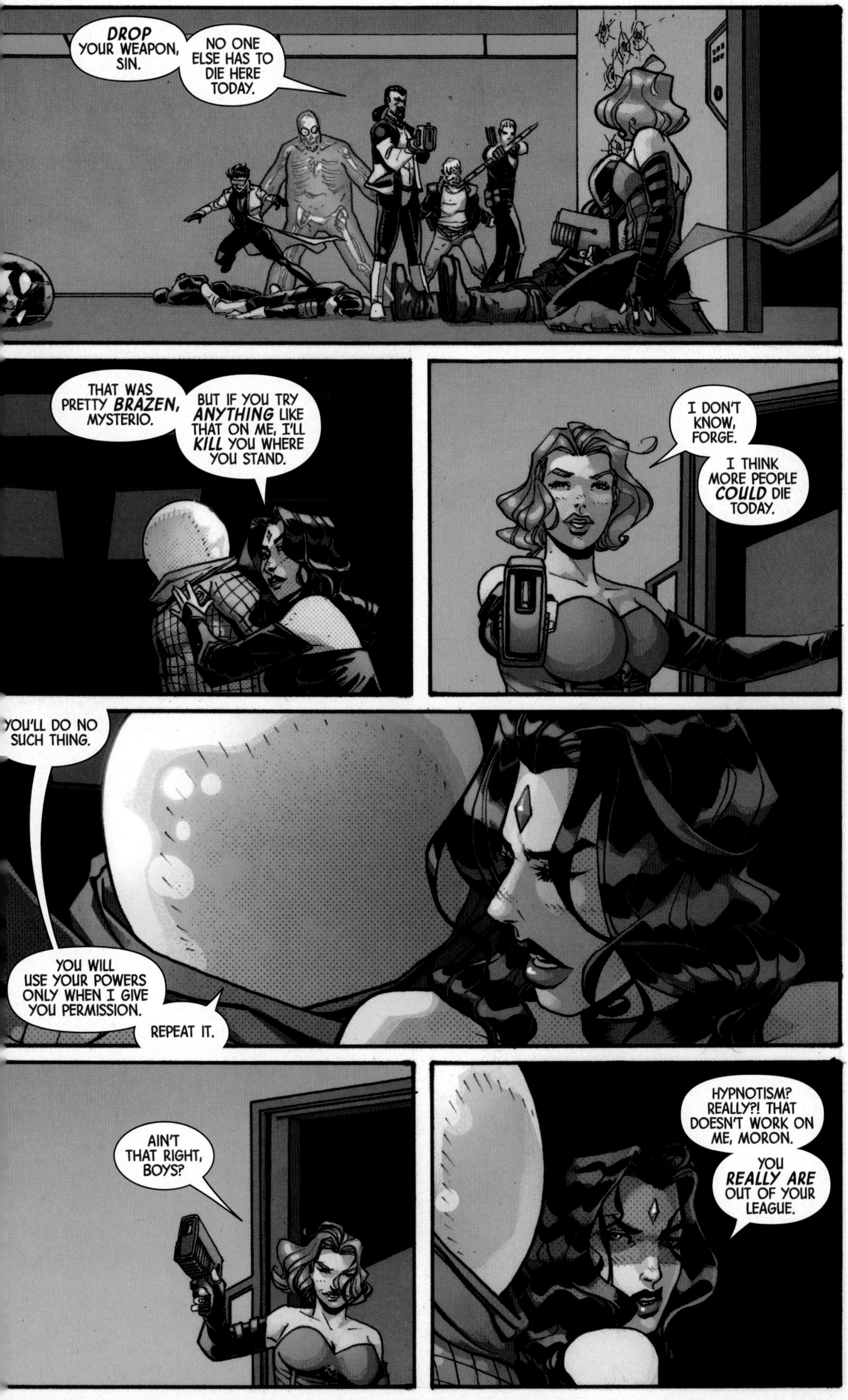
DROP YOUR WEAPON, SIN.
NO ONE ELSE HAS TO DIE HERE TODAY.
THAT WAS PRETTY BRAZEN, MYSTERIO.
BUT IF YOU TRY ANYTHING LIKE THAT ON ME, I'LL KILL YOU WHERE YOU STAND.
I DON'T KNOW, FORGE.
I THINK MORE PEOPLE COULD DIE TODAY.
YOU'LL DO NO SUCH THING.
YOU WILL USE YOUR POWERS ONLY WHEN I GIVE YOU PERMISSION.
REPEAT IT.
AIN'T THAT RIGHT, BOYS?
HYPNOTISM? REALLY?! THAT DOESN'T WORK ON ME, MORON.
YOU REALLY ARE OUT OF YOUR LEAGUE.

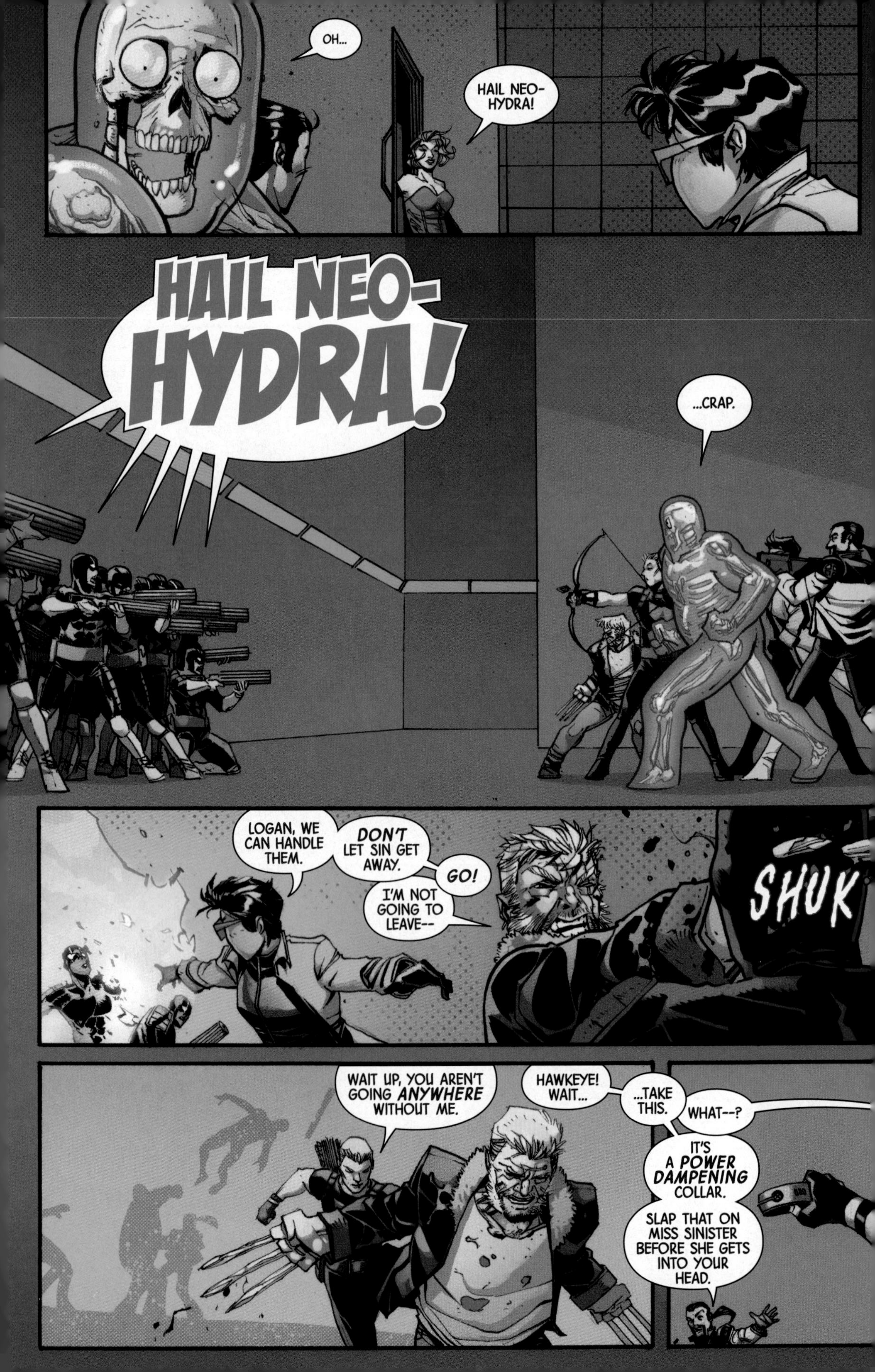
OH...
HAIL NEO-HYDRA!
HAIL NEO-HYDRA!
...CRAP.
LOGAN, WE CAN HANDLE THEM.
DON'T LET SIN GET AWAY.
GO!
I'M NOT GOING TO LEAVE--
SHUK
WAIT UP, YOU AREN'T GOING ANYWHERE WITHOUT ME.
HAWKEYE! WAIT...
...TAKE THIS.
WHAT--?
IT'S A POWER DAMPENING COLLAR.
SLAP THAT ON MISS SINISTER BEFORE SHE GETS INTO YOUR HEAD.

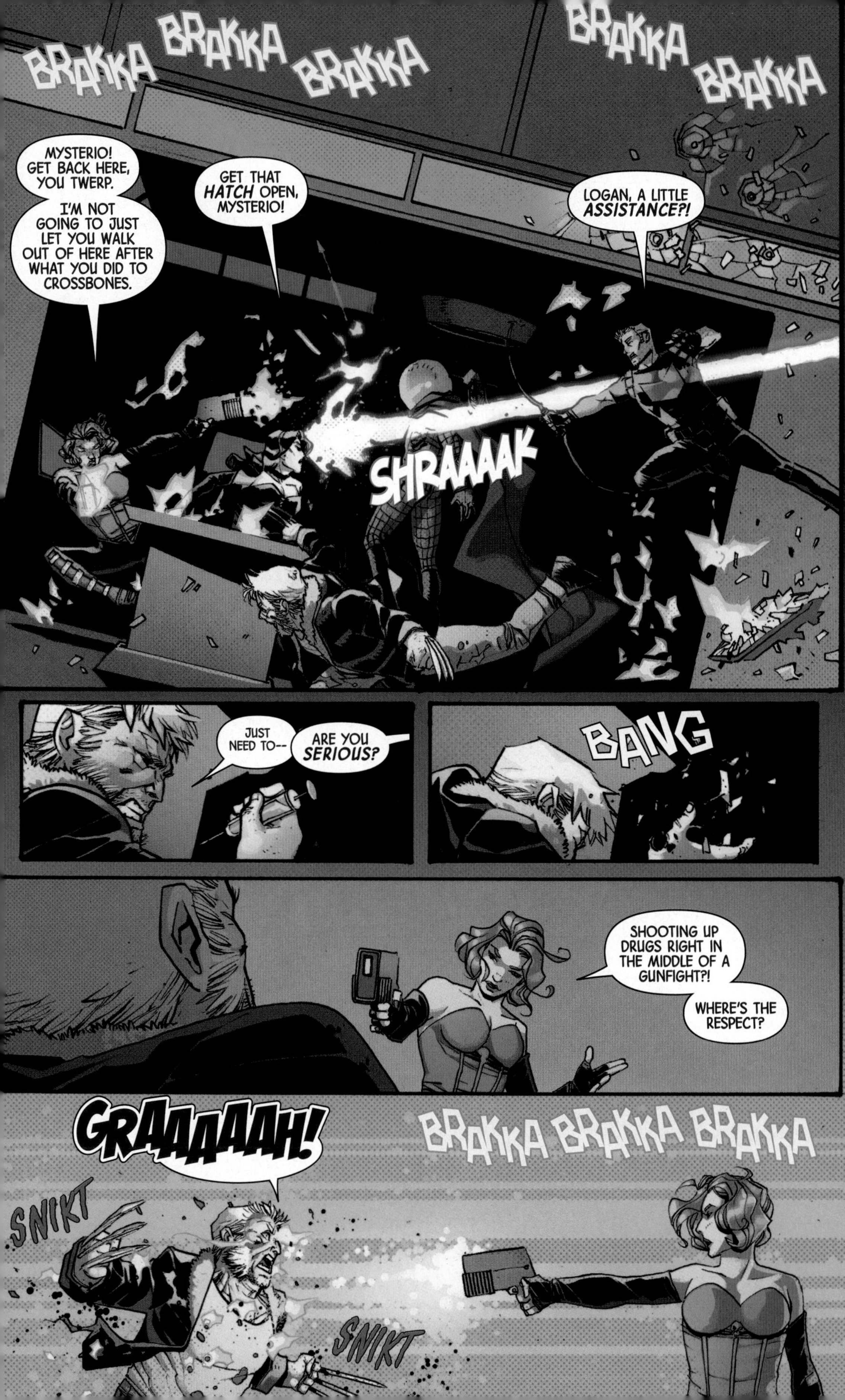
BRAKKA BRAKKA BRAKKA
BRAKKA BRAKKA
MYSTERIO! GET BACK HERE, YOU TWERP.
I'M NOT GOING TO JUST LET YOU WALK OUT OF HERE AFTER WHAT YOU DID TO CROSSBONES.
GET THAT HATCH OPEN, MYSTERIO!
LOGAN, A LITTLE ASSISTANCE?!
SHRAAAAK
JUST NEED TO--
ARE YOU SERIOUS?
BANG
SHOOTING UP DRUGS RIGHT IN THE MIDDLE OF A GUNFIGHT?!
WHERE'S THE RESPECT?
GRAAAAAH!
BRAKKA BRAKKA BRAKKA
SNIKT
SNIKT

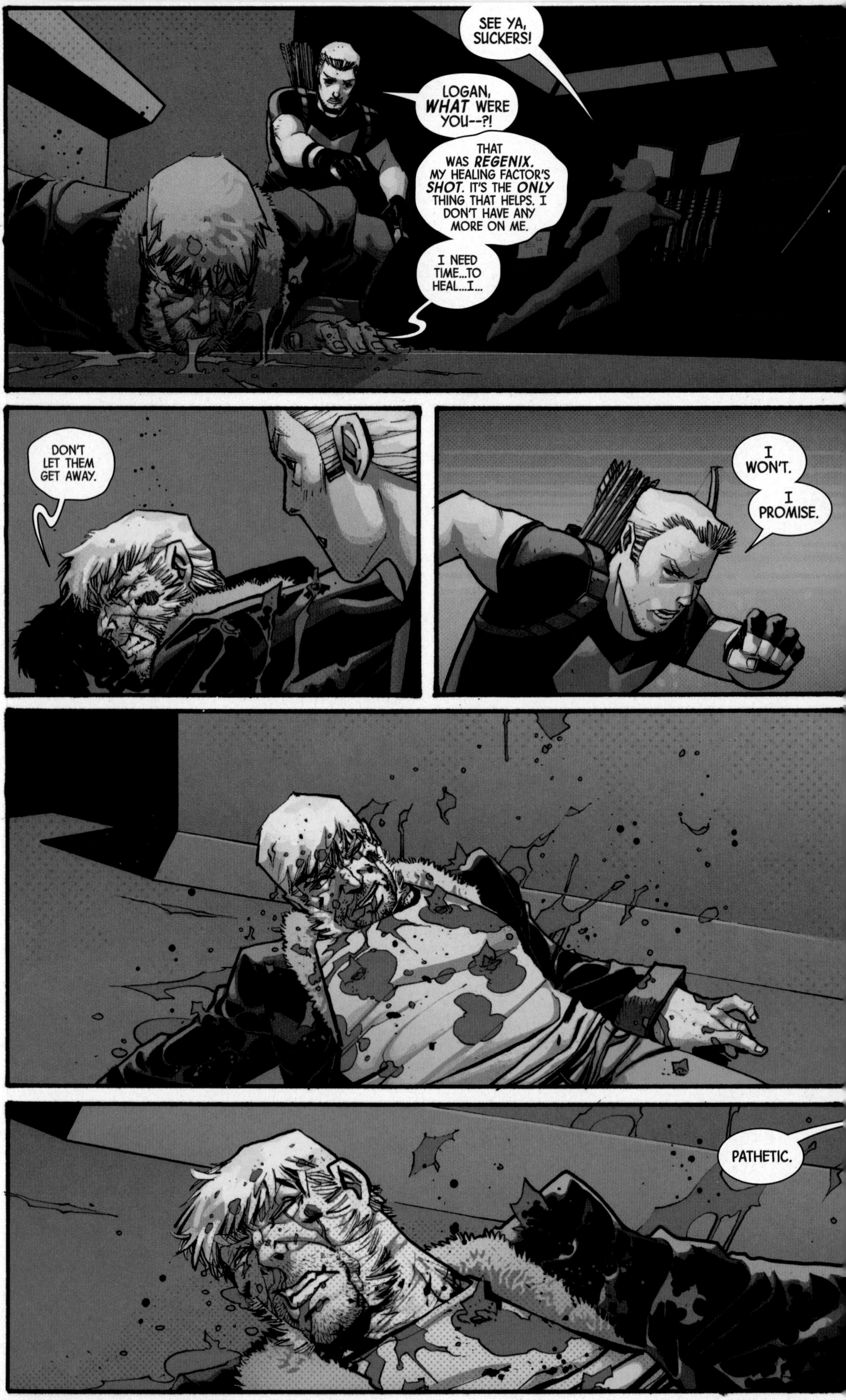
SEE YA, SUCKERS!
LOGAN, WHAT WERE YOU--?!
THAT WAS REGENIX. MY HEALING FACTOR'S SHOT. IT'S THE ONLY THING THAT HELPS. I DON'T HAVE ANY MORE ON ME.
I NEED TIME...TO HEAL...I...
DON'T LET THEM GET AWAY.
I WON'T.
I PROMISE.
PATHETIC.

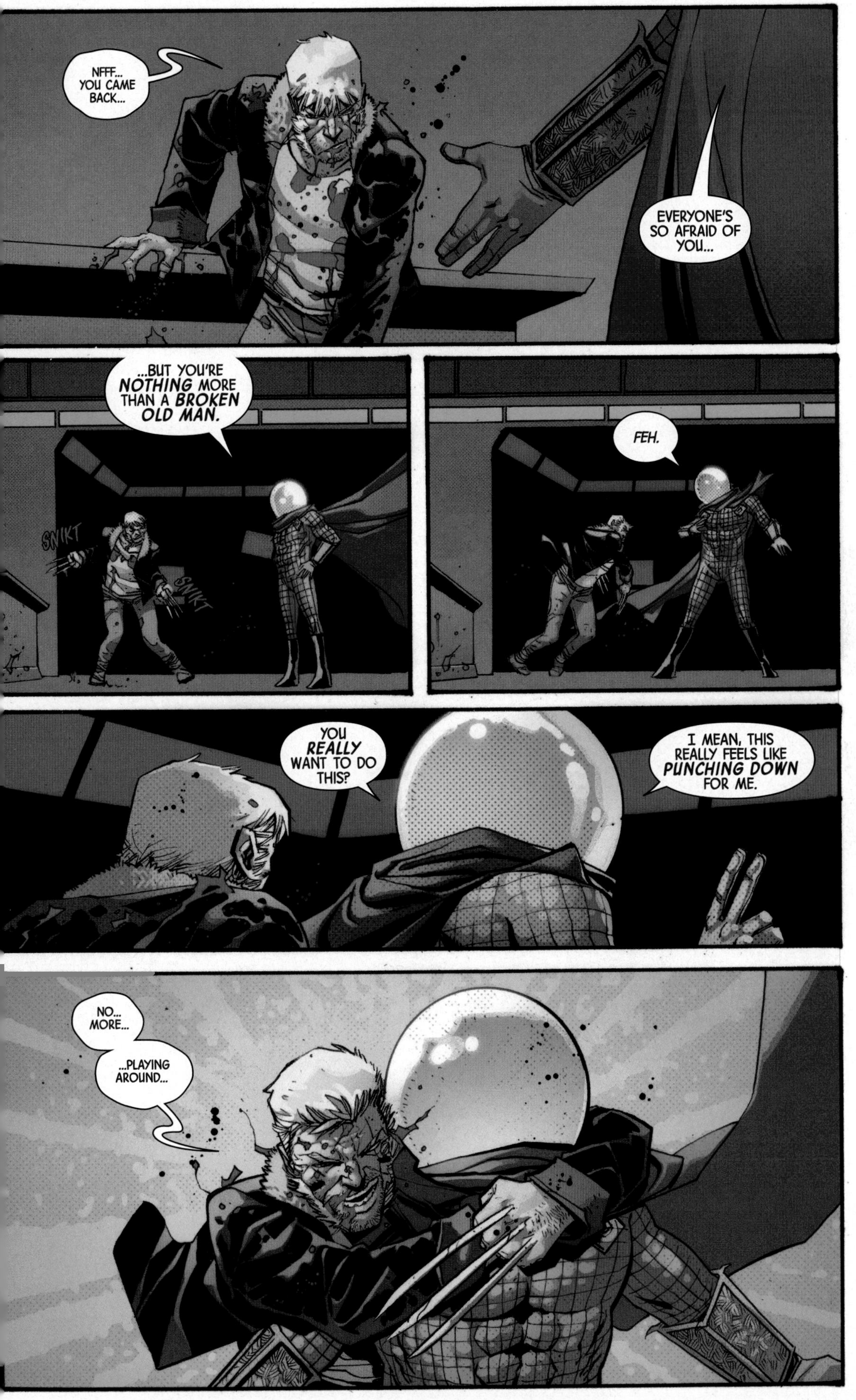
NFFF... YOU CAME BACK...
EVERYONE'S SO AFRAID OF YOU...
...BUT YOU'RE NOTHING MORE THAN A BROKEN OLD MAN.
SNIKT
SNIKT
FEH.
YOU REALLY WANT TO DO THIS?
I MEAN, THIS REALLY FEELS LIKE PUNCHING DOWN FOR ME.
NO... MORE...
...PLAYING AROUND...

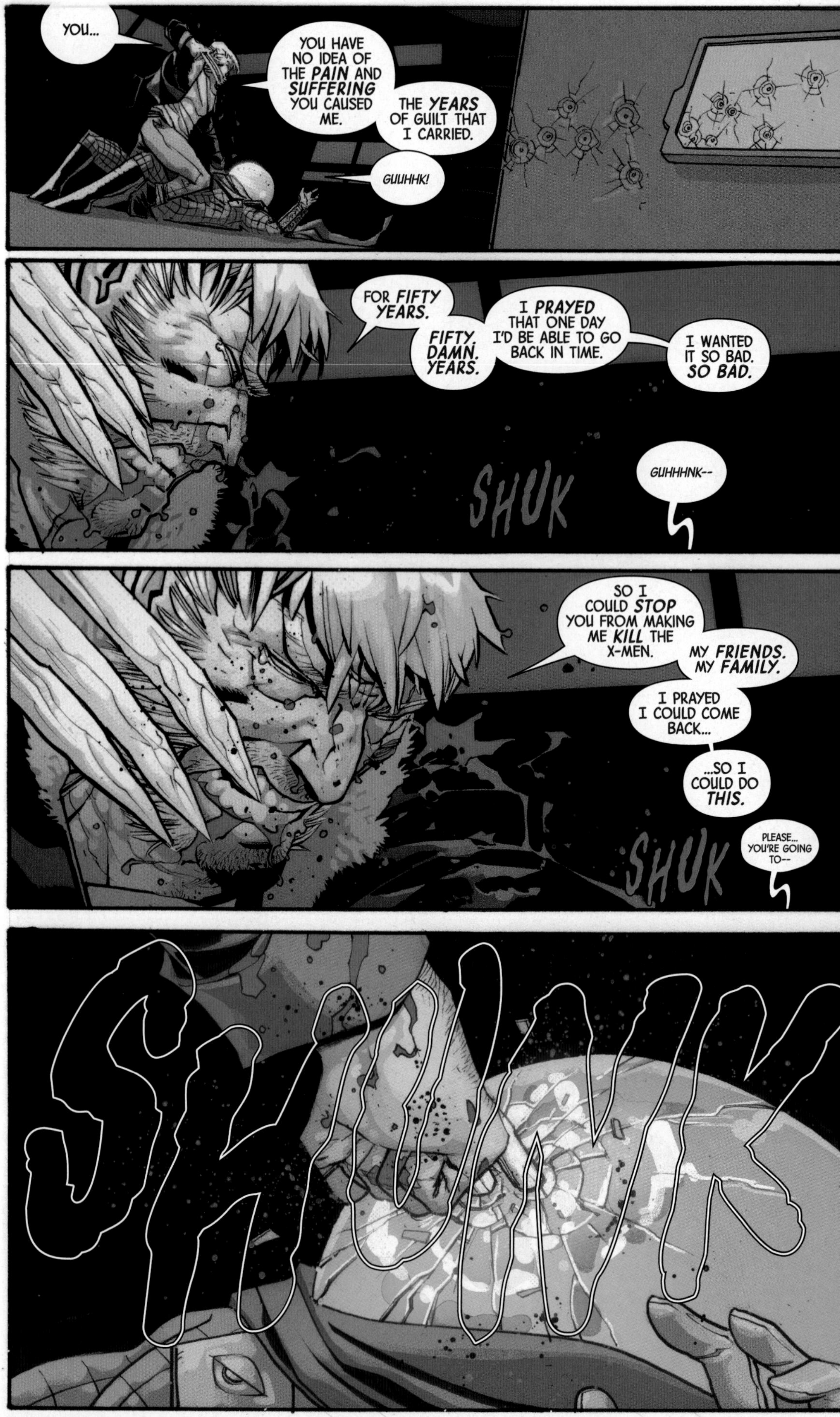
YOU...
YOU HAVE NO IDEA OF THE PAIN AND SUFFERING YOU CAUSED ME.
THE YEARS OF GUILT THAT I CARRIED.
GUUHHK!
FOR FIFTY YEARS.
FIFTY. DAMN. YEARS.
I PRAYED THAT ONE DAY I'D BE ABLE TO GO BACK IN TIME.
I WANTED IT SO BAD. SO BAD.
SHUK
GUHHHNK--
SO I COULD STOP YOU FROM MAKING ME KILL THE X-MEN.
MY FRIENDS. MY FAMILY.
I PRAYED I COULD COME BACK...
...SO I COULD DO THIS.
SHUK
PLEASE... YOU'RE GOING TO--
SHUNK

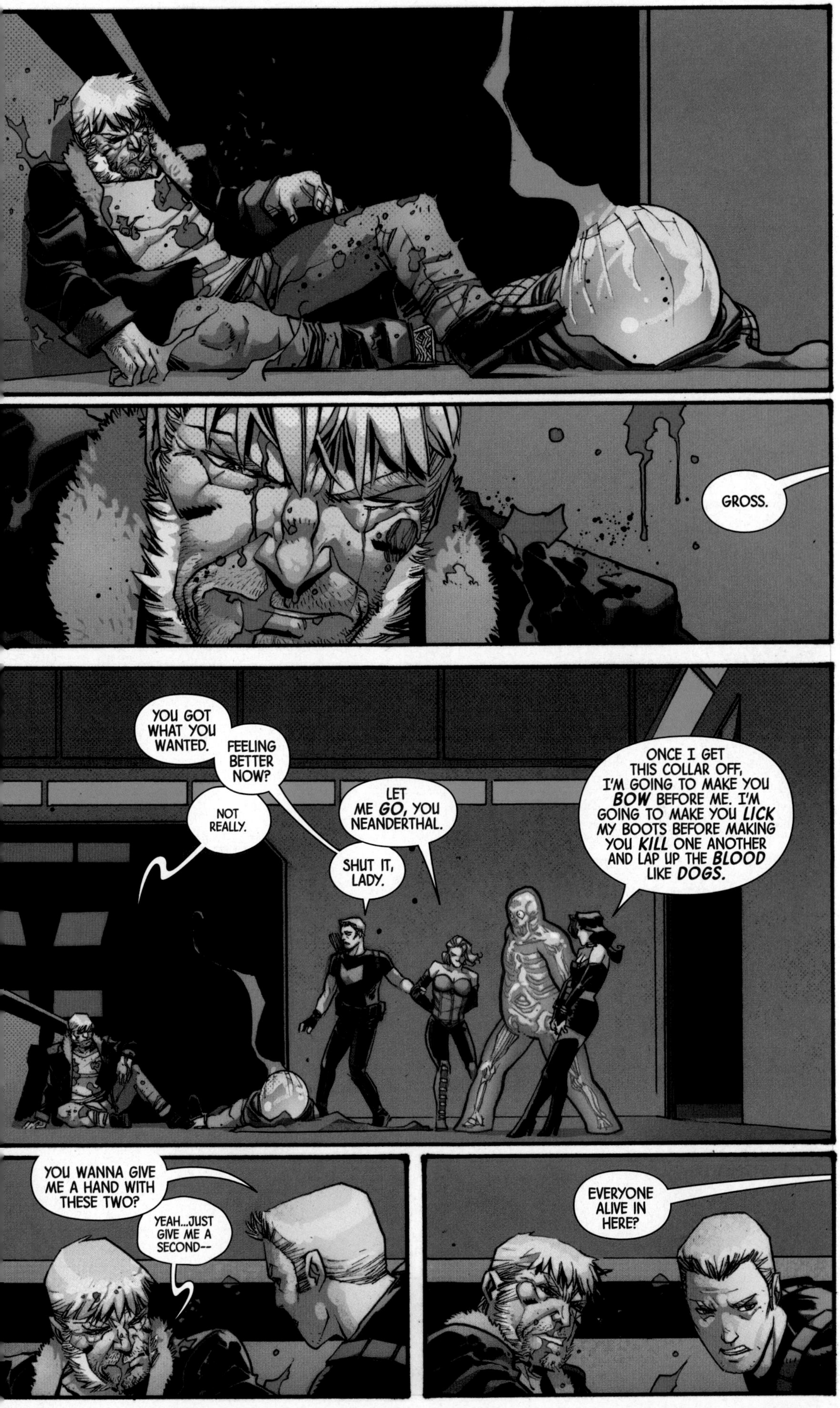
GROSS.
YOU GOT WHAT YOU WANTED.
FEELING BETTER NOW?
NOT REALLY.
LET ME GO, YOU NEANDERTHAL.
SHUT IT, LADY.
ONCE I GET THIS COLLAR OFF, I'M GOING TO MAKE YOU BOW BEFORE ME. I'M GOING TO MAKE YOU LICK MY BOOTS BEFORE MAKING YOU KILL ONE ANOTHER AND LAP UP THE BLOOD LIKE DOGS.
YOU WANNA GIVE ME A HAND WITH THESE TWO?
YEAH...JUST GIVE ME A SECOND--
EVERYONE ALIVE IN HERE?

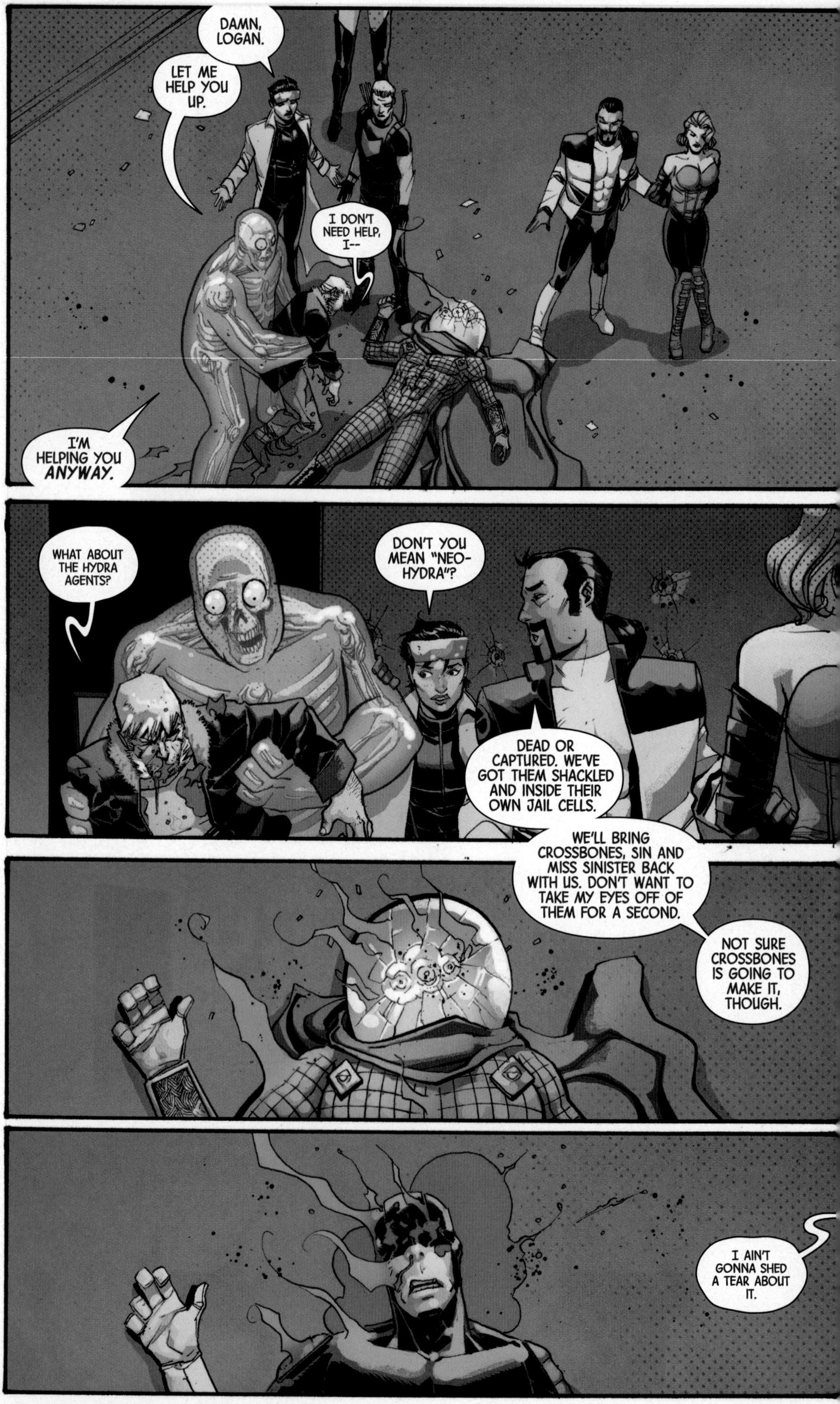
DAMN, LOGAN.
LET ME HELP YOU UP.
I DON'T NEED HELP, I--
I'M HELPING YOU ANYWAY.
WHAT ABOUT THE HYDRA AGENTS?
DON'T YOU MEAN "NEO-HYDRA"?
DEAD OR CAPTURED. WE'VE GOT THEM SHACKLED AND INSIDE THEIR OWN JAIL CELLS.
WE'LL BRING CROSSBONES, SIN AND MISS SINISTER BACK WITH US. DON'T WANT TO TAKE MY EYES OFF OF THEM FOR A SECOND.
NOT SURE CROSSBONES IS GOING TO MAKE IT, THOUGH.
I AIN'T GONNA SHED A TEAR ABOUT IT.

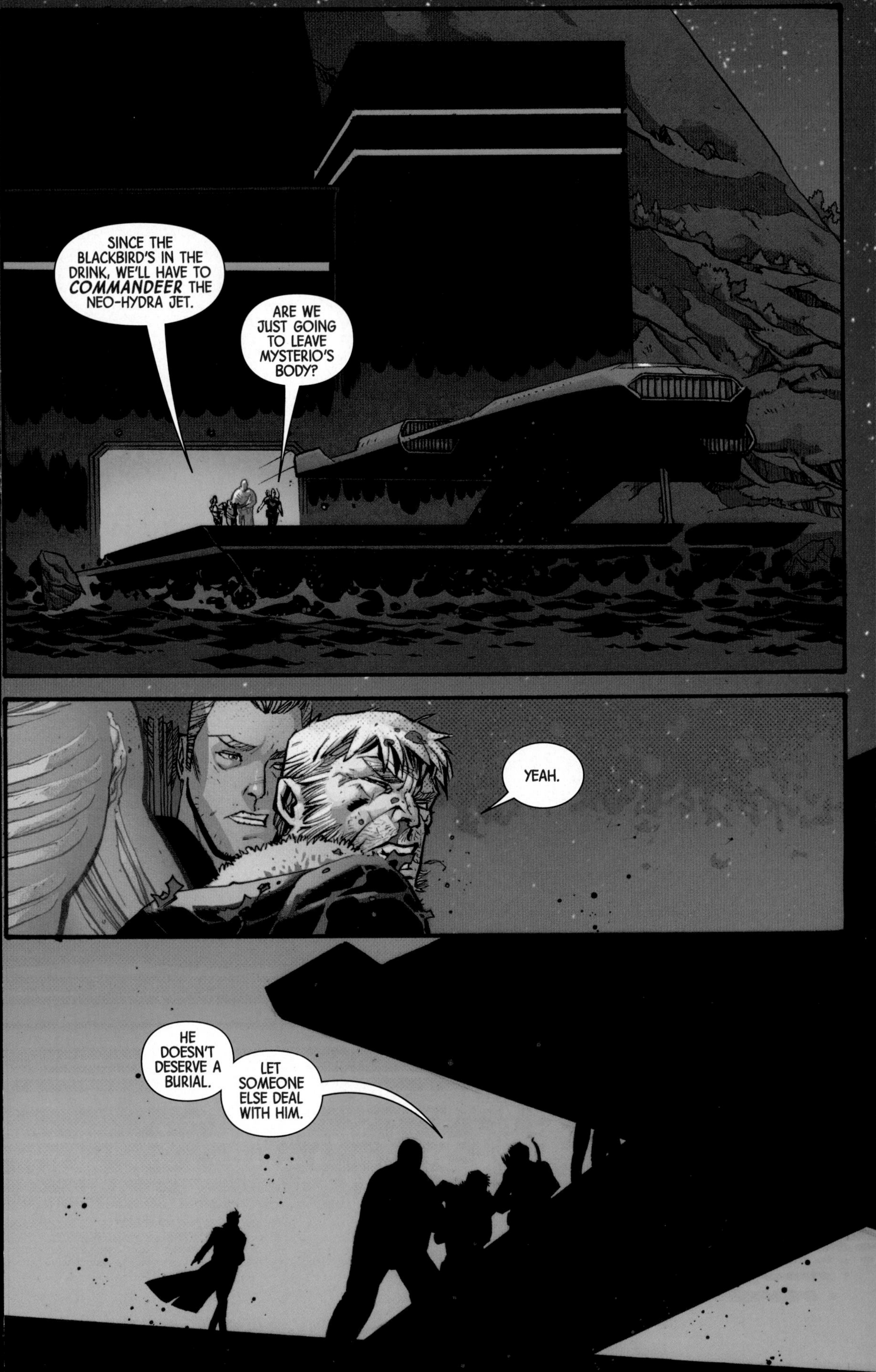
SINCE THE BLACKBIRD'S IN THE DRINK, WE'LL HAVE TO COMMANDEER THE NEO-HYDRA JET.
ARE WE JUST GOING TO LEAVE MYSTERIO'S BODY?
YEAH.
HE DOESN'T DESERVE A BURIAL.
LET SOMEONE ELSE DEAL WITH HIM.

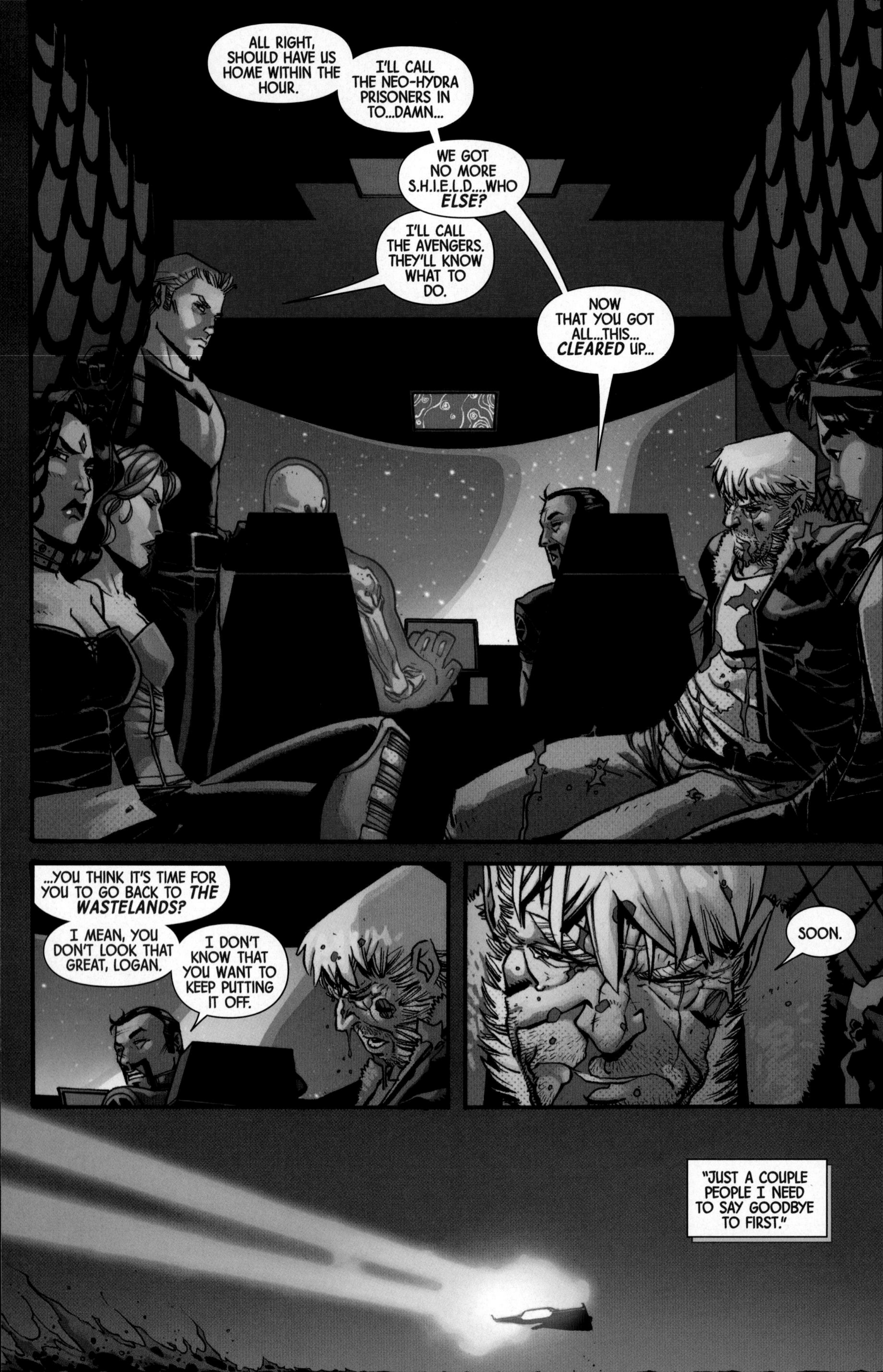
ALL RIGHT, SHOULD HAVE US HOME WITHIN THE HOUR.
I'LL CALL THE NEO-HYDRA PRISONERS IN TO...DAMN...
WE GOT NO MORE S.H.I.E.L.D....WHO ELSE?
I'LL CALL THE AVENGERS. THEY'LL KNOW WHAT TO DO.
NOW THAT YOU GOT ALL...THIS... CLEARED UP...
...YOU THINK IT'S TIME FOR YOU TO GO BACK TO THE WASTELANDS?
I MEAN, YOU DON'T LOOK THAT GREAT, LOGAN.
I DON'T KNOW THAT YOU WANT TO KEEP PUTTING IT OFF.
SOON.
"JUST A COUPLE PEOPLE I NEED TO SAY GOODBYE TO FIRST."

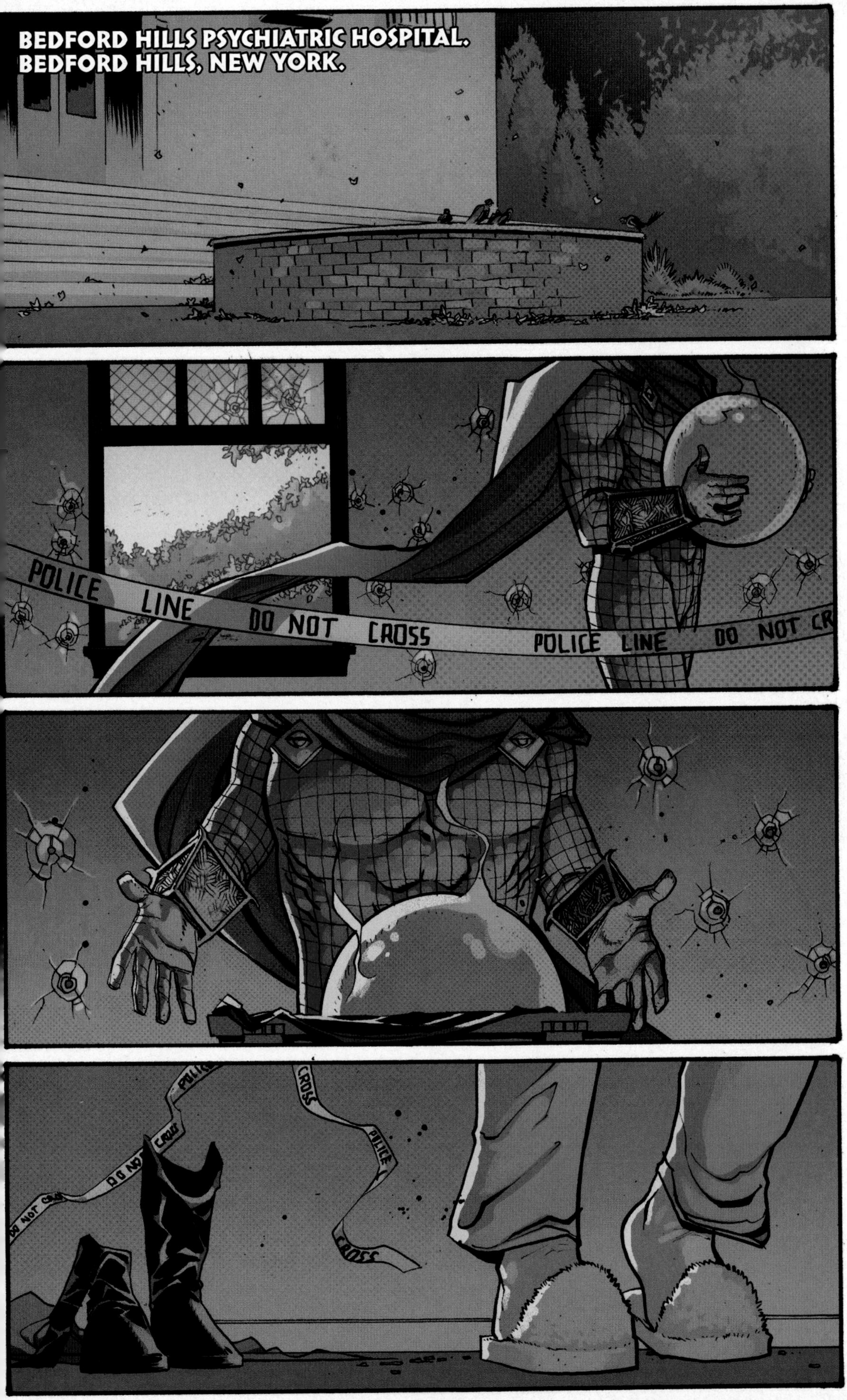
BEDFORD HILLS PSYCHIATRIC HOSPITAL.
BEDFORD HILLS, NEW YORK.
POLICE LINE DO NOT CROSS POLICE LINE DO NOT CR
DO NOT CROSS
POLICE
CROSS

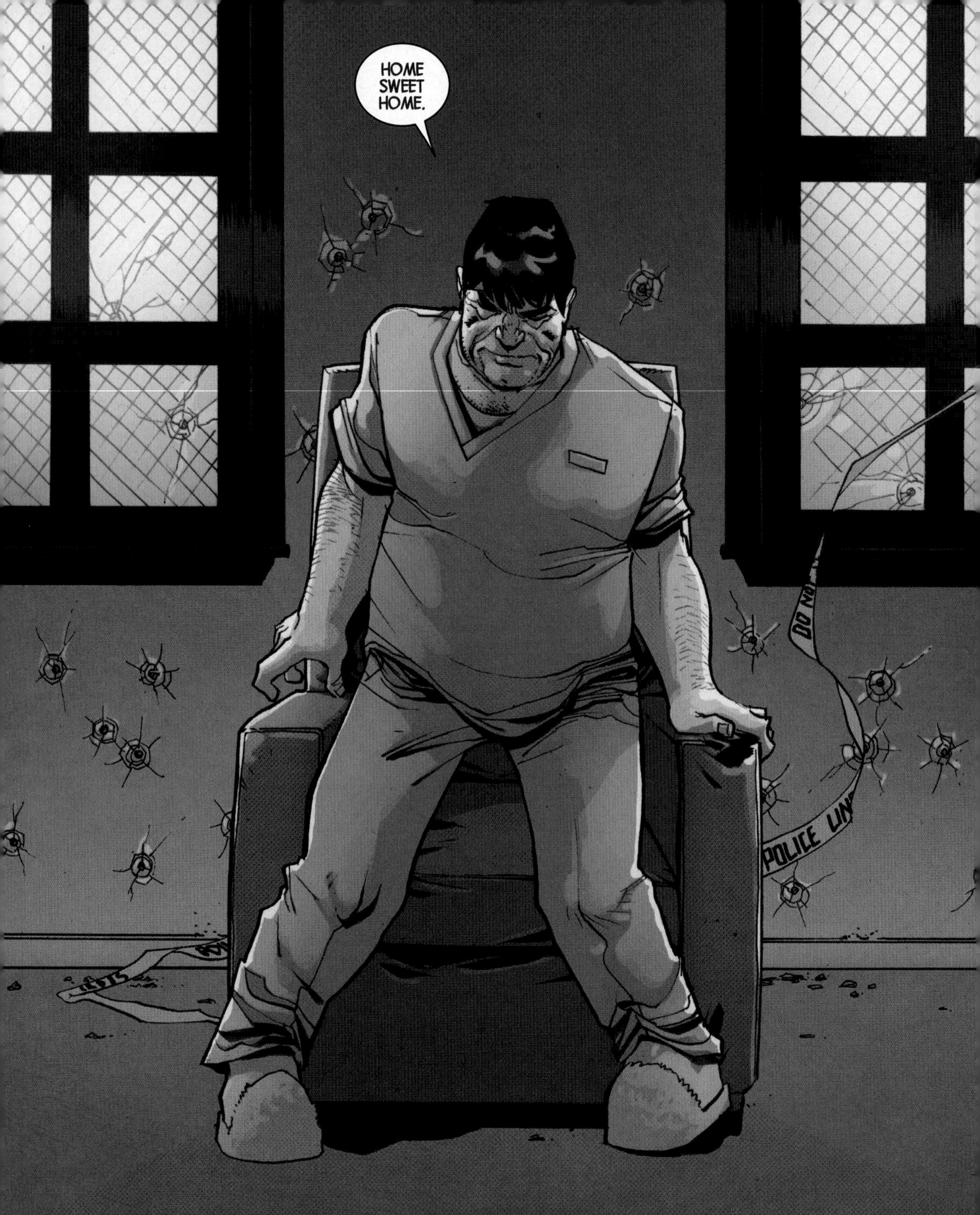
HOME SWEET HOME.

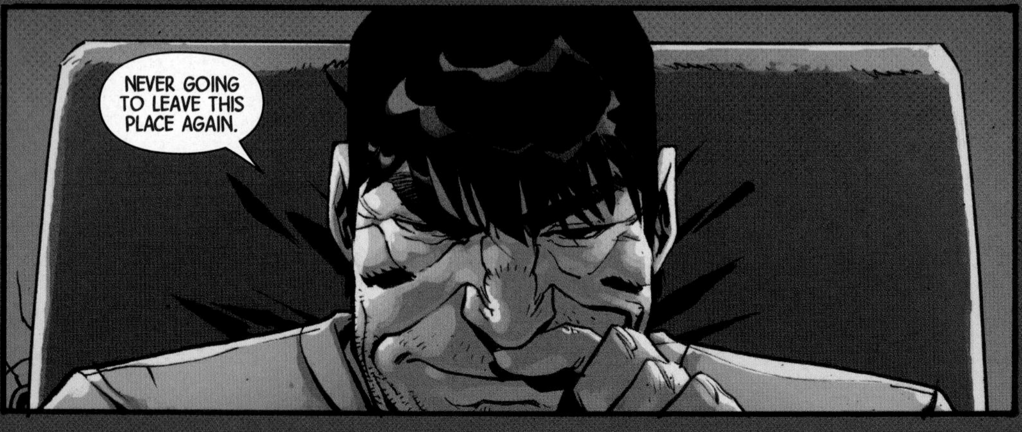
NEVER GOING TO LEAVE THIS PLACE AGAIN.

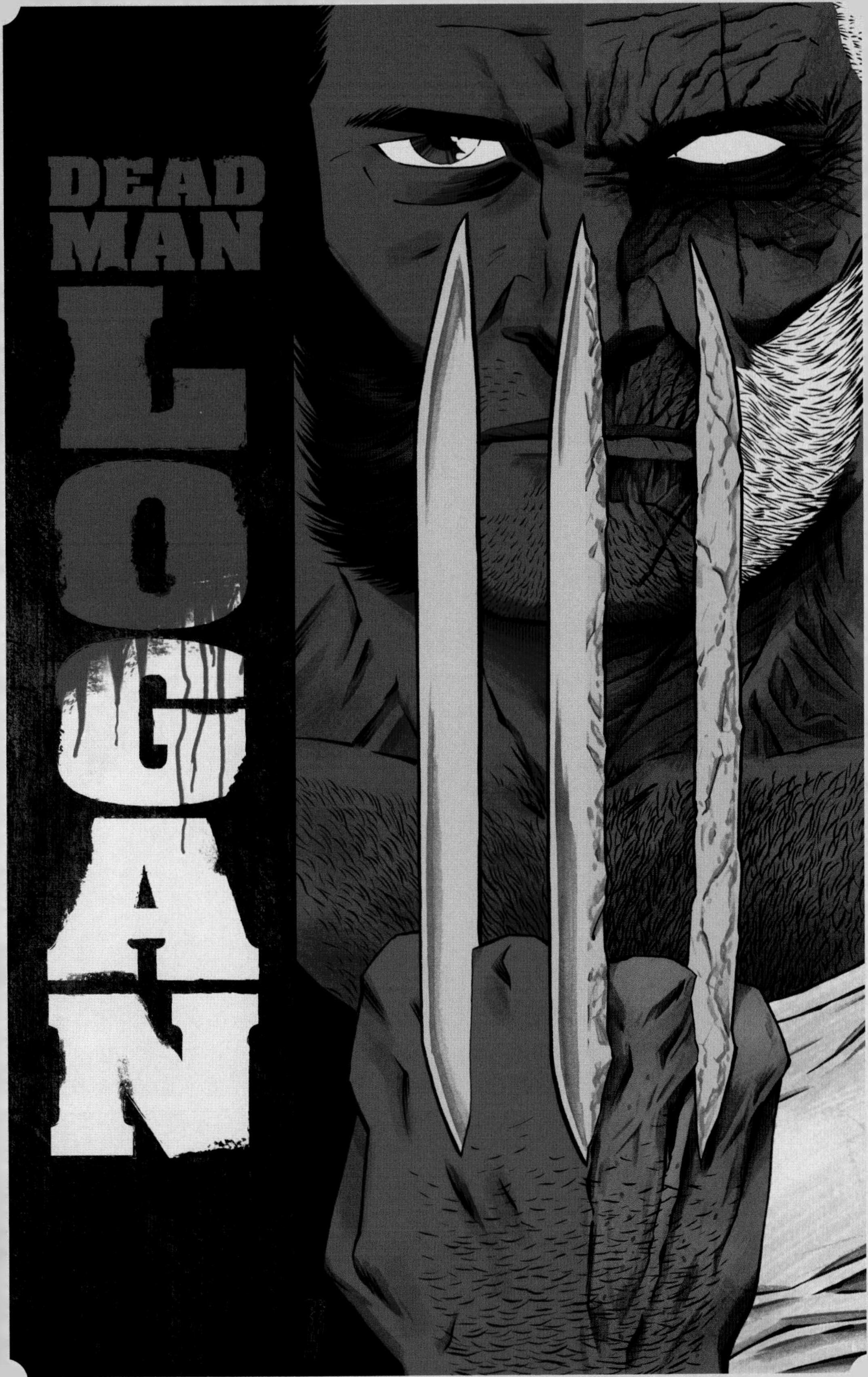
DEAD
MAN
LOGAN

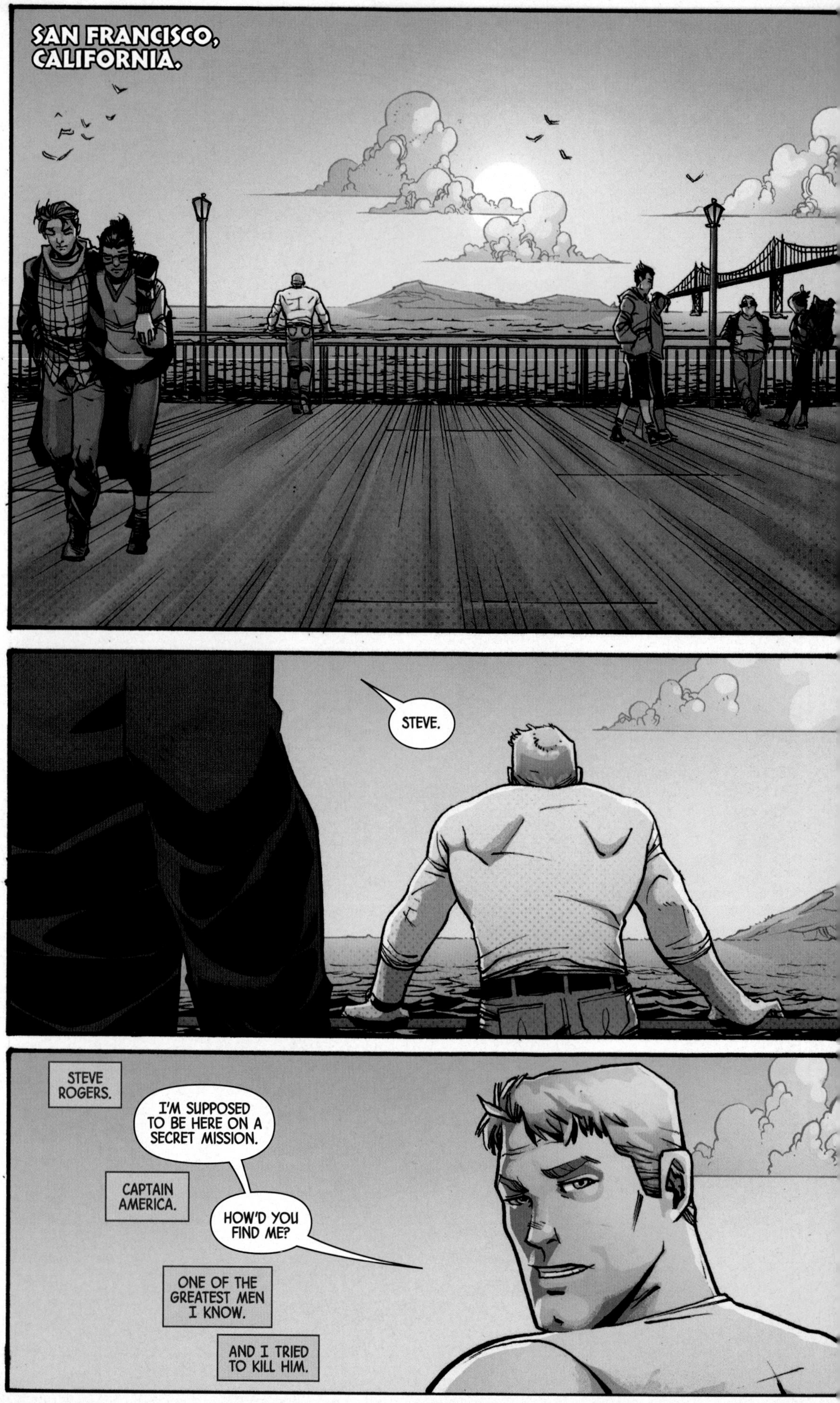
SAN FRANCISCO, CALIFORNIA.
STEVE.
STEVE ROGERS.
I'M SUPPOSED TO BE HERE ON A SECRET MISSION.
CAPTAIN AMERICA.
HOW'D YOU FIND ME?
ONE OF THE GREATEST MEN I KNOW.
AND I TRIED TO KILL HIM.

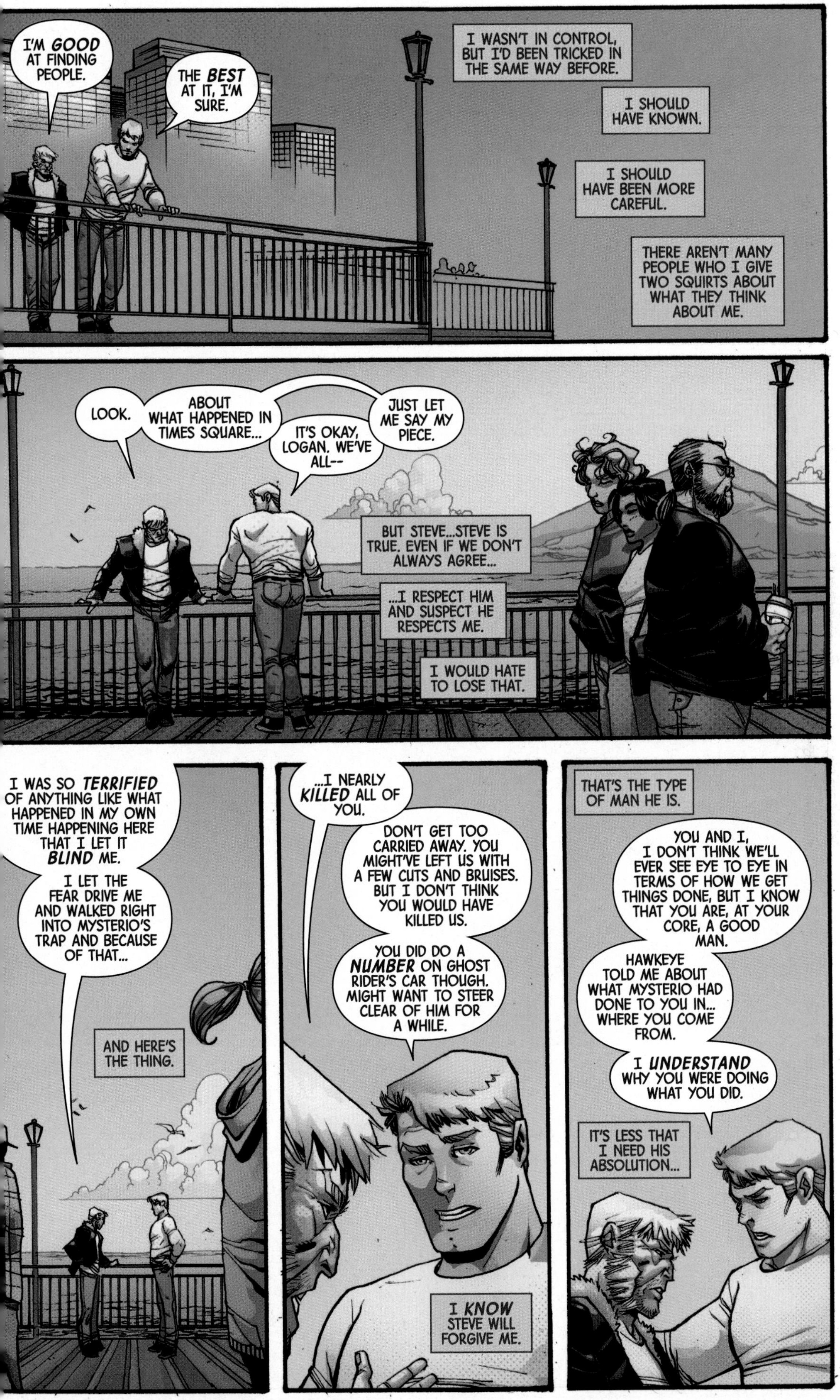
I'M GOOD AT FINDING PEOPLE.
THE BEST AT IT, I'M SURE.
I WASN'T IN CONTROL, BUT I'D BEEN TRICKED IN THE SAME WAY BEFORE.
I SHOULD HAVE KNOWN.
I SHOULD HAVE BEEN MORE CAREFUL.
THERE AREN'T MANY PEOPLE WHO I GIVE TWO SQUIRTS ABOUT WHAT THEY THINK ABOUT ME.
LOOK.
ABOUT WHAT HAPPENED IN TIMES SQUARE...
JUST LET ME SAY MY PIECE.
IT'S OKAY, LOGAN. WE'VE ALL--
BUT STEVE...STEVE IS TRUE. EVEN IF WE DON'T ALWAYS AGREE...
...I RESPECT HIM AND SUSPECT HE RESPECTS ME.
I WOULD HATE TO LOSE THAT.
I WAS SO TERRIFIED OF ANYTHING LIKE WHAT HAPPENED IN MY OWN TIME HAPPENING HERE THAT I LET IT BLIND ME.
I LET THE FEAR DRIVE ME AND WALKED RIGHT INTO MYSTERIO'S TRAP AND BECAUSE OF THAT...
AND HERE'S THE THING.
...I NEARLY KILLED ALL OF YOU.
DON'T GET TOO CARRIED AWAY. YOU MIGHT'VE LEFT US WITH A FEW CUTS AND BRUISES. BUT I DON'T THINK YOU WOULD HAVE KILLED US.
YOU DID DO A NUMBER ON GHOST RIDER'S CAR THOUGH. MIGHT WANT TO STEER CLEAR OF HIM FOR A WHILE.
I KNOW STEVE WILL FORGIVE ME.
THAT'S THE TYPE OF MAN HE IS.
YOU AND I, I DON'T THINK WE'LL EVER SEE EYE TO EYE IN TERMS OF HOW WE GET THINGS DONE, BUT I KNOW THAT YOU ARE, AT YOUR CORE, A GOOD MAN.
HAWKEYE TOLD ME ABOUT WHAT MYSTERIO HAD DONE TO YOU IN... WHERE YOU COME FROM.
I UNDERSTAND WHY YOU WERE DOING WHAT YOU DID.
IT'S LESS THAT I NEED HIS ABSOLUTION...

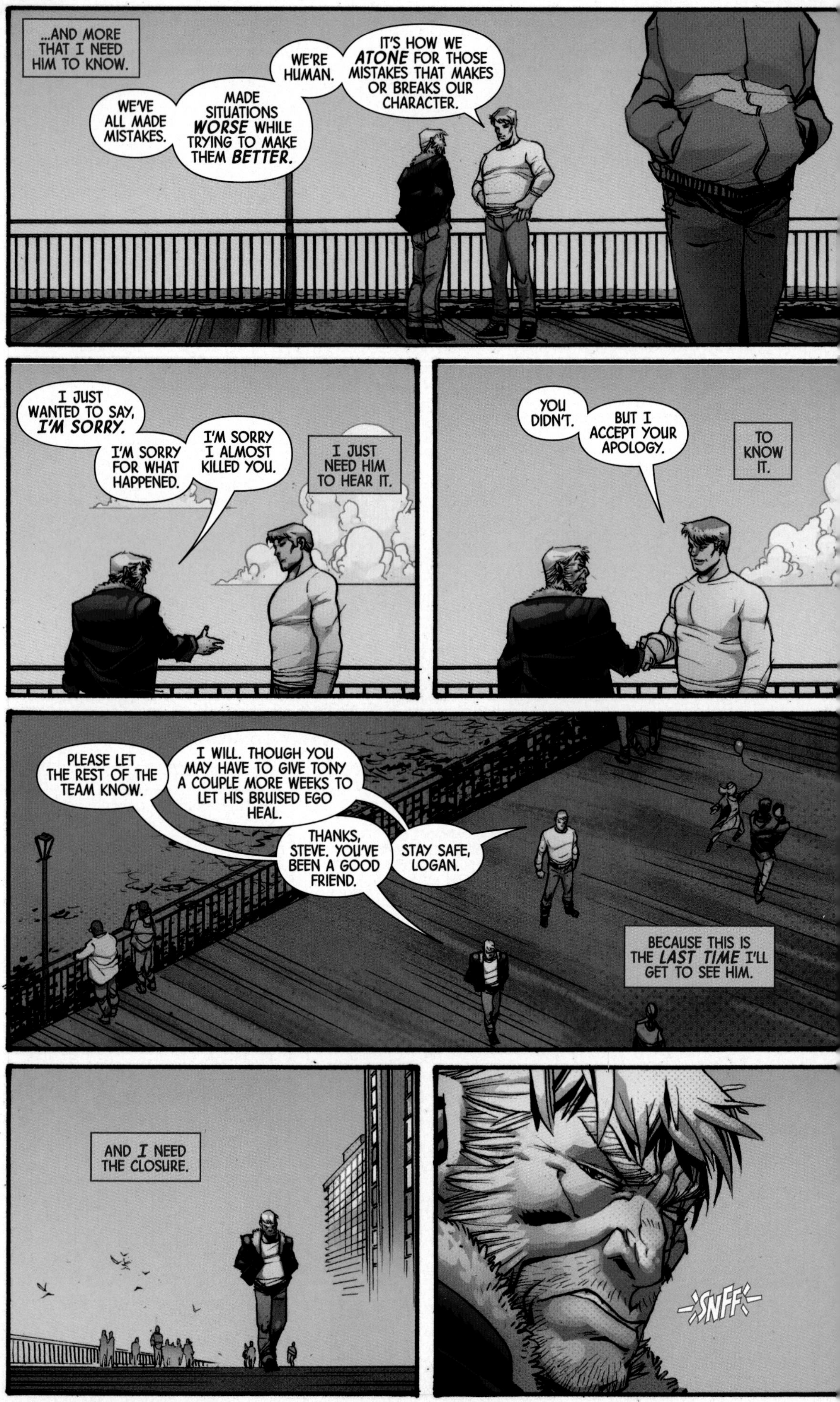
...AND MORE THAT I NEED HIM TO KNOW.
WE'VE ALL MADE MISTAKES.
MADE SITUATIONS WORSE WHILE TRYING TO MAKE THEM BETTER.
WE'RE HUMAN.
IT'S HOW WE ATONE FOR THOSE MISTAKES THAT MAKES OR BREAKS OUR CHARACTER.
I JUST WANTED TO SAY, I'M SORRY.
I'M SORRY FOR WHAT HAPPENED.
I'M SORRY I ALMOST KILLED YOU.
I JUST NEED HIM TO HEAR IT.
YOU DIDN'T.
BUT I ACCEPT YOUR APOLOGY.
TO KNOW IT.
PLEASE LET THE REST OF THE TEAM KNOW.
I WILL. THOUGH YOU MAY HAVE TO GIVE TONY A COUPLE MORE WEEKS TO LET HIS BRUISED EGO HEAL.
THANKS, STEVE. YOU'VE BEEN A GOOD FRIEND.
STAY SAFE, LOGAN.
BECAUSE THIS IS THE LAST TIME I'LL GET TO SEE HIM.
AND I NEED THE CLOSURE.
SNFF

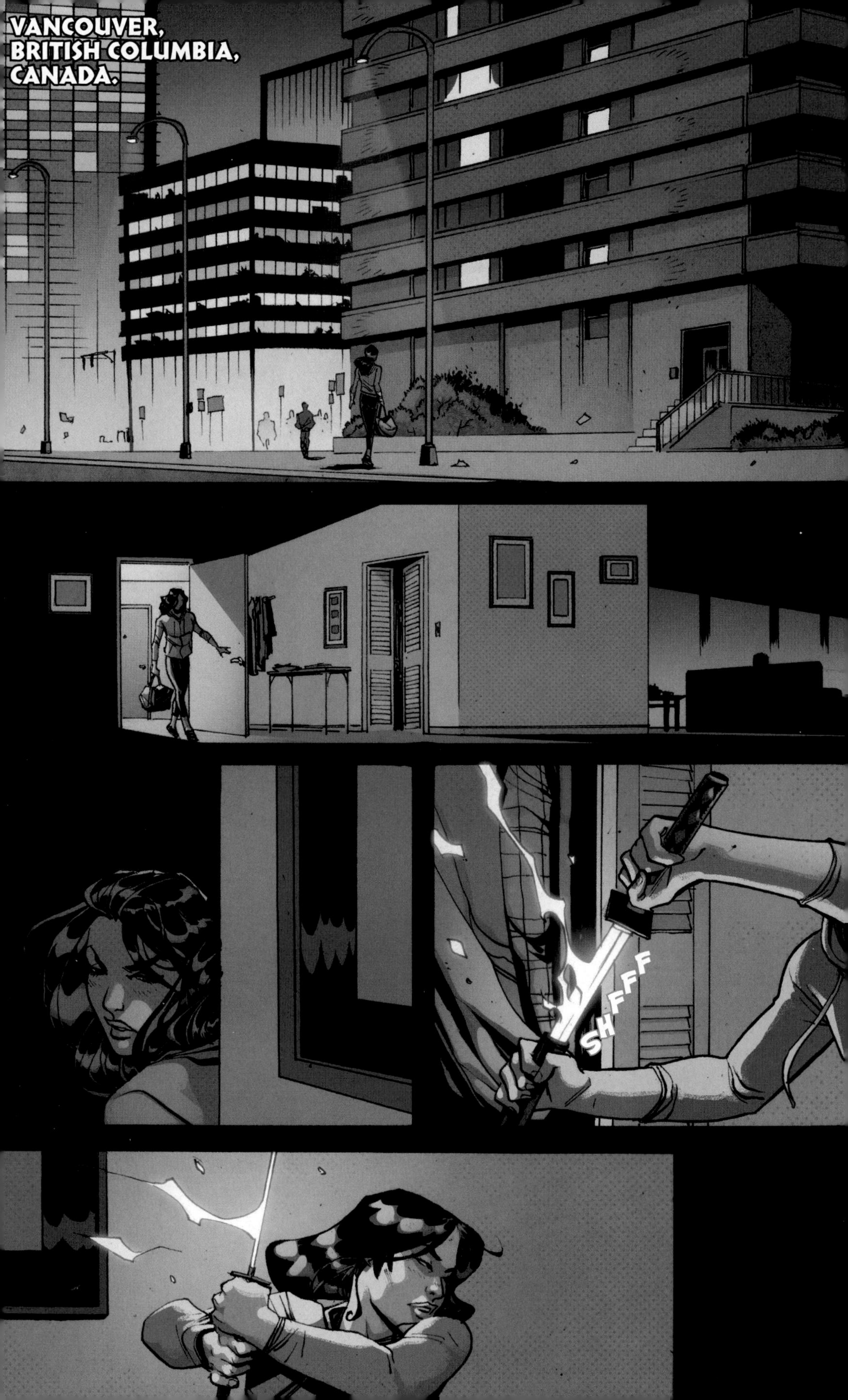
VANCOUVER, BRITISH COLUMBIA, CANADA.
SHFFF

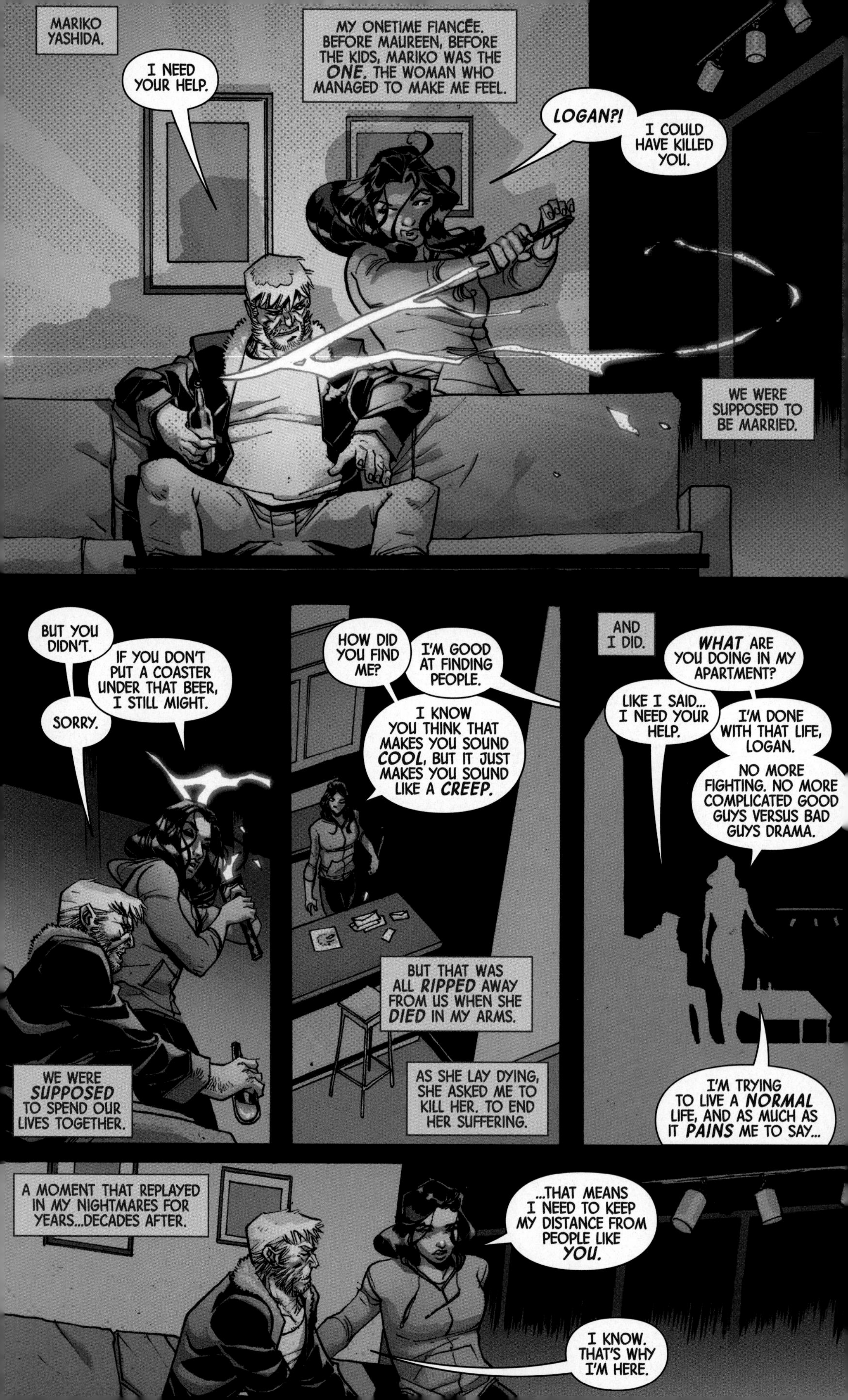
MARIKO YASHIDA.
I NEED YOUR HELP.
MY ONETIME FIANCÉE. BEFORE MAUREEN, BEFORE THE KIDS, MARIKO WAS THE ONE. THE WOMAN WHO MANAGED TO MAKE ME FEEL.
LOGAN?!
I COULD HAVE KILLED YOU.
WE WERE SUPPOSED TO BE MARRIED.
BUT YOU DIDN'T.
IF YOU DON'T PUT A COASTER UNDER THAT BEER, I STILL MIGHT.
SORRY.
WE WERE SUPPOSED TO SPEND OUR LIVES TOGETHER.
HOW DID YOU FIND ME?
I'M GOOD AT FINDING PEOPLE.
I KNOW YOU THINK THAT MAKES YOU SOUND COOL, BUT IT JUST MAKES YOU SOUND LIKE A CREEP.
BUT THAT WAS ALL RIPPED AWAY FROM US WHEN SHE DIED IN MY ARMS.
AS SHE LAY DYING, SHE ASKED ME TO KILL HER. TO END HER SUFFERING.
AND I DID.
WHAT ARE YOU DOING IN MY APARTMENT?
LIKE I SAID... I NEED YOUR HELP.
I'M DONE WITH THAT LIFE, LOGAN.
NO MORE FIGHTING. NO MORE COMPLICATED GOOD GUYS VERSUS BAD GUYS DRAMA.
I'M TRYING TO LIVE A NORMAL LIFE, AND AS MUCH AS IT PAINS ME TO SAY...
A MOMENT THAT REPLAYED IN MY NIGHTMARES FOR YEARS...DECADES AFTER.
...THAT MEANS I NEED TO KEEP MY DISTANCE FROM PEOPLE LIKE YOU.
I KNOW. THAT'S WHY I'M HERE.

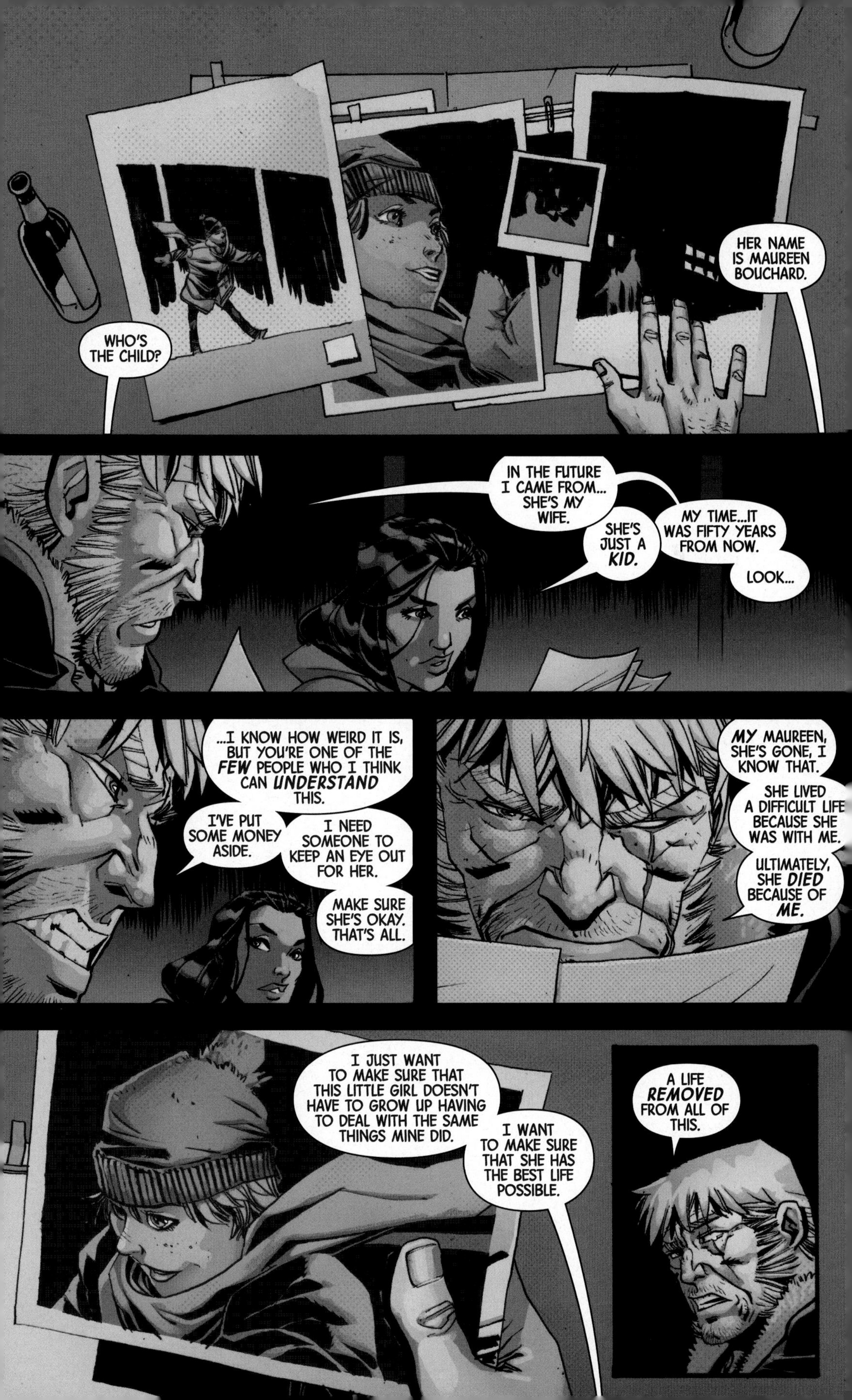
WHO'S THE CHILD?
HER NAME IS MAUREEN BOUCHARD.
IN THE FUTURE I CAME FROM... SHE'S MY WIFE.
SHE'S JUST A KID.
MY TIME...IT WAS FIFTY YEARS FROM NOW.
LOOK...
...I KNOW HOW WEIRD IT IS, BUT YOU'RE ONE OF THE FEW PEOPLE WHO I THINK CAN UNDERSTAND THIS.
I'VE PUT SOME MONEY ASIDE.
I NEED SOMEONE TO KEEP AN EYE OUT FOR HER.
MAKE SURE SHE'S OKAY. THAT'S ALL.
MY MAUREEN, SHE'S GONE, I KNOW THAT.
SHE LIVED A DIFFICULT LIFE BECAUSE SHE WAS WITH ME.
ULTIMATELY, SHE DIED BECAUSE OF ME.
I JUST WANT TO MAKE SURE THAT THIS LITTLE GIRL DOESN'T HAVE TO GROW UP HAVING TO DEAL WITH THE SAME THINGS MINE DID.
I WANT TO MAKE SURE THAT SHE HAS THE BEST LIFE POSSIBLE.
A LIFE REMOVED FROM ALL OF THIS.

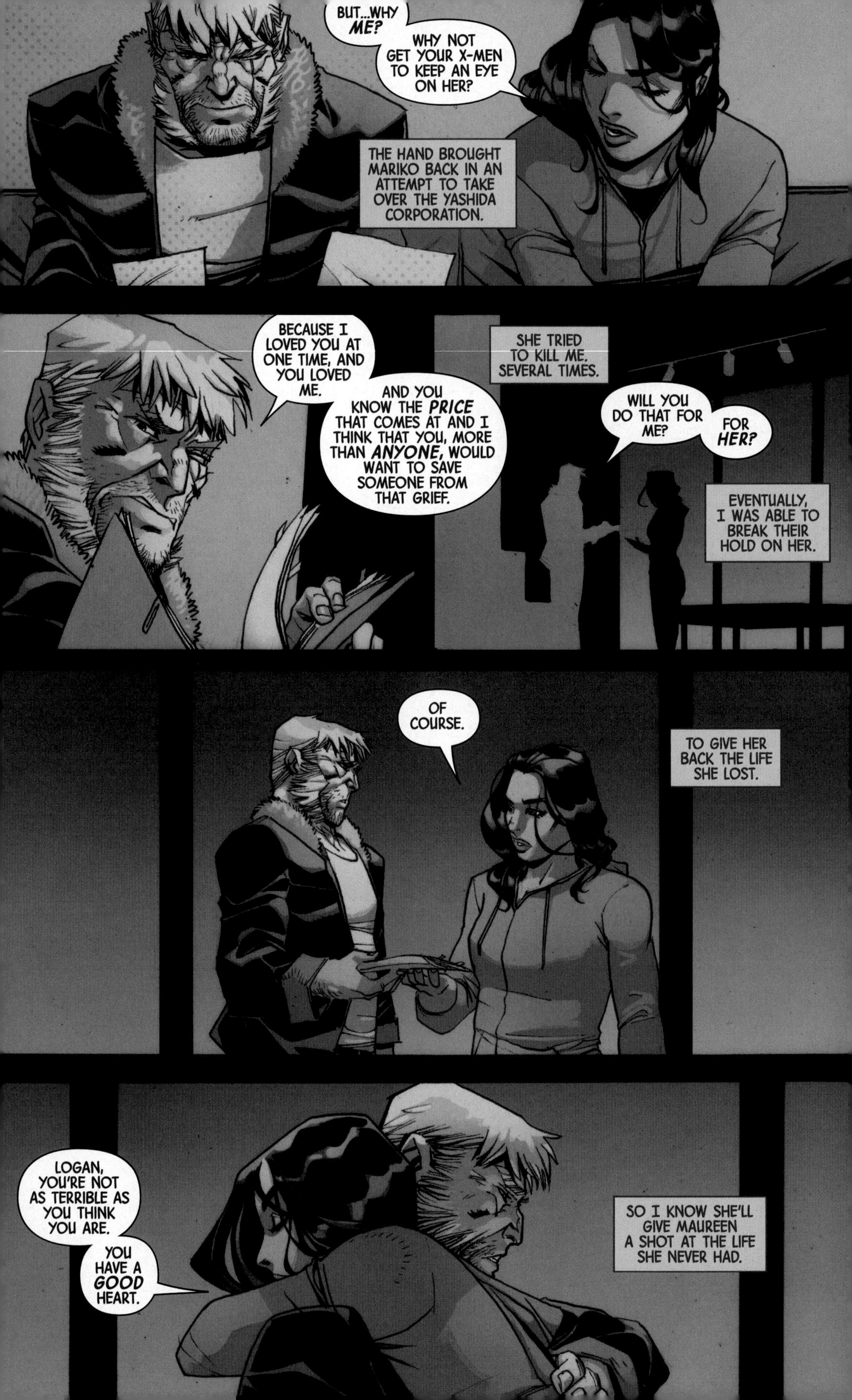

BUT...WHY ME?
WHY NOT GET YOUR X-MEN TO KEEP AN EYE ON HER?
THE HAND BROUGHT MARIKO BACK IN AN ATTEMPT TO TAKE OVER THE YASHIDA CORPORATION.
BECAUSE I LOVED YOU AT ONE TIME, AND YOU LOVED ME.
AND YOU KNOW THE PRICE THAT COMES AT AND I THINK THAT YOU, MORE THAN ANYONE, WOULD WANT TO SAVE SOMEONE FROM THAT GRIEF.
SHE TRIED TO KILL ME. SEVERAL TIMES.
WILL YOU DO THAT FOR ME?
FOR HER?
EVENTUALLY, I WAS ABLE TO BREAK THEIR HOLD ON HER.
OF COURSE.
TO GIVE HER BACK THE LIFE SHE LOST.
LOGAN, YOU'RE NOT AS TERRIBLE AS YOU THINK YOU ARE.
YOU HAVE A GOOD HEART.
SO I KNOW SHE'LL GIVE MAUREEN A SHOT AT THE LIFE SHE NEVER HAD.

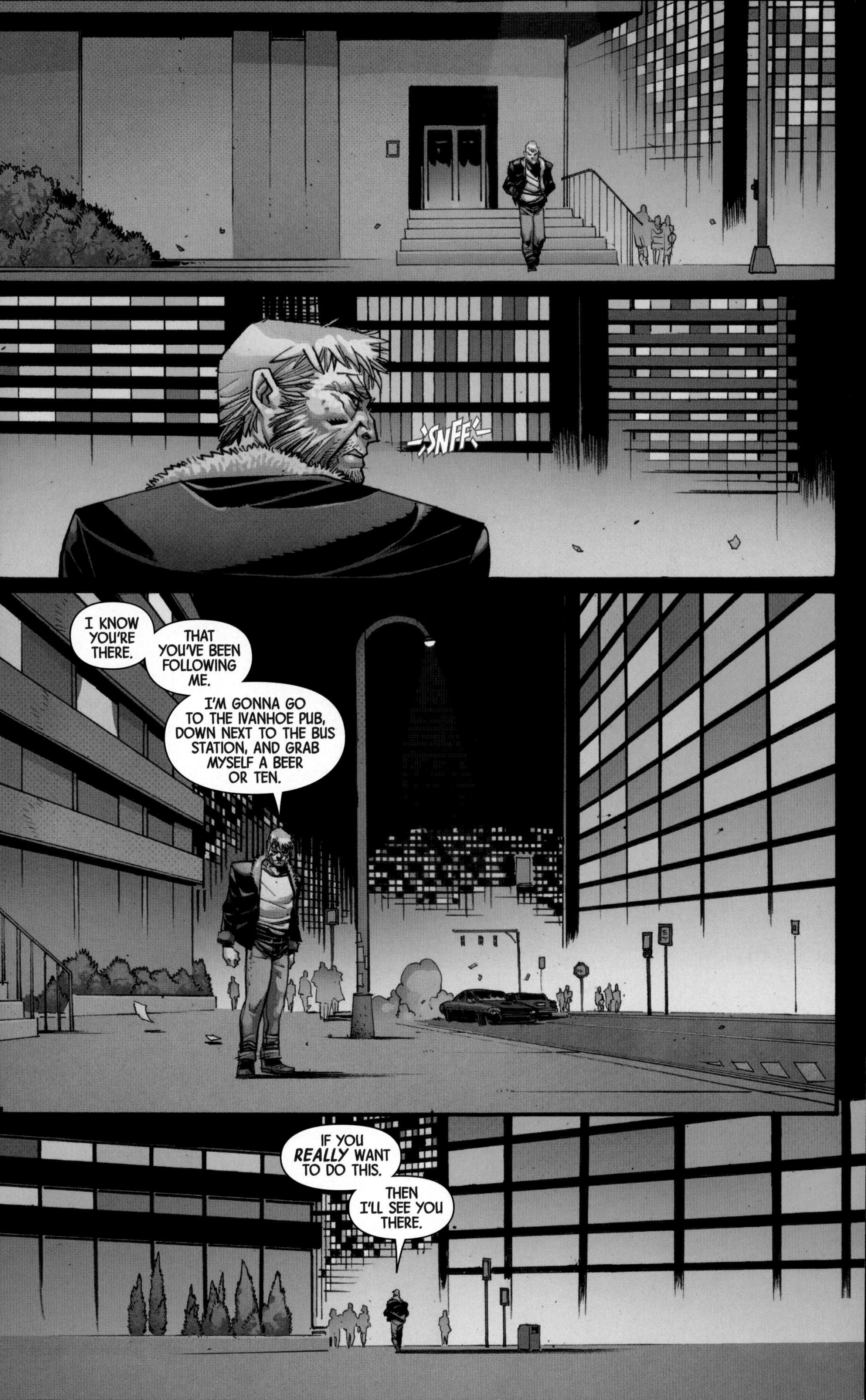
SNFF
I KNOW YOU'RE THERE.
THAT YOU'VE BEEN FOLLOWING ME.
I'M GONNA GO TO THE IVANHOE PUB, DOWN NEXT TO THE BUS STATION, AND GRAB MYSELF A BEER OR TEN.
IF YOU *REALLY* WANT TO DO THIS.
THEN I'LL SEE YOU THERE.

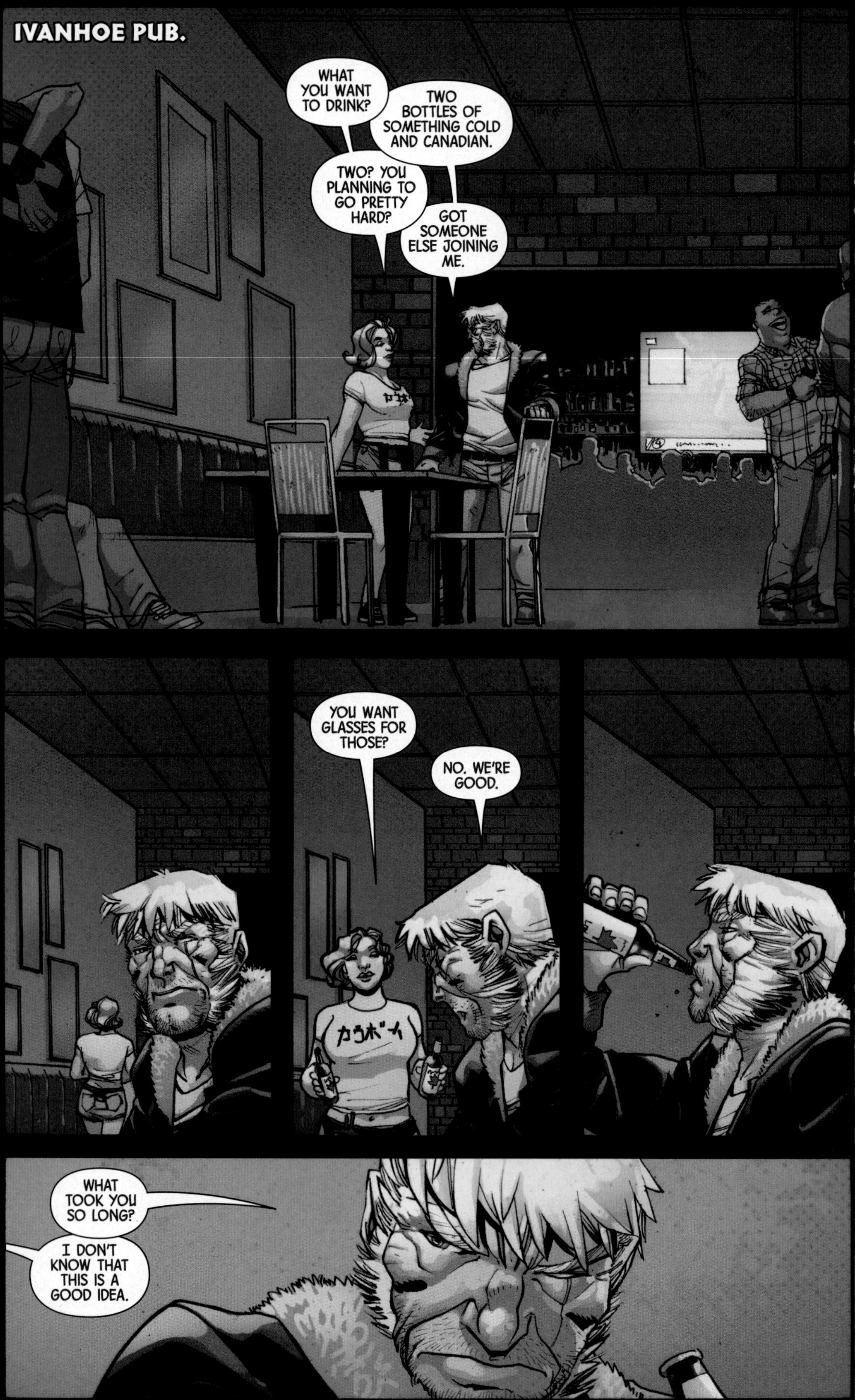
IVANHOE PUB.
WHAT YOU WANT TO DRINK?
TWO BOTTLES OF SOMETHING COLD AND CANADIAN.
TWO? YOU PLANNING TO GO PRETTY HARD?
GOT SOMEONE ELSE JOINING ME.
YOU WANT GLASSES FOR THOSE?
NO. WE'RE GOOD.
カウボーイ
WHAT TOOK YOU SO LONG?
I DON'T KNOW THAT THIS IS A GOOD IDEA.

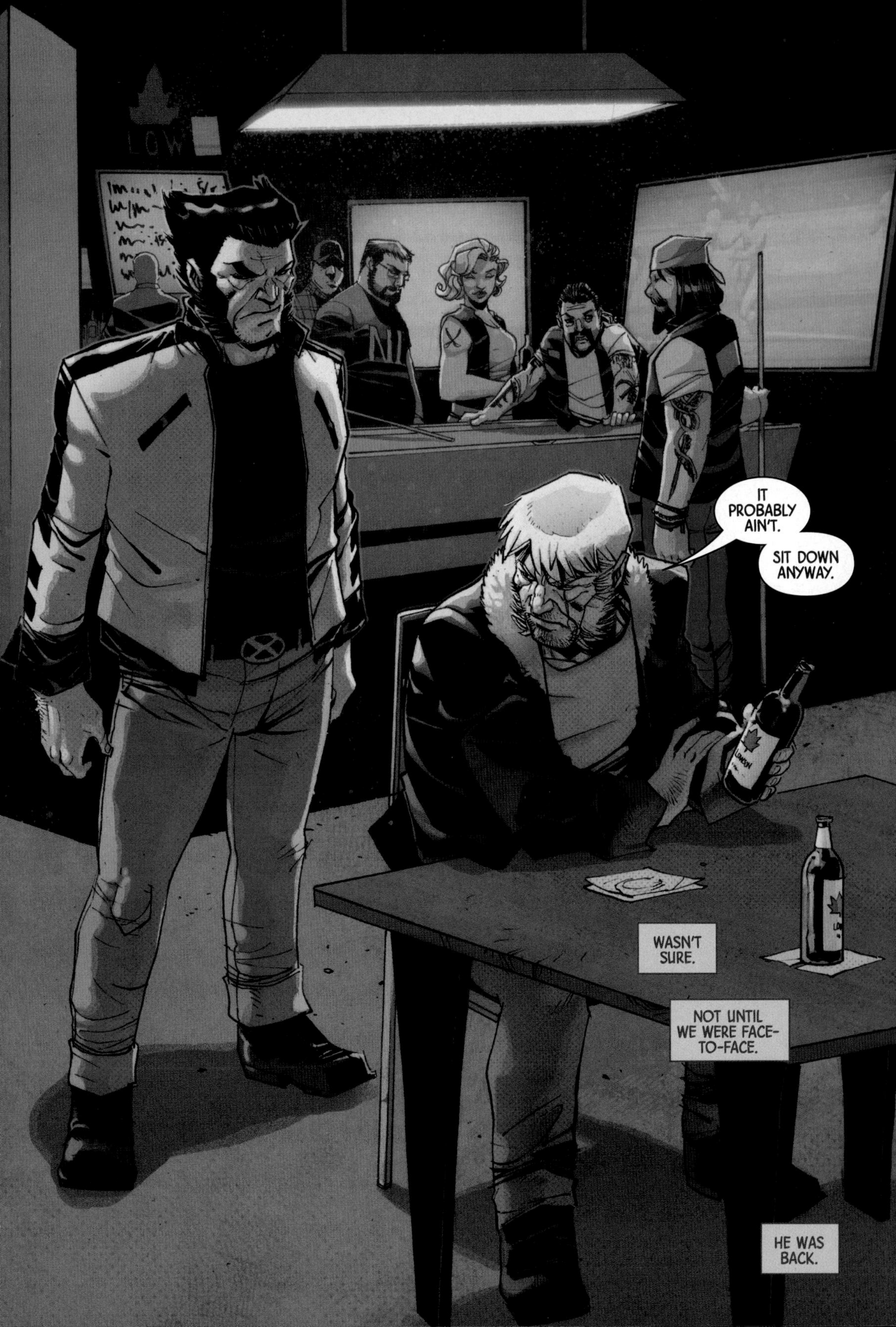
IT PROBABLY AIN'T.
SIT DOWN ANYWAY.
WASN'T SURE.
NOT UNTIL WE WERE FACE-TO-FACE.
HE WAS BACK.

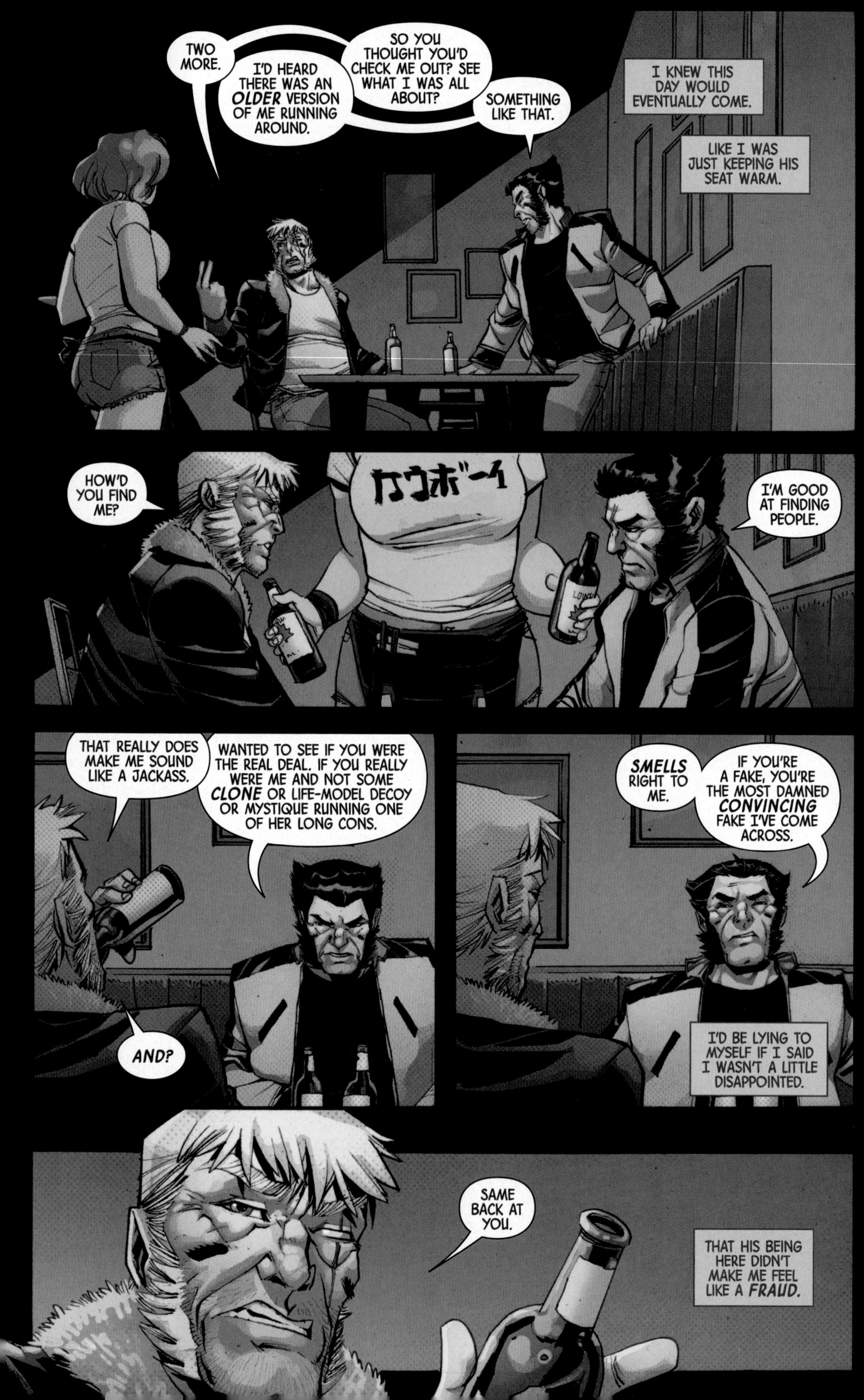

TWO MORE.
I'D HEARD THERE WAS AN OLDER VERSION OF ME RUNNING AROUND.
SO YOU THOUGHT YOU'D CHECK ME OUT? SEE WHAT I WAS ALL ABOUT?
SOMETHING LIKE THAT.
I KNEW THIS DAY WOULD EVENTUALLY COME.
LIKE I WAS JUST KEEPING HIS SEAT WARM.
HOW'D YOU FIND ME?
カウボーイ
I'M GOOD AT FINDING PEOPLE.
THAT REALLY DOES MAKE ME SOUND LIKE A JACKASS.
WANTED TO SEE IF YOU WERE THE REAL DEAL. IF YOU REALLY WERE ME AND NOT SOME CLONE OR LIFE-MODEL DECOY OR MYSTIQUE RUNNING ONE OF HER LONG CONS.
AND?
SMELLS RIGHT TO ME.
IF YOU'RE A FAKE, YOU'RE THE MOST DAMNED CONVINCING FAKE I'VE COME ACROSS.
I'D BE LYING TO MYSELF IF I SAID I WASN'T A LITTLE DISAPPOINTED.
SAME BACK AT YOU.
THAT HIS BEING HERE DIDN'T MAKE ME FEEL LIKE A FRAUD.

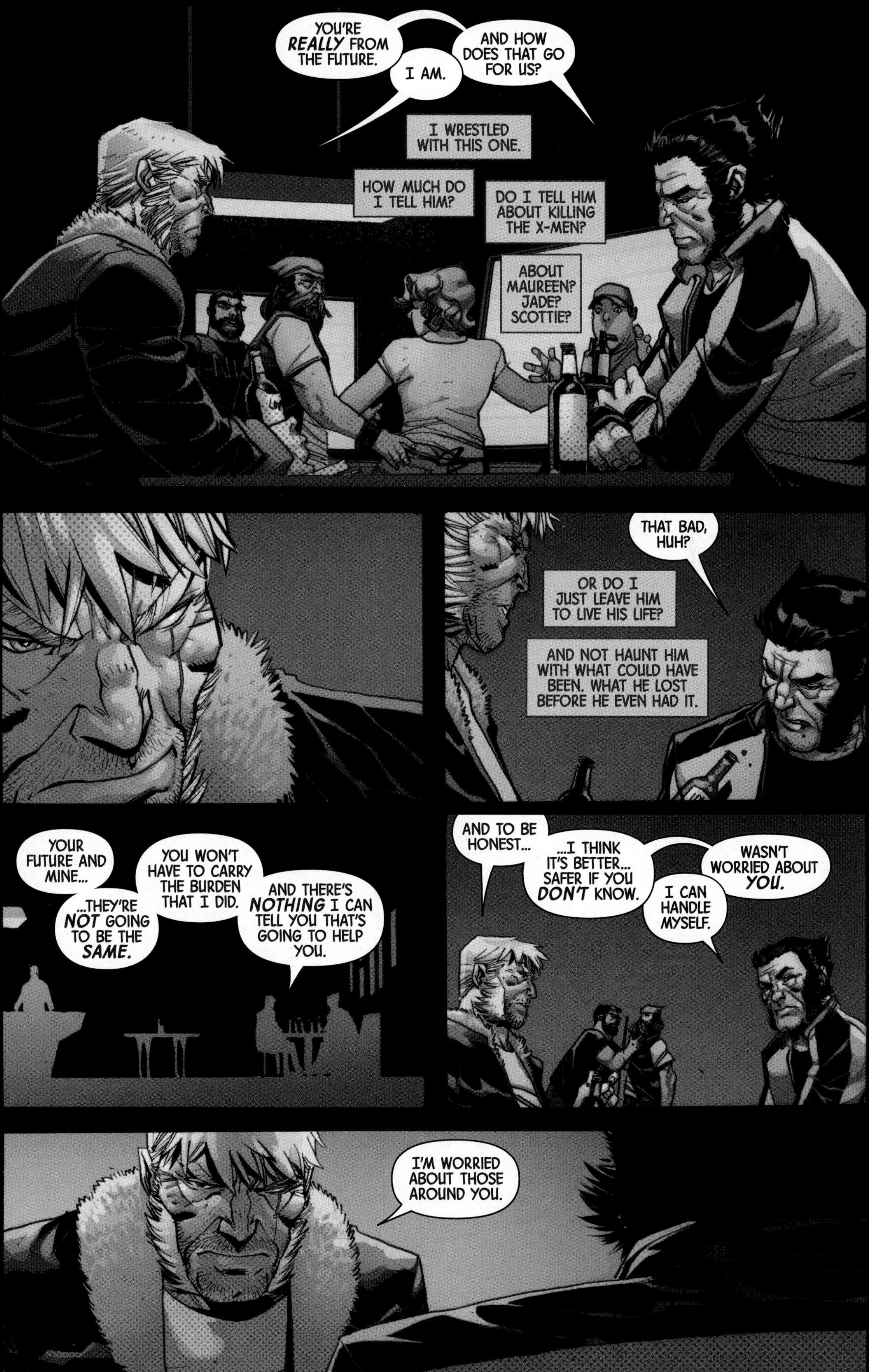
YOU'RE REALLY FROM THE FUTURE.
I AM.
AND HOW DOES THAT GO FOR US?
I WRESTLED WITH THIS ONE.
HOW MUCH DO I TELL HIM?
DO I TELL HIM ABOUT KILLING THE X-MEN?
ABOUT MAUREEN? JADE? SCOTTIE?
OR DO I JUST LEAVE HIM TO LIVE HIS LIFE?
AND NOT HAUNT HIM WITH WHAT COULD HAVE BEEN. WHAT HE LOST BEFORE HE EVEN HAD IT.
THAT BAD, HUH?
YOUR FUTURE AND MINE...
...THEY'RE NOT GOING TO BE THE SAME.
YOU WON'T HAVE TO CARRY THE BURDEN THAT I DID.
AND THERE'S NOTHING I CAN TELL YOU THAT'S GOING TO HELP YOU.
AND TO BE HONEST...
...I THINK IT'S BETTER... SAFER IF YOU DON'T KNOW.
WASN'T WORRIED ABOUT YOU.
I CAN HANDLE MYSELF.
I'M WORRIED ABOUT THOSE AROUND YOU.

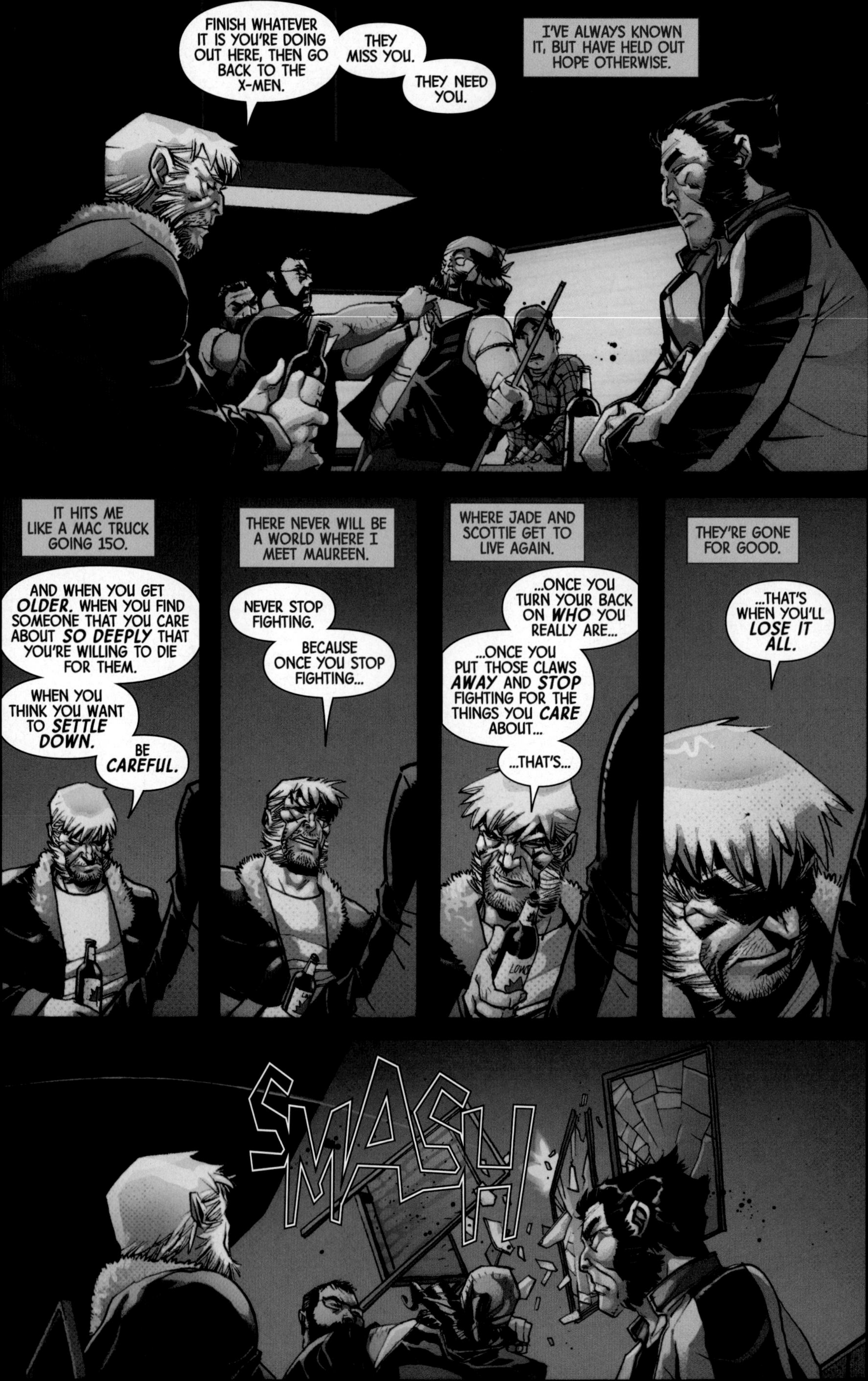

FINISH WHATEVER IT IS YOU'RE DOING OUT HERE, THEN GO BACK TO THE X-MEN.
THEY MISS YOU.
THEY NEED YOU.
I'VE ALWAYS KNOWN IT, BUT HAVE HELD OUT HOPE OTHERWISE.
IT HITS ME LIKE A MAC TRUCK GOING 150.
AND WHEN YOU GET OLDER. WHEN YOU FIND SOMEONE THAT YOU CARE ABOUT SO DEEPLY THAT YOU'RE WILLING TO DIE FOR THEM.
WHEN YOU THINK YOU WANT TO SETTLE DOWN.
BE CAREFUL.
THERE NEVER WILL BE A WORLD WHERE I MEET MAUREEN.
NEVER STOP FIGHTING.
BECAUSE ONCE YOU STOP FIGHTING...
WHERE JADE AND SCOTTIE GET TO LIVE AGAIN.
...ONCE YOU TURN YOUR BACK ON WHO YOU REALLY ARE...
...ONCE YOU PUT THOSE CLAWS AWAY AND STOP FIGHTING FOR THE THINGS YOU CARE ABOUT...
...THAT'S...
THEY'RE GONE FOR GOOD.
...THAT'S WHEN YOU'LL LOSE IT ALL.
SMASH

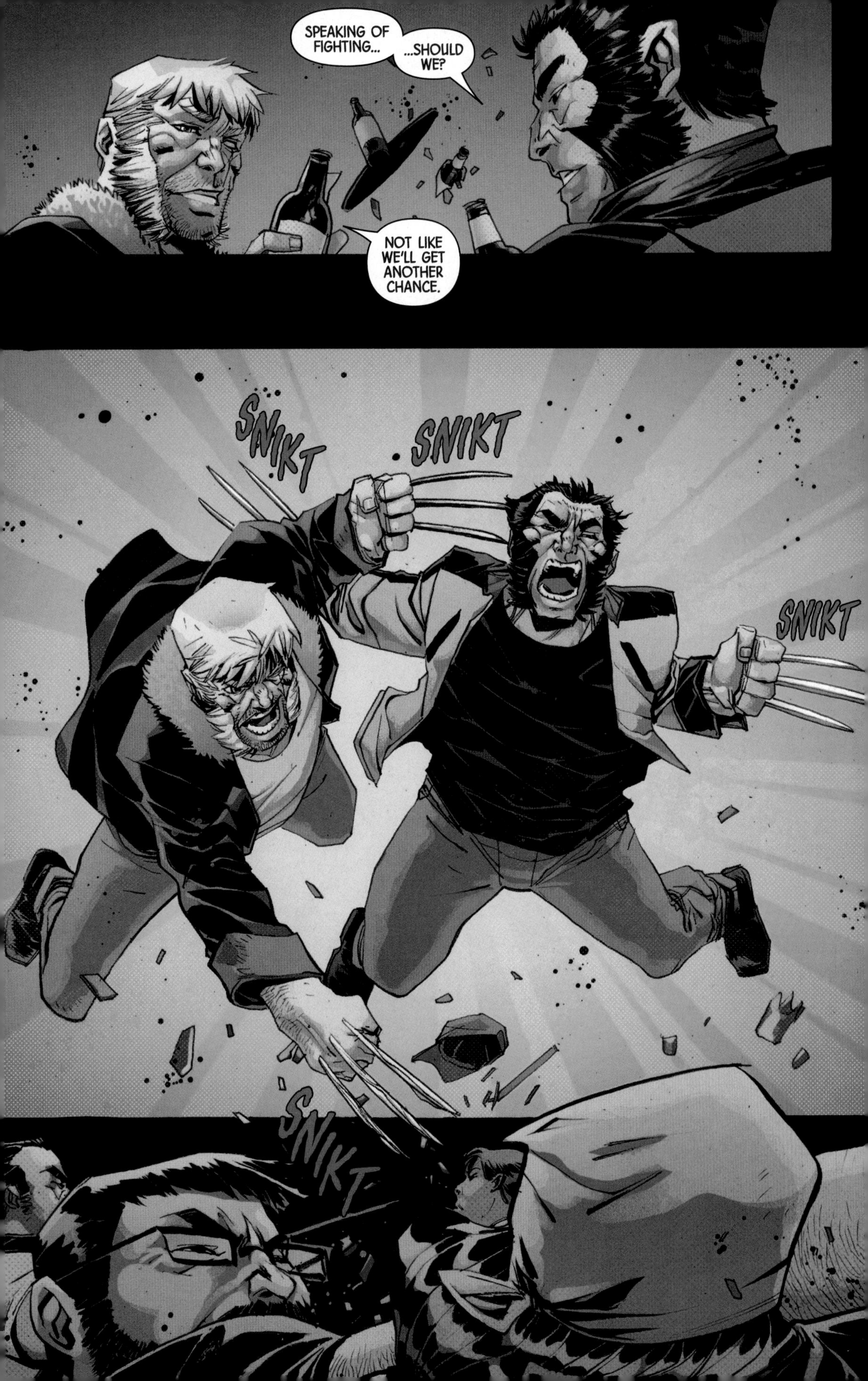

SPEAKING OF FIGHTING...
...SHOULD WE?
NOT LIKE WE'LL GET ANOTHER CHANCE.
SNIKT
SNIKT
SNIKT
SNIKT

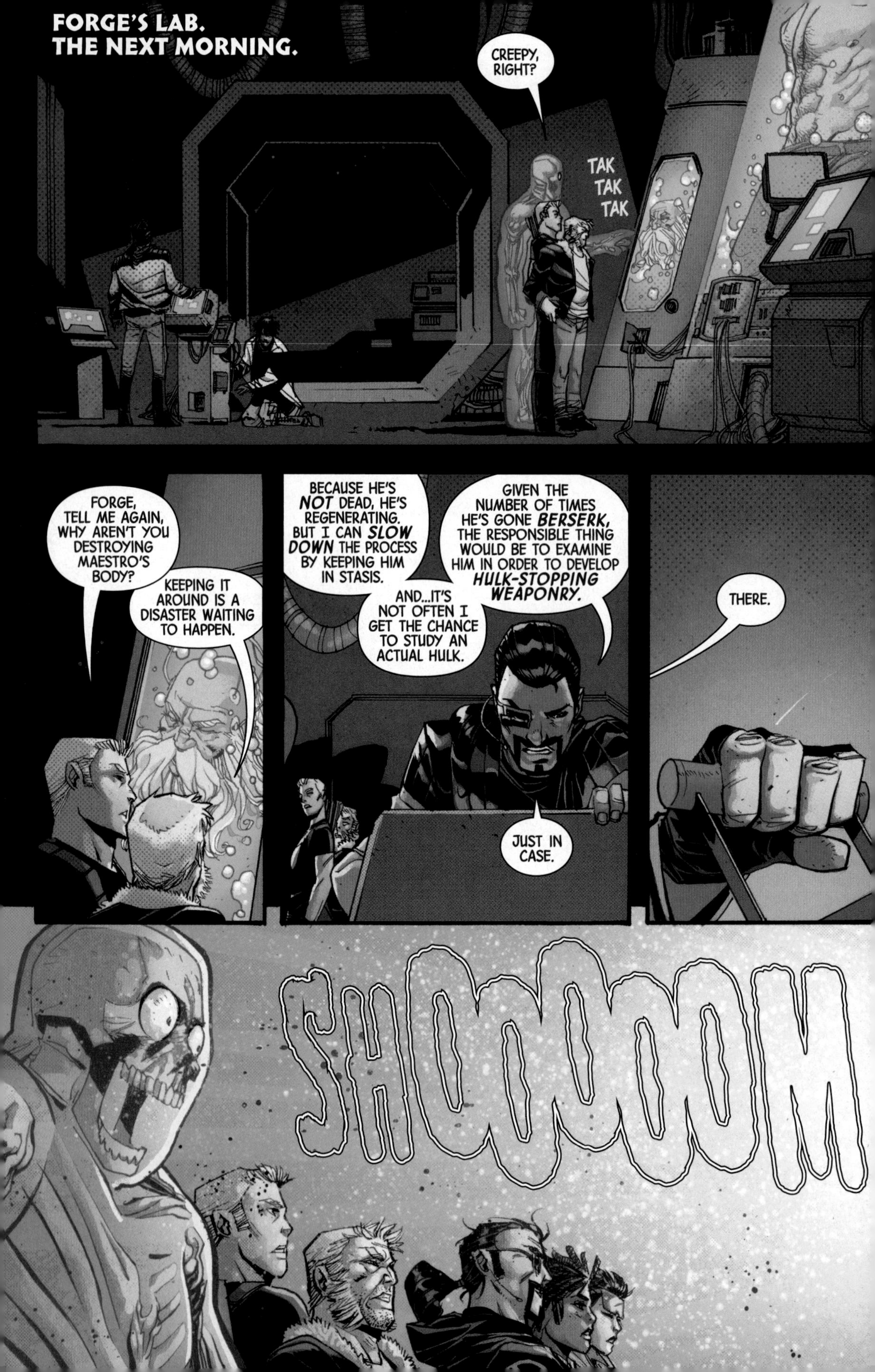
FORGE'S LAB.
THE NEXT MORNING.
CREEPY, RIGHT?
TAK TAK TAK
FORGE, TELL ME AGAIN, WHY AREN'T YOU DESTROYING MAESTRO'S BODY?
KEEPING IT AROUND IS A DISASTER WAITING TO HAPPEN.
BECAUSE HE'S NOT DEAD, HE'S REGENERATING. BUT I CAN SLOW DOWN THE PROCESS BY KEEPING HIM IN STASIS.
AND...IT'S NOT OFTEN I GET THE CHANCE TO STUDY AN ACTUAL HULK.
GIVEN THE NUMBER OF TIMES HE'S GONE BERSERK, THE RESPONSIBLE THING WOULD BE TO EXAMINE HIM IN ORDER TO DEVELOP HULK-STOPPING WEAPONRY.
JUST IN CASE.
THERE.
SHOOOOOOM

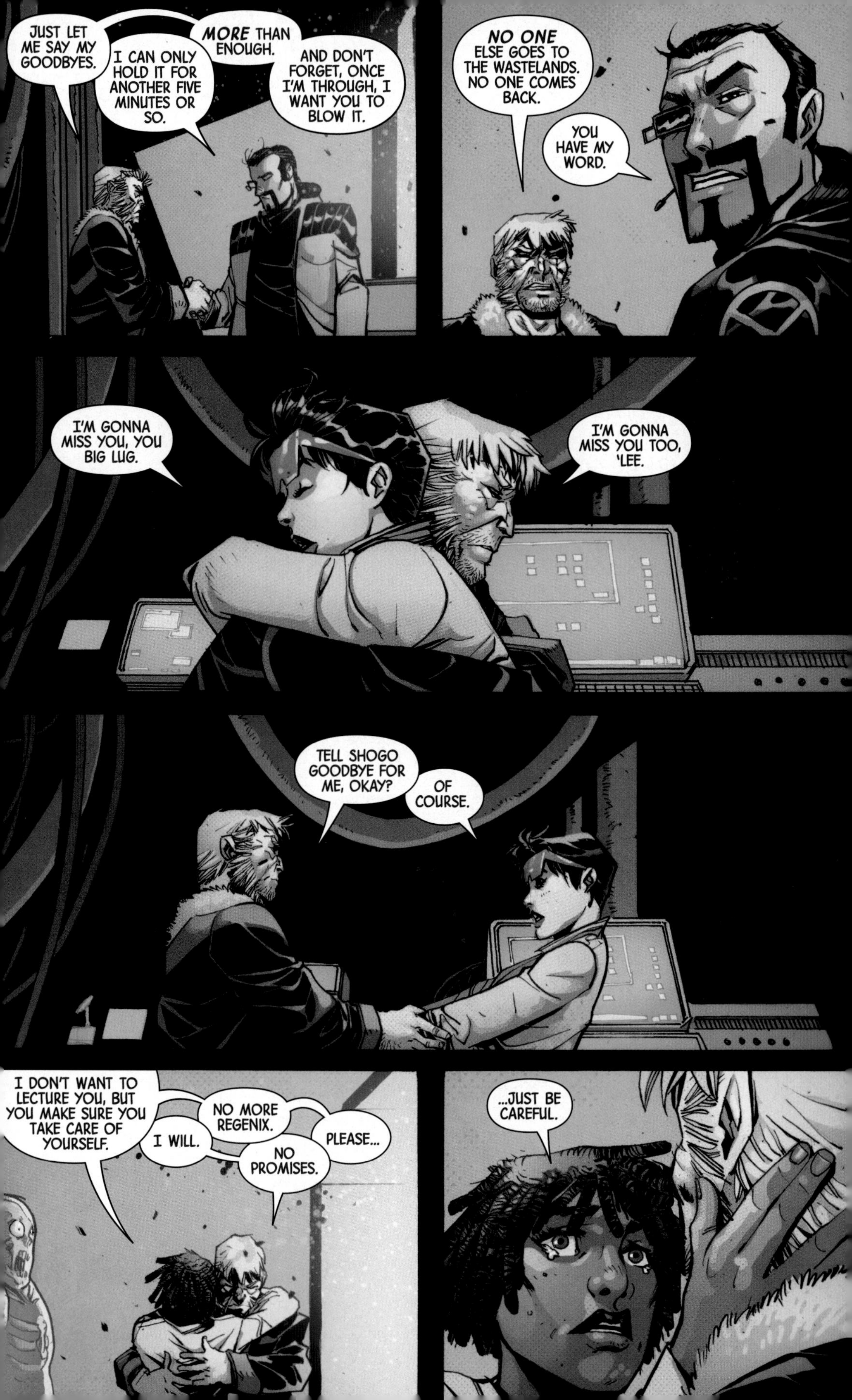
JUST LET ME SAY MY GOODBYES.
MORE THAN ENOUGH.
I CAN ONLY HOLD IT FOR ANOTHER FIVE MINUTES OR SO.
AND DON'T FORGET, ONCE I'M THROUGH, I WANT YOU TO BLOW IT.
NO ONE ELSE GOES TO THE WASTELANDS. NO ONE COMES BACK.
YOU HAVE MY WORD.
I'M GONNA MISS YOU, YOU BIG LUG.
I'M GONNA MISS YOU TOO, 'LEE.
TELL SHOGO GOODBYE FOR ME, OKAY?
OF COURSE.
I DON'T WANT TO LECTURE YOU, BUT YOU MAKE SURE YOU TAKE CARE OF YOURSELF.
I WILL.
NO MORE REGENIX.
NO PROMISES.
PLEASE...
...JUST BE CAREFUL.

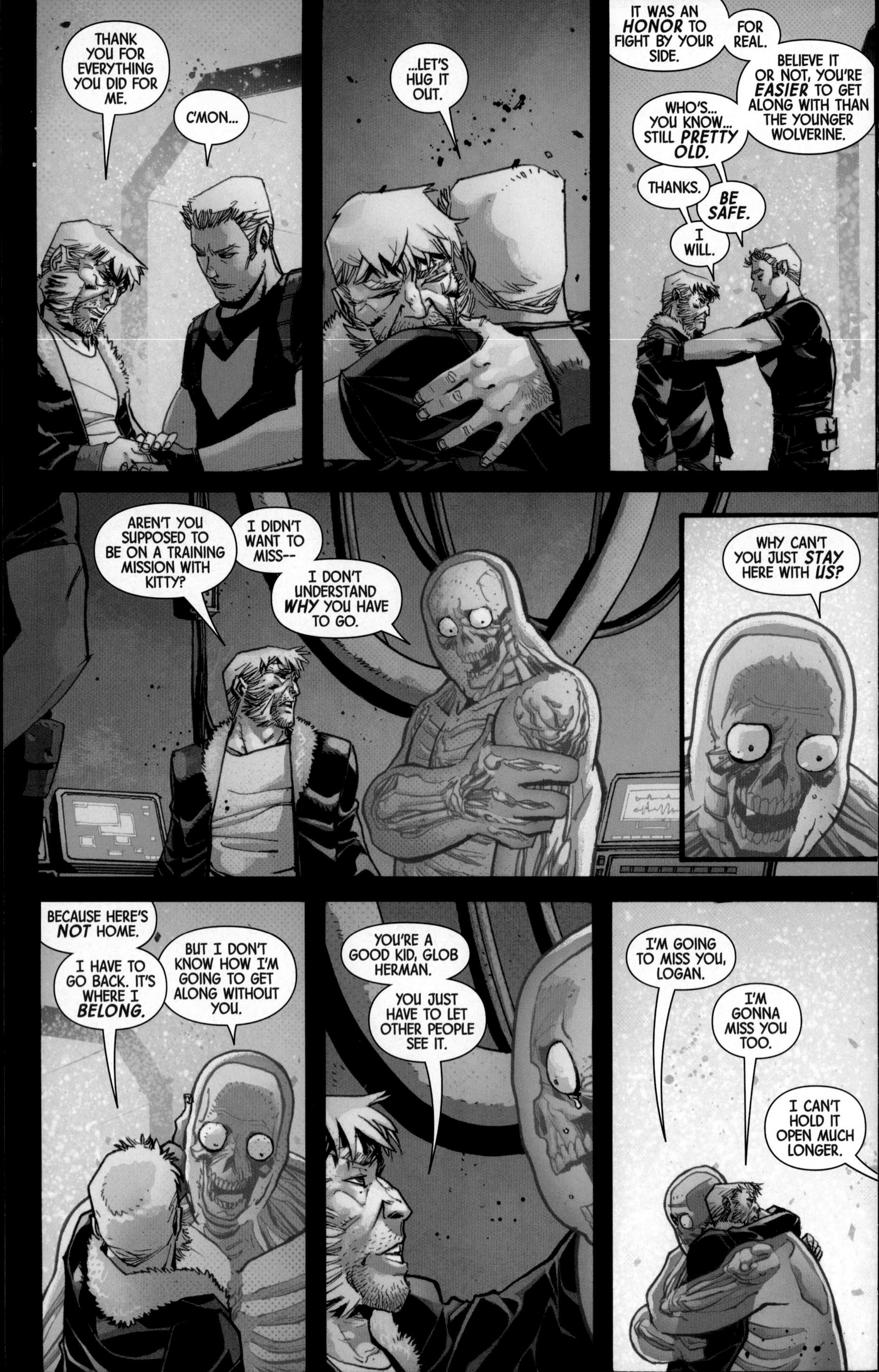
THANK YOU FOR EVERYTHING YOU DID FOR ME.
C'MON...
...LET'S HUG IT OUT.
IT WAS AN HONOR TO FIGHT BY YOUR SIDE.
FOR REAL.
BELIEVE IT OR NOT, YOU'RE EASIER TO GET ALONG WITH THAN THE YOUNGER WOLVERINE.
WHO'S... YOU KNOW... STILL PRETTY OLD.
THANKS.
BE SAFE.
I WILL.
AREN'T YOU SUPPOSED TO BE ON A TRAINING MISSION WITH KITTY?
I DIDN'T WANT TO MISS--
I DON'T UNDERSTAND WHY YOU HAVE TO GO.
WHY CAN'T YOU JUST STAY HERE WITH US?
BECAUSE HERE'S NOT HOME.
I HAVE TO GO BACK. IT'S WHERE I BELONG.
BUT I DON'T KNOW HOW I'M GOING TO GET ALONG WITHOUT YOU.
YOU'RE A GOOD KID, GLOB HERMAN.
YOU JUST HAVE TO LET OTHER PEOPLE SEE IT.
I'M GOING TO MISS YOU, LOGAN.
I'M GONNA MISS YOU TOO.
I CAN'T HOLD IT OPEN MUCH LONGER.

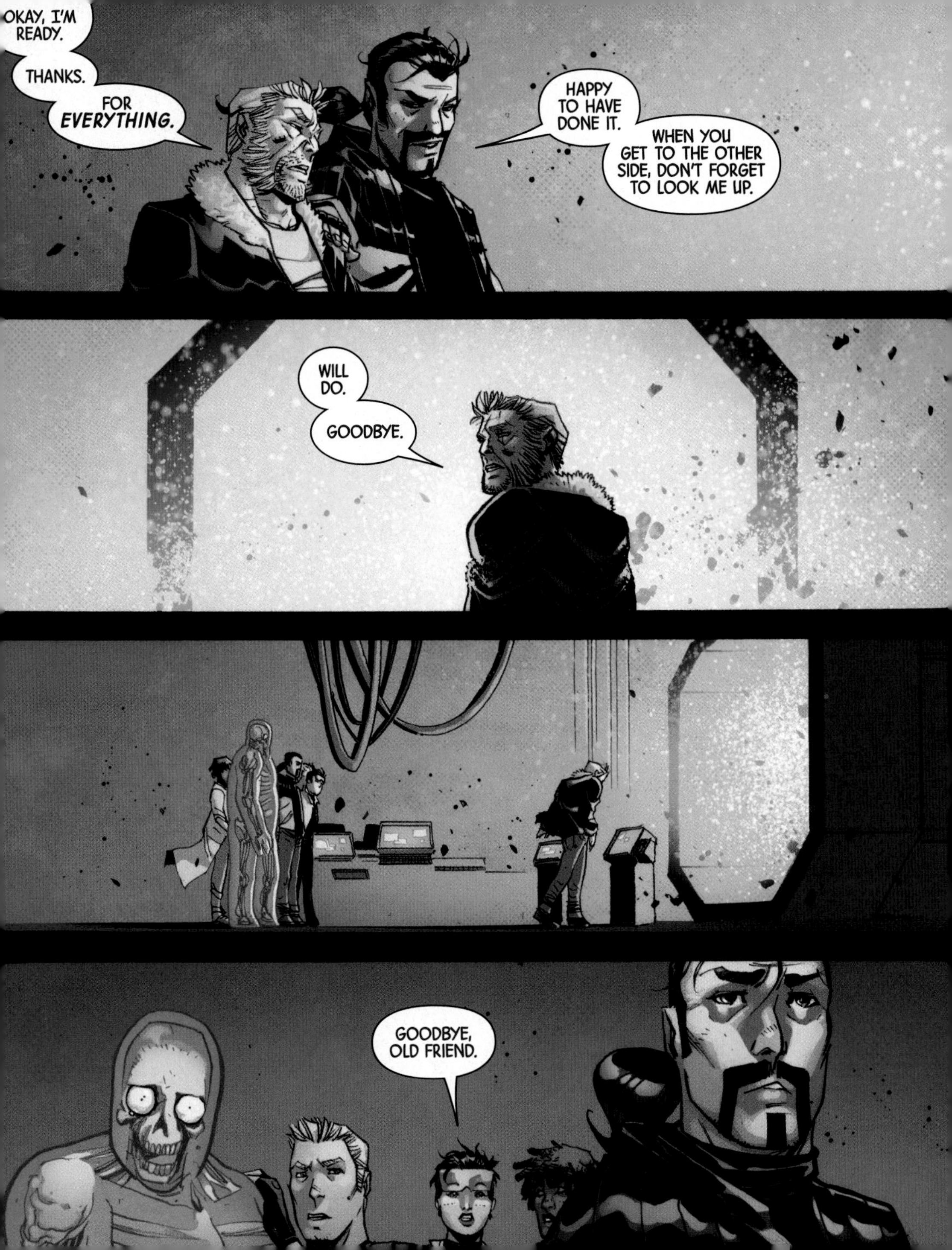
OKAY, I'M READY.
THANKS.
FOR *EVERYTHING.*
HAPPY TO HAVE DONE IT.
WHEN YOU GET TO THE OTHER SIDE, DON'T FORGET TO LOOK ME UP.
WILL DO.
GOODBYE.
GOODBYE, OLD FRIEND.

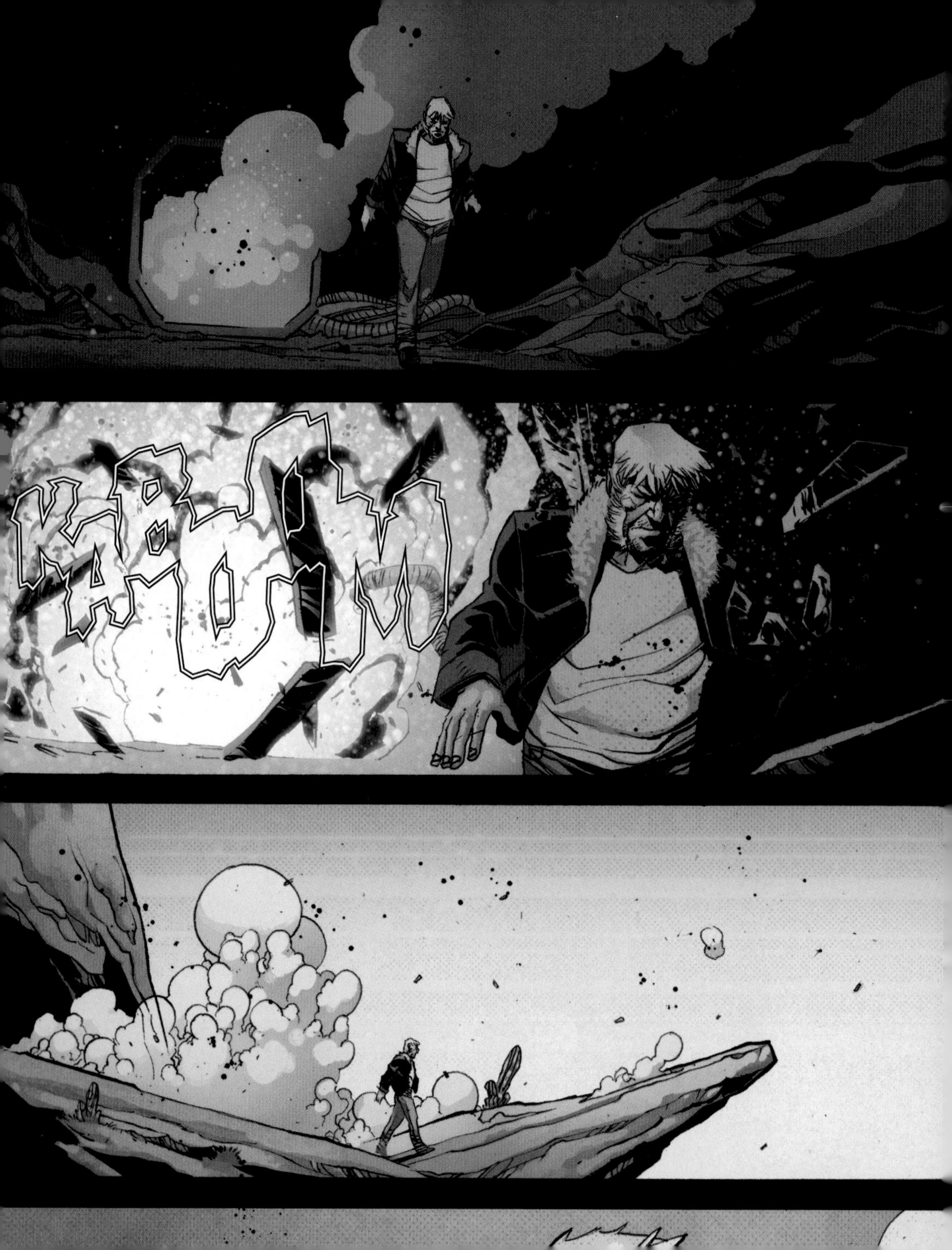
KABOOM

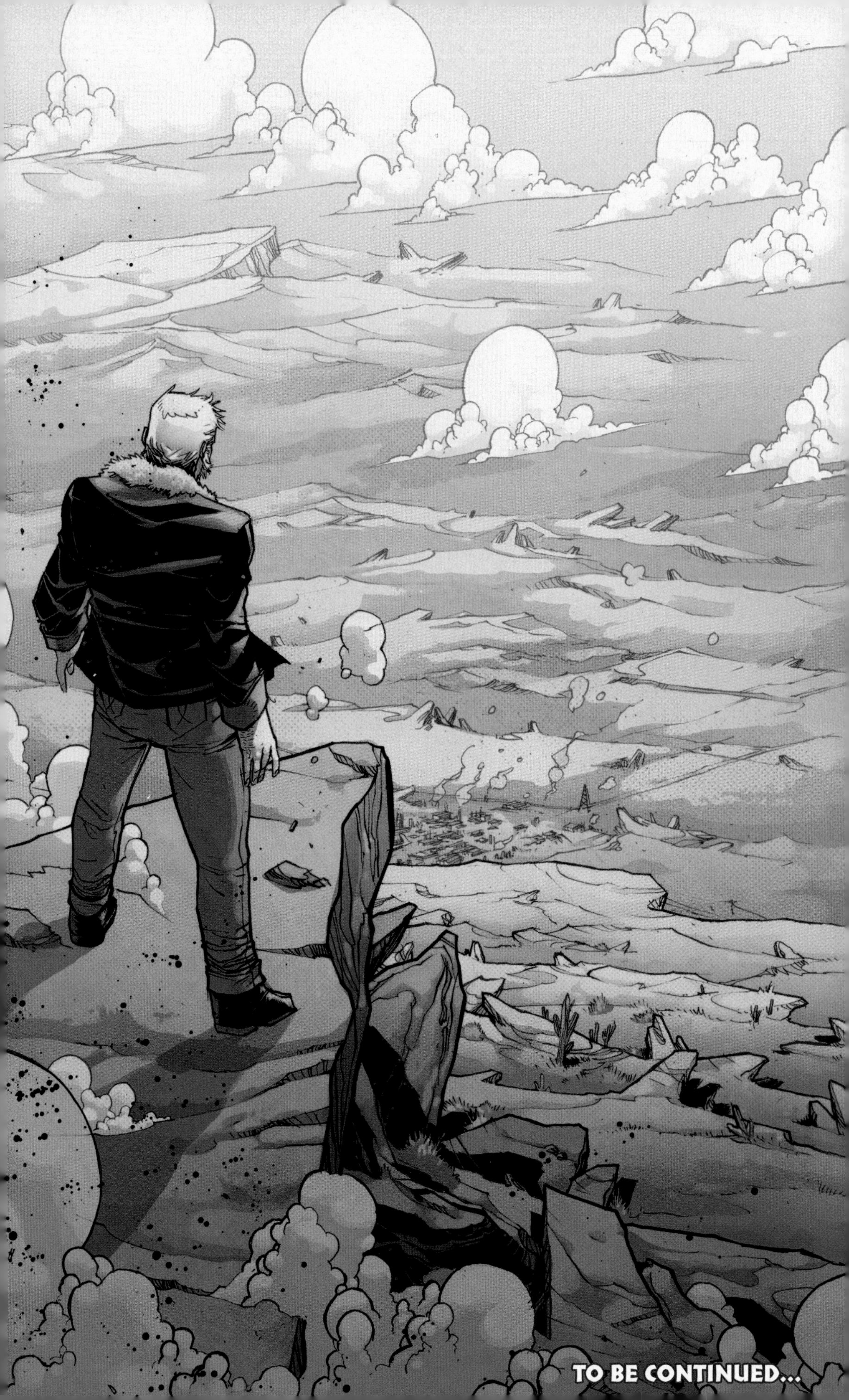
TO BE CONTINUED...

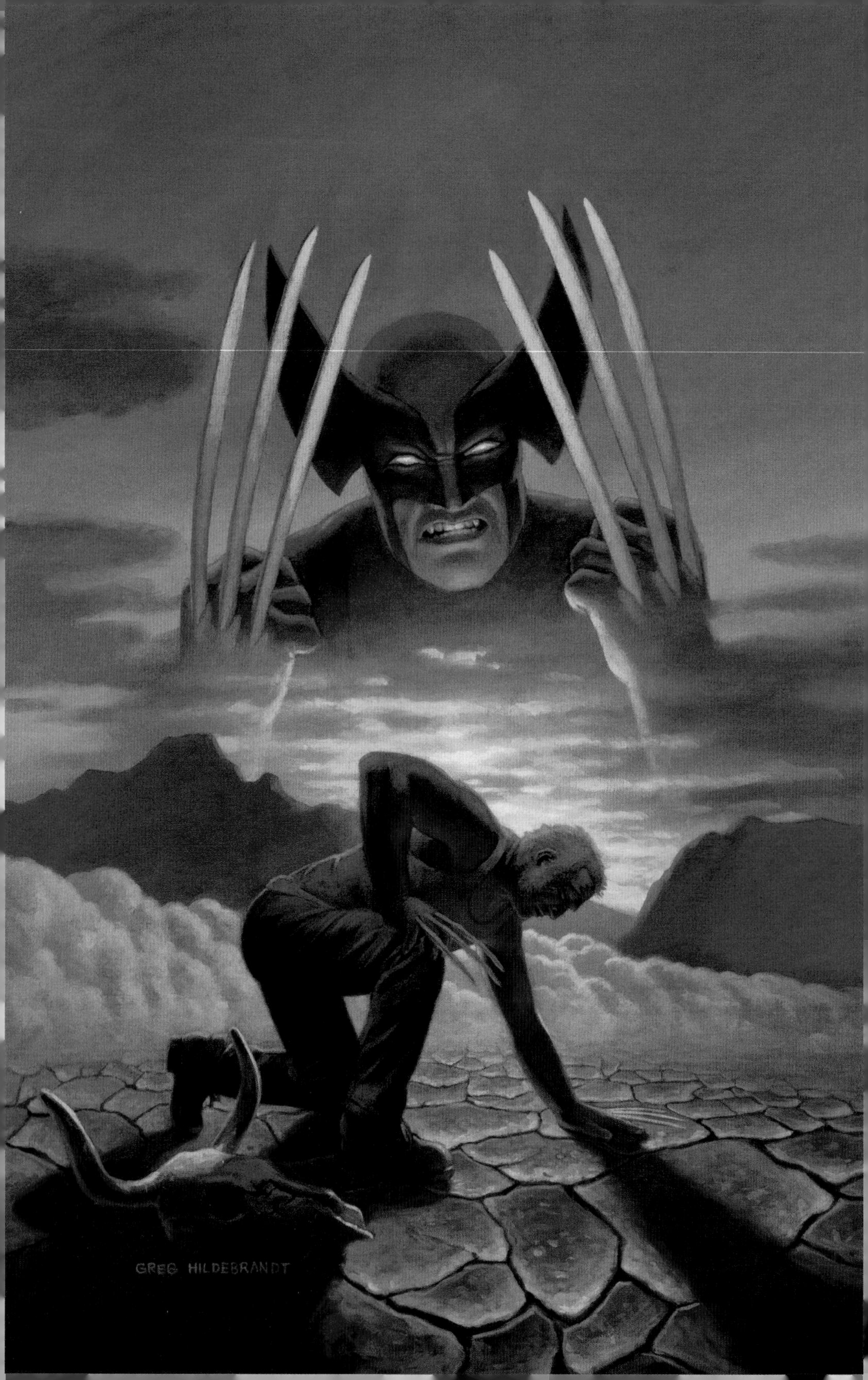
GREG HILDEBRANDT

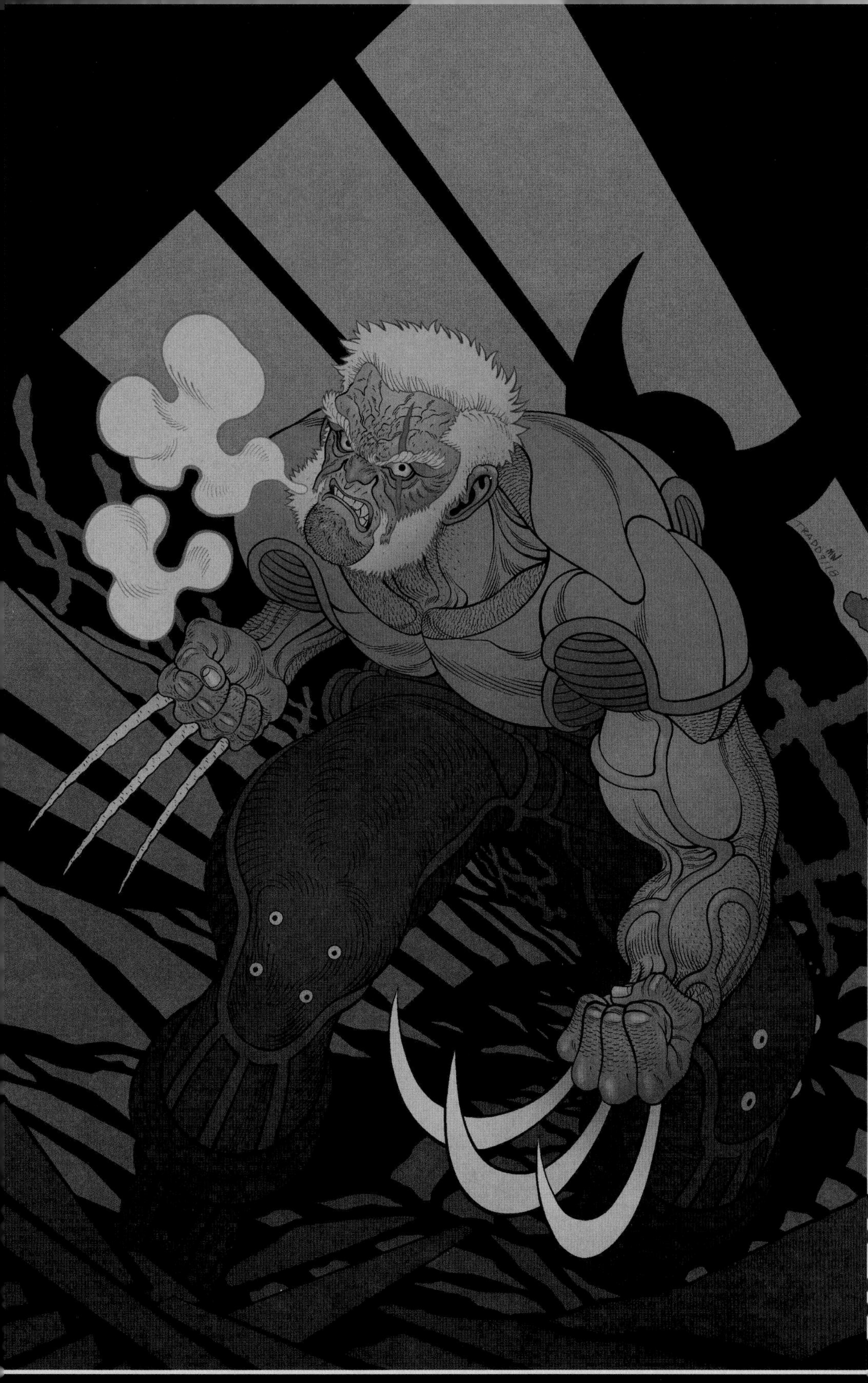

#1 VARIANT BY
TRADD MOORE & MATTHEW WILSON

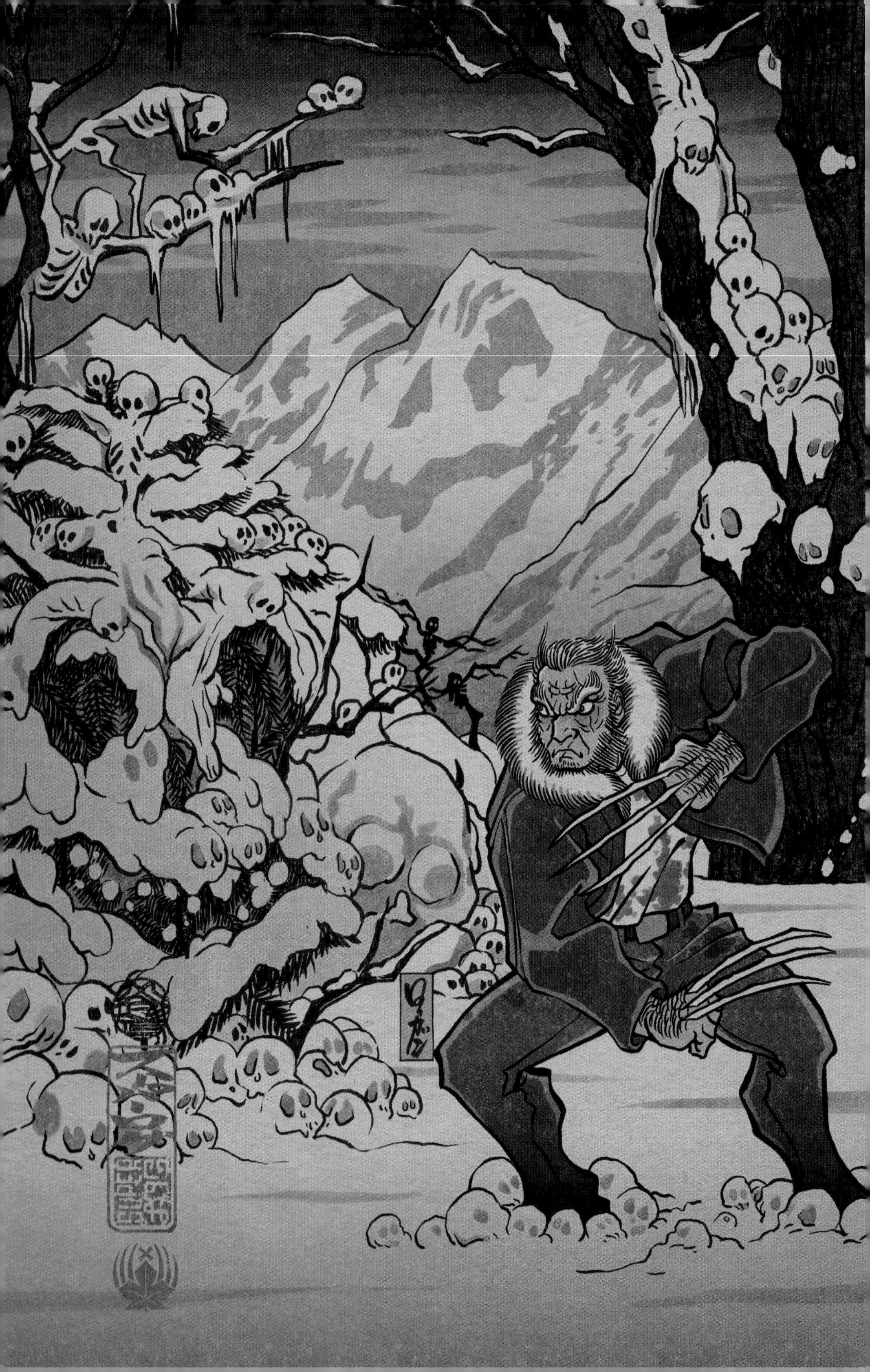

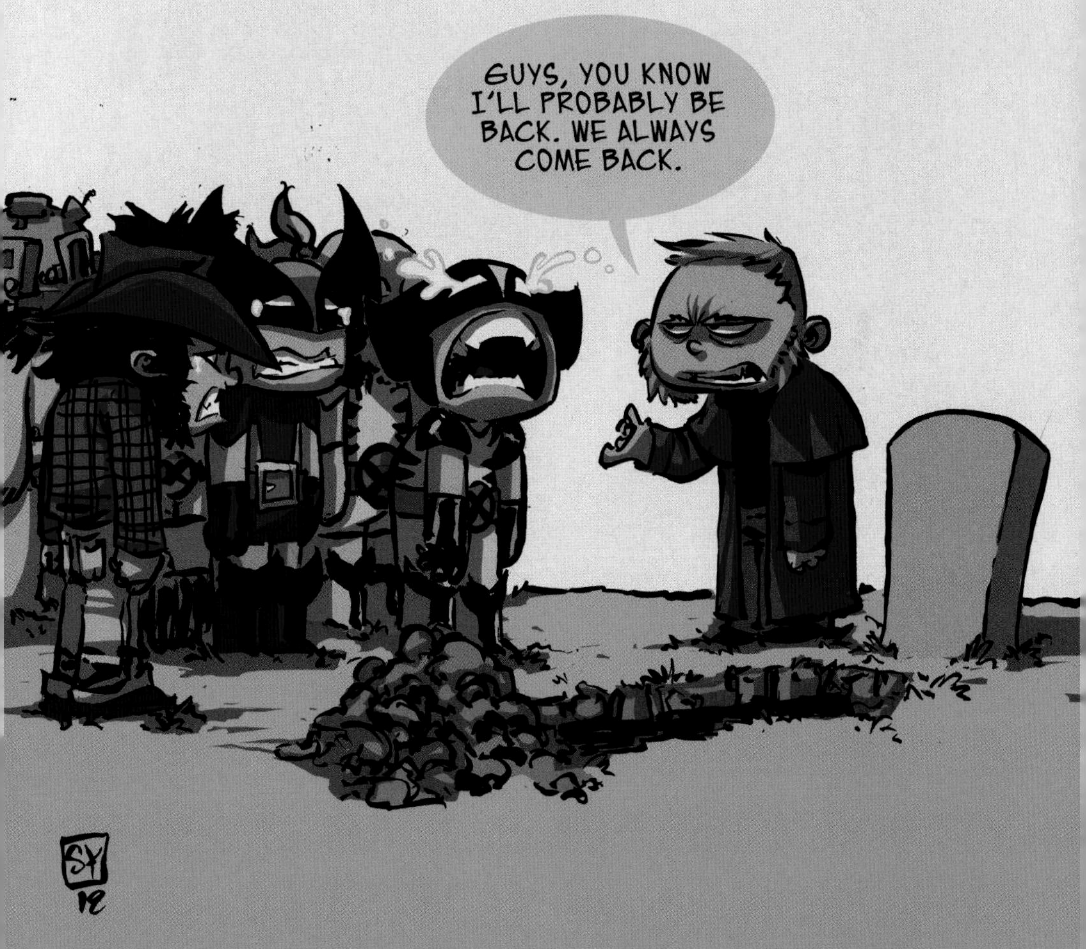
GUYS, YOU KNOW I'LL PROBABLY BE BACK. WE ALWAYS COME BACK.
SY 12

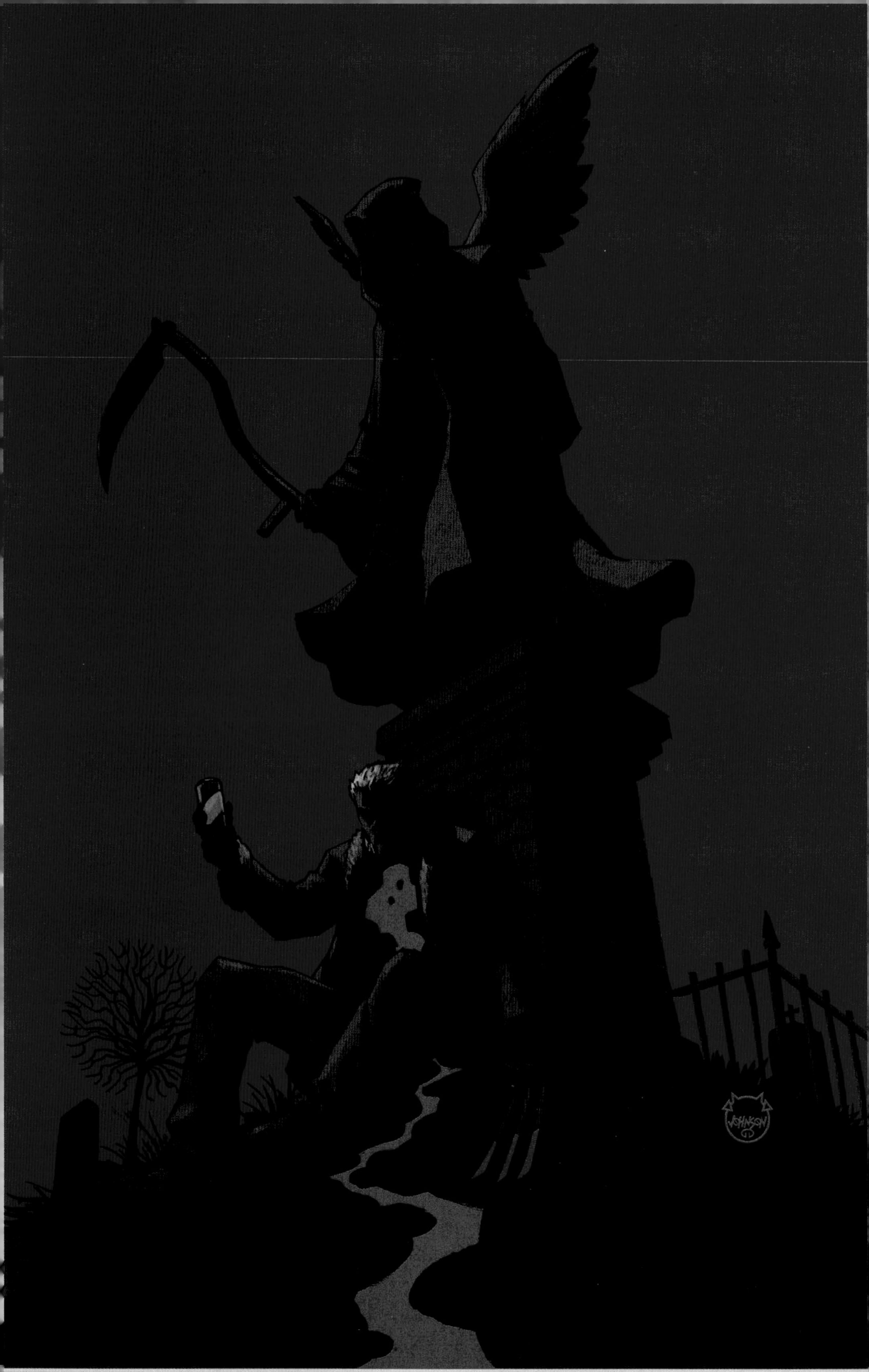
JOHNSON

#2 VARIANT BY
DAVE JOHNSON

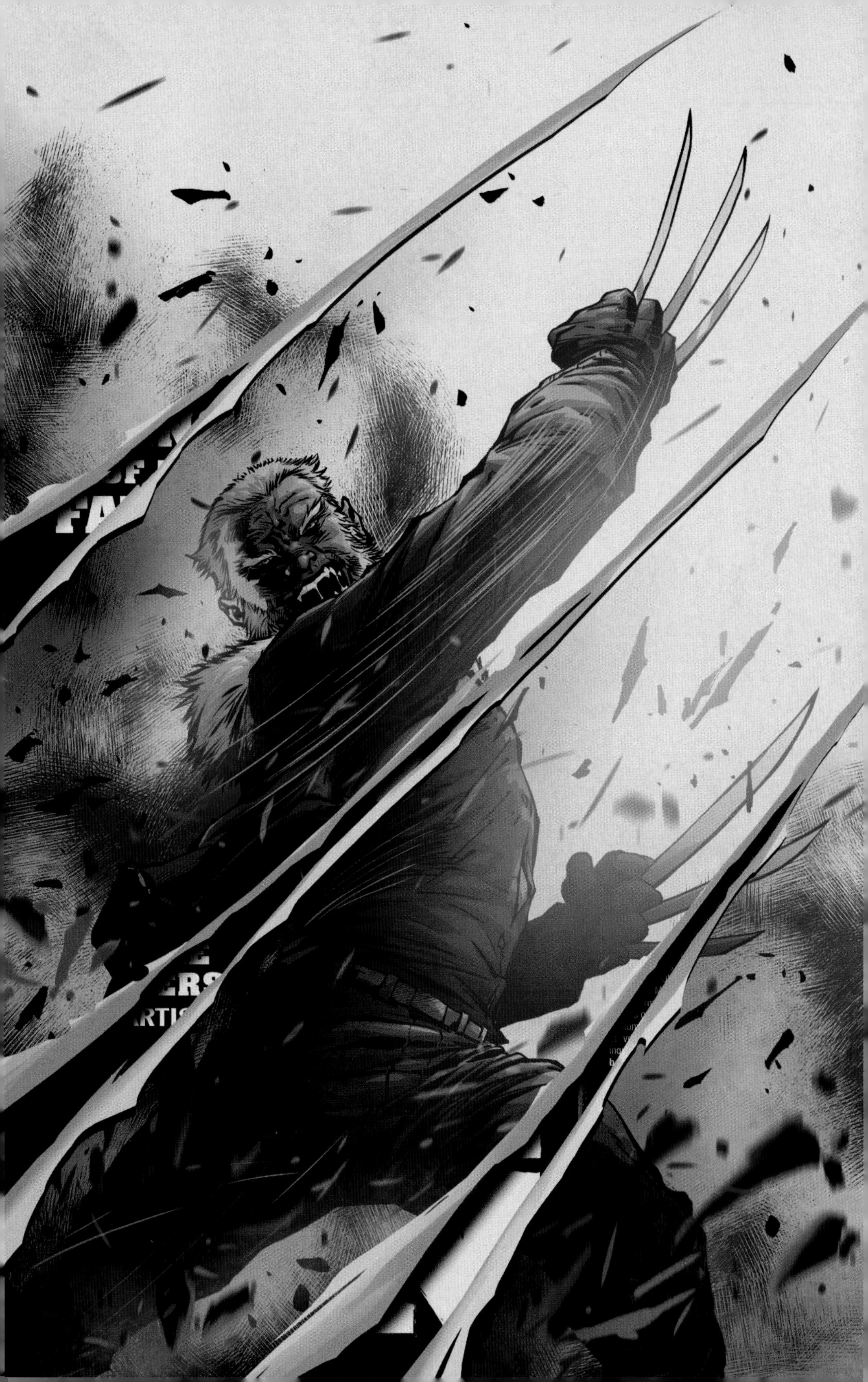

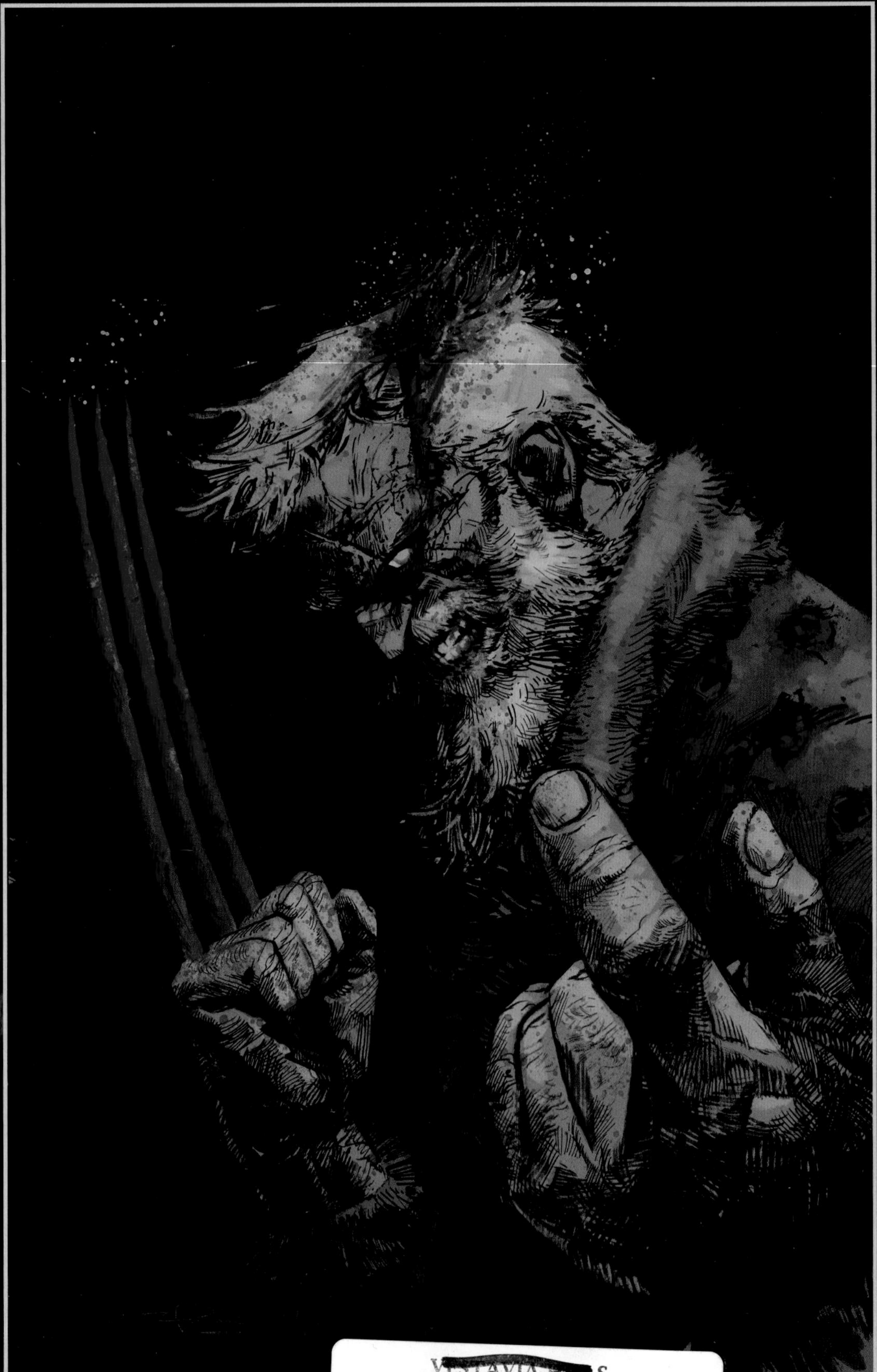

#4 VARIANT BY
GERARDO ZAFFINO